Merz to Emigre and Beyond:

Avant-Garde
Magazine Design
of the
Twentieth Century

Merz to Emigre and Beyond:

Avant-Garde
Magazine Design
of the
Twentieth Century
Steven Heller

This book is dedicated to Elaine Lustig Cohen

Research
J P Roth

Phaidon Press Limited
Regent's Wharf
All Saints Street
London N1 9PA

Phaidon Press Inc.
180 Varick Street
New York, NY 10014

www.phaidon.com

First published 2003
© 2003 Phaidon Press Limited

ISBN 0 7148 3927 2

A CIP catalogue record of this book is available from the
British Library.

Designed by HDR Visual Communication
Printed in Hong Kong

Above: **Zijeme**, vol.1 no.6, 1931, cover by Ladislav Sutnar. Published by Druzstevní Prace (Cooperative Works).

Frontispiece: **Minotaure**, no.7, 1935, cover by Joan Miró. Edited by Albert Skira and E Tériade.

This book surveys the 'paper' stage of twentieth-century avant-garde periodical publishing, specifically the design and typography of numerous magazines, newspapers, reviews and journals that in various ways have challenged the sanctity of art, politics, society and culture. Over the past decade, the Internet has had a major impact on the transmission of popular and unpopular ideas to large audiences all over the globe. Yet, before the digital era, paper was the most interactive of mediums and the avant-garde periodicals discussed in the following pages were agents of cultural upheaval.

Without paper there could, arguably, be no avant-garde, but without an avant-garde, paper would be less volatile. None the less, electronic – and especially digital – media is currently usurping some of paper's role as a medium of provocation, and it will continue to do so as technology advances. Artists and propagandists in concert with technicians and programmers routinely test the boundaries of various new media, developing ingenious software to infiltrate the public mind while advancing their aims. The future of paperless communication is as yet untold, but paper's usability options are increasingly proscribed in today's multimedia environment. It is, consequently, difficult to think now of paper as the main delivery system for radical ideas, although it would be foolhardy to believe that a transformation to another medium will be complete and absolute in the very near future because the twentieth-century avant-garde relied so heavily on paper. However, periodicals will doubtless change with the new media, and the avant-garde by definition will lead the way. So, as the next epoch takes shape, this book takes stock of the paper avant-garde to examine what is truly radical about the journals produced by progressive individuals, groups

and movements and why they became wellsprings of unprecedented art and design.

The term 'avant-garde' means the advance guard of unconventional ideas, especially in the arts, though not divorced from politics or society. The vanguard produces work that challenges the status quo despite the occasional threat of severe penalty. So an avant-garde is the instrument of radical change for better or worse, but always in opposition to the prevailing power structure. In whatever guise it appears, and however flawed it may be, the avant-garde is used (tacitly or otherwise) by societies as a means to trigger progress by disrupting complacency and promoting unacceptability. Because change can be frightening and, therefore, unwelcome, leaders of entrenched institutions often instinctively thwart the avant-garde whenever possible. Bertrand Russell wrote in *Unpopular Essays*, 'Change is indubitable, whereas progress is a matter of controversy.'[1] And controversy invariably follows avant-gardes around whenever they materialize.

An avant-garde is rebellious in intent, and the job of rebels is to make trouble. Of course, trouble might be viewed as a dubious achievement, depending on one's allegiance and status within a particular system, but ultimately challenging the norms of any cultural establishment by attacking existing traditions and values encourages re-evaluation of the culture as a whole – a shift that is necessary to avoid social stagnation. Virtually every society has avant-gardes whose actions provoke, in this order, grave concern, concession and co-option – a fairly common evolutionary cycle except where societies have puritanical or dictatorial regimes that routinely expunge opposition and control behaviour. Generally, avant-gardes have a small window of unacceptability, when the most radical characteristics are filtered out leaving only a veneer of

Introduction:
The Paper Avant-Garde

insurrection in the form of popular style and taste, before their extremist ideas are adopted as 'New Wave'. This is what happened with the Nineties music/culture magazine *Ray Gun* which spawned followers like *Huh*, *Speak* and *Lava*, each astutely borrowing the unconventional typographic codes and ultimately mining the radical 'style' of the originator to establish their own markets.

The term avant-garde, like *au courant*, has a modish ring to it, but must not be affixed like a designer fashion label on every attempt to transcend propriety – as commercial marketing departments are wont to do in their quest for the 'next big thing'. Many periodicals look radical because they adopt type and layout that connotes radicalism, but in reality this is merely a veil. Just because something looks dangerous does not mean that it is – it could be pandering to an audience that believes certain typographies and images afford a 'cool' status. A magazine that is raunchy, obscene or tasteless is not necessarily avant-garde either, unless the purpose is clearly defined. Dada, in the early part of the twentieth century, and the Underground sex press during the later part, eschewed conventional notions of taste and decorum as an integral part of their respective missions. Periodicals

that aggressively (and perhaps even dangerously) ignite rebellion with a view to challenging cultural complacency may be considered avant-garde, but not all manifestations of the avant-garde are violent.

Movements are formed around a core – an idea, ideal or ideology – and avant-garde publications serve as rallying points that reflect, through word and picture, the principles on which the respective movements are founded. Publications can be the headquarters or the expeditionary forces – the base or the outreach – of such movements. The American journal *Resistance*, for example, was a clearing house (or base) of anarchist ideology targeted exclusively at its adherents, while the Scandinavian *Social Kunst* was a compendium (or outreach) of radical political artists, aimed at a larger audience.

It is also axiomatic that members of such inherently contentious avant-garde movements as Expressionism, Dadaism and De Stijl are often at odds with one another over esoteric issues and their internecine battles are revealed in the pages of their respective publications. For example, the Dutch painter Piet Mondrian (1872–1944), who worked with only primary colours – red, yellow, blue and black – broke with the De Stijl movement, which he founded

Below from left: **Resistance**, vol.6 no.4, August 1947. Politics was a principal theme in radical periodicals of the early to mid-twentieth century. *Resistance* propagated a Communist agenda through polemical drawings and woodcuts as shown on the cover of this issue.

Social Kunst, no.8, 1932. Published by Mondes Forlag in Copenhagen, *Social Kunst* was a siphon and showcase for left-wing political imagery from Europe and America in the Thirties. The cover montage shown here is by John Heartfield.

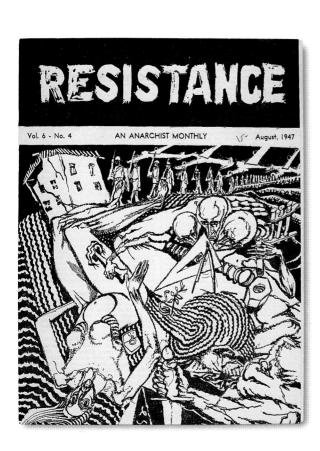

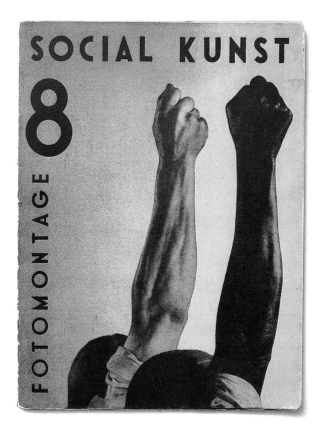

with the artist and architect Theo van Doesburg in 1917, over a disagreement concerning the latter's introduction of the diagonal. Mondrian felt that Van Doesburg had betrayed the movement's fundamental purist principles regarding the static immutability achieved through the maintenance of stable verticals and horizontals. He argued that retaining the equilibrium of the grid was the only way to find truth in plastic art. This seemingly inconsequential argument was rife with philosophical implications on the essence of art. The artists conducted their feud within the pages of journals like *De Stijl*, where they aired their views and attacked each other.

Without avant-garde periodicals, such critiques or other manifestos might not have reached targeted audiences. These periodicals served two vital functions for their movements: to signal a cultural position, through content and design, and to attract new adherents to the fold. Unlike mass-market magazines and newspapers, avant-garde publications have therefore done more than simply inform or entertain: they have influenced social or cultural action, often through provocation. Magazines like the Russian *Artists' Brigade* of the Thirties, for instance, inspired Soviet artists to use their art to promote the ideals of the continuous revolution and the German *Die International* sparked political action in the name of Communist ideology.

Some avant-gardes were, in hindsight, actually regressive yet promulgated what, in their own periods, appeared to be progressive ideas. In fact, radical movements are not always inherently good. Vanguards are suspect because they disrupt, and disruption is abhorred by keepers of the status quo. The Italian Fascists were called 'vanguardista', and promoted themselves as a cultural shock troop that assaulted antiquity, destroyed continuity and raped convention. Well and good, but their message was ultimately tyrannical, dogmatic and corrupt. The Italian Futurist movement, a cultural vanguard that was in sympathy with the Fascist Party, was truly avant-garde because its proponents reinvented poetry, art and graphic design. Yet, given its creed of cultural disruption, it actively supported oppressive Fascist policies which led to Italy's occupation by the Nazis in World War II. Today Futurist art is a revolutionary paradigm but its underlying ideology remains unsavoury, as evidenced by the scores of periodicals issued under the Futurist banner.

Many avant-gardes may resolutely represent their respective Zeitgeist but circumspection may shine a more negative light on their once viable philosophy and ideals after the era has passed into history. The Sixties hippie obsession with drugs and free love, as projected through the first psychedelic Underground paper *The Oracle*, has certainly come under fire because of the adverse psychotropic effects that were levied on a generation during the decade of peace and love. So, the goal of an avant-garde at its moment of inception is to destroy all existing value systems, and radical periodicals provide a touchstone.

However, for cultural transformations to have lasting resonance they cannot be innocuous, no matter how damaging their influence may be in the long run, so it is important to distinguish between an avant-garde and a cultural fad. Consumer society has come to accept and cheerfully anticipate the ethic known as 'forced obsolescence' – the commercially motivated, periodic alteration of form and style of goods – as a means of revitalizing activity in the market-place, but this is not to be confused with avant-gardism. A true avant-garde will not overtly appeal to mass taste, and indeed encourages *bad* taste as a means to replace the sanctified with the unholy. An avant-garde has to produce such unpleasant alternatives to the status quo that it will be unequivocally and avidly shunned by all but those few who adhere to it. An avant-garde must make noise.

Avant-gardes can be likened to gangs of cultural thugs that force their way through the safeguards of the social infrastructure and use art and the media as a means of ramming home unorthodox ideas. Twentieth-century avant-garde periodicals were more or less the apparatus of disobedience designed to rally the faithful and to offend the compliant. And in this critical mass of radical thought and deed, *design* is key. Although words are the building blocks of meaning, visual ideas can be expressed much more persuasively through the medium of graphic design (the marriage of typography, layout and image); it is a code that telegraphs intent. One might argue that radical ideas must appear vanguard to *be* vanguard. Harsh words on a tame page cannot have the same impact as a boisterous layout. The impression portrayed through design must be unsettling, if only at first, in order to provoke the reaction of readers. The design of most Dada publications produced during the early Twenties purposefully disrupted established professional norms by redirecting traditional sight and reading patterns in order to send a signal that nothing of the past, not even the most neutral or transparent of typefaces, would remain unscathed. Revolution is meaningless unless it discomfits the *ancien régime*.

Opposite: **Artists' Brigade**, no.4, 1931. Published by the Federation of Workers in Three Dimensional Arts, *Artists' Brigade* promoted artists' participation in politics, culture and agitprop. This cover features a photomontage by El Lissitzky.

Avant-gardes attack the status quo through many art forms – painting, sculpture, theatre, music, film, video, dance, poetry and even clothing. So, while periodicals are by no means their only medium, owing to the immediacy (and ephemeral nature) of magazines and newspapers they have served both as a channel for ideas and – in the spirit of Marshall McLuhan's mantra of medium as message – as the ideas themselves. The periodicals surveyed here have fulfilled these two roles with varying degrees of success, and at different levels of intensity. Some have fought existing power structures at the expense of their own freedoms (*Mother Earth*, the American magazine edited by Emma Goldman, was banned after the Americans entered World War I in 1917 and Goldman, a Russian national, was later deported back to the Soviet Union); others were able to push limits because they were not suppressed by (or did not threaten) the establishment (the Underground paper *New York Ace*, for example, engaged in left-wing rabble-rousing but managed to stay inches clear of censorship). Some were Trojan horses, designed in benign skins so as to sneak into respectable quarters (the American magazine *Evergreen Review* was professionally designed, partly to veil its charged content). Others looked as flagrantly extremist as their philosophies demanded (the Mexican magazine *El Corno Emplumado* [The Plumed Horn] exemplified the radical spectrum of erotic, Surrealist art).

Examining many of these reviews today in the light of seemingly more radical developments in new media, one might wonder what all the fuss was about. The degree of shock needed to cause outrage these days, and to disrupt the equilibrium of the body politic, has long since risen to the most absurd levels of abomination that far exceed the capacity of mere periodicals printed on paper. With all that is transmitted electronically, what is printed on paper must do a lot to make the world take notice. But this is exactly why these artefacts are so fascinating. Once upon a time print on paper could unlock passions, ignite emotions, and change the world, if only for brief moments. Here is the evidence of that power.

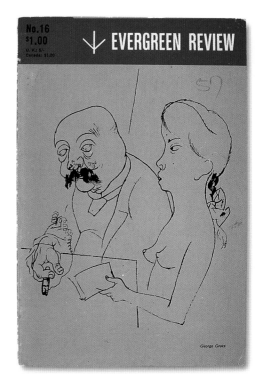

Opposite, from left:

Mother Earth, vol.9 no.6, August 1914. Edited by Emma Goldman, *Mother Earth* was an outlet for socialist ideology in the US until it was suspended in 1917 as seditious. On this cover a brush drawing by Man Ray portrays the evils of capitalism and government.

New York Ace, vol.1 no.3, 25 January 1972. *New York Ace,* edited by Rex Weiner and art directed by Steven Heller, took a jaundiced view of mainstream journalism. This absurdist cover illustration by Brad Holland critically comments on urban life.

Evergreen Review, no.16, 1960. Published by Grove Press and edited by Barney Rossett, *Evergreen Review* began in the early Sixties as an arts and literary review that published taboo writing and images. Rossett believed that George Grosz's art, as shown on this cover, was as relevant in the Sixties as it was in the Twenties.

Right: **El Corno Emplumado**, no.27, July 1968. This Mexican Surrealist review was published during the early Sixties. This cover montage of Jean Genet as a cyclops, by Robert David Cohen, represents the multinational range of avant-garde magazines.

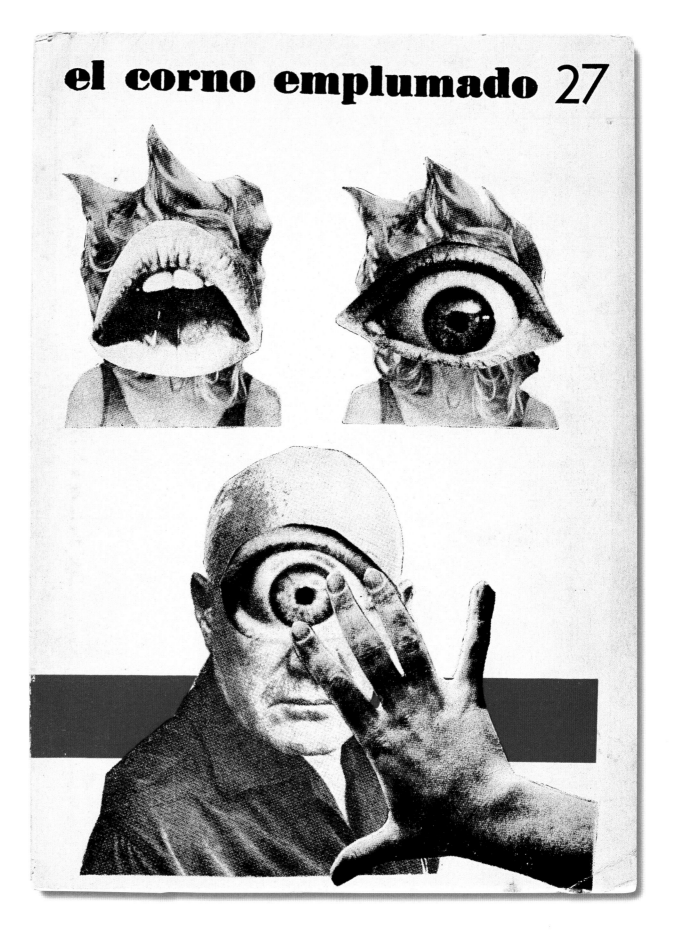

el corno emplumado 27

SO

LES

L

L'ASSIETTE AU BEURRE

N° 19 — 8 Août 1901.

—

30 Centimes.

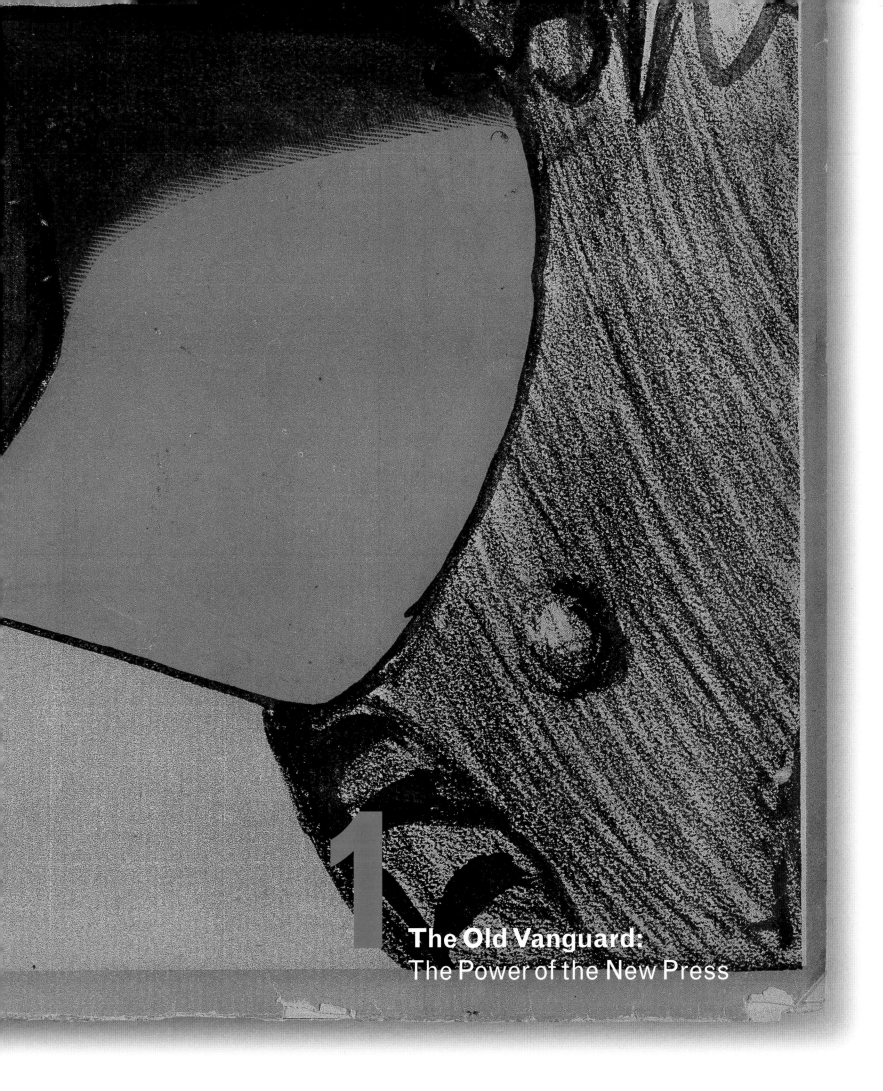

The Old Vanguard:
The Power of the New Press

When did artists, writers and editors become the vanguard of the avant-garde? Perhaps this dates back to ancient Egypt when slaves scrawled anthropomorphic caricatures of slave-masters on tiny bits of papyrus. Legend has it that these were surreptitiously passed around, and since this was unsanctioned art, dire punishment was probably meted out if it was found in their possession. If this was not the actual wellspring, then certainly Johann Gutenberg's mid-fifteenth-century invention, mechanizing the production of printing type, opened the floodgates for the future of serially produced missives, some of which indeed attacked convention and authority. By the eighteenth century the ability to print on paper in comparatively large quantities made periodical publications the most important of all new, critical media. Ultimately, by the early nineteenth century, the invention of high-speed printing presses, which had the capacity to reproduce faithful images, spawned what became an anti-establishment (or opposition) publishing genre known as the satiric (or comic) periodical.

Satiric presses emerged in France, Germany, Italy, England, Russia and the United States as the century progressed. But the most incendiary of all developed in Paris of the 1830s, where a score of biting satirical journals were published during the rise of the pseudo-republican Citizen King, Louis Philippe. The most obstreperous of

these, founded in 1831 by the illustrator Charles Philipon (1802–62), were *Le Charivari* (Disturbance) and *La Caricature*, large, tabloid-sized, letterpress-printed pictorial newspapers with black-and-white lithographic illustrations that cruelly satirized the *comédie humaine*.

Philipon employed France's most acerbic draughtsmen as commentators. Honoré Daumier, J J Grandville, and Gustave Doré, among others, used their incomparable drawing skills as weapons in an attack against the restoration of a French king who advocated a free press and republican principles but, in truth, through his corrupt reign, made a mockery of these ideals. Louis Philippe's censorious regime and obsequious parliament was at best a disappointment, and at worst a crime, to proponents of republicanism. Graphic depictions of 'Le Poire' (the Pear), a term of ridicule that demystified the corpulent monarch, created by Philipon and his colleagues were outlawed under hastily penned censorship decrees. Although these periodicals were routinely confiscated and the artists detained and imprisoned, such acts served to bolster the satirists' resolve to find ever more inventive means of challenging authority. Daumier, for instance, created thousands of iconic dissenting images – both symbolic and realistic, comic and tragic – that continue to have resonance more than a century-and-a-half after the fact.

Previous page: **L'Assiette au Beurre**, detail of no.19, 8 August 1901, cover by Thomaz Leal Da Camara.

Right: **Le Charivari**, cover of vol.16 no.1, 1 January 1847. **La Caricature**, no.15, 9 January 1834, inside page illustration by Honoré Daumier.

Published and edited by Charles Philipon, *La Caricature* and *Le Charivari* were Philipon's most daring satiric journals. They were designed by anonymous printers who followed the standard typographic style – stark simple logo and columns of grey text type – but the cartoons and caricatures were radical for their style and content. The lithographic drawings were reproduced on full pages for maximum impact.

Opposite: **Punch**, cover and inside page of vol.83 no.2144, 12 August 1882. *Punch*, the leading English satiric periodical, was not designed in a radical fashion. The typographic design inside was staid and the cartoons were the main attraction. Its ornately illustrated cover by Richard Doyle, featuring Mr Punch, was the same every week. The *Punch* style was mimicked by other English and American comic journals.

These large, tabloid-size publications had strikingly illustrated front pages (topped with bold mastheads set in a serif poster type). Inside were full pages of tightly composed, uninterrupted text adjacent to full-page lithographs, which was the conventional format for newspapers of the day. None the less, the marriage of text and pictures served as a model for opposition presses in other nations and became the archetype of modern anti-establishment rhetoric.

A decade after the first issues of *Le Charivari* and *La Caricature*, England's *Punch* was founded, in 1841, and it remained in print until recently. It was not the country's first upstart publication but it was a paradigm for what followed. Its format differed significantly from French periodicals in that it was smaller than a tabloid; its cover art has never changed, each and every issue carrying the same humorous motif with a drawing of Mr Punch, and nor has the interior with its tightly-packed type interrupted by drawings.

With *Punch*, the roots of acceptable unacceptability dug deep. Eventually *Punch* moved from a place on the fringe into its niche as a British institution. Yet during the early years, *Punch* was in competition with the more radical satirical journals from countries in which democracy had yet to get a foothold. From its inception, *Punch* was known as *The London Charivari*, its purpose being to remind those from both high and low society that they needed lessons in civility, if not morality, from time to time. *Punch* offered outspoken commentaries on despotism abroad and injustice at home. The early nineteenth century marked the infancy of the Industrial Revolution and *Punch* benefited from advances in steam-powered printing technology, yet its contributors also lambasted the deleterious impact of industrialization on society, such as the terrible living conditions of the poor, exploitation in the sweatshops, and pollution in the River Thames. However, *Punch* was comparatively moderate in its attacks against the Crown and, compared to the earlier French periodicals, was downright supportive of the monarchy. While this does not imply that the magazine or its artists were benign in their satires, it underlines the fact that England was a constitutional monarchy and its need for satiric expression as a tool of social disruption was therefore markedly different from those nations with more despotic monarchies. *Punch* none the less played a role in pushing graphic humour beyond safe conventions and gave satire one truly significant innovation.

The word 'cartoon' in the modern sense was a *Punch* coinage. During the reign of Charles I, the common phrase in England for a satiric image was 'a mad designe'. In the time of George II it was known as a 'hieroglyphic'. Throughout the golden age of the great eighteenth-century British satirists, James Gilray, William Hogarth and George Cruikshank, the term was 'caricature', and the word 'pencillings' referred to

early-nineteenth-century satiric tableaux. It was not until July 1843, however, when the first public exhibition of cartoons (or preliminary sketches for grand paintings and murals) for the ceilings and walls of the new Houses of Parliament was held, that *Punch* started its own sarcastic series of critical 'cartoons'. These parodies attacked the aesthetic indulgence of the official cartoons and gave new meaning to the old word. But *Punch* did more than merely change the terminology. These cartoons were visual *and* verbal with gag-lines – witty sayings or dialogue – that commented on the unsettling happenings in Europe at the time and the social concerns at home. *Punch* inspired other comic journals, *Fliegende Blätter* and *Kladderadatsch* in Germany, *Petit Journal pour Rire* in France, and *Life*, *Puck* and *Judge* in the United States, which were the primary, mass critical media of the nineteenth and early twentieth centuries.

By 1848, Europe was in the first of its modern political upheavals. France, for one, had rejected the monarchy in favour of a Second Republic that rekindled the spirit of social reform. Yet, within a short time, conservatives and reactionaries enabled the rise of a new empire under the rule of the despotic emperor Louis Napoleon. For the brief period before his rise to power, the press was freer to criticize the government and its officials, thus proportionally increasing the number of publications to meet demand until Napoleon instituted draconian censorship decrees that reined in such freedoms. The sands shifted once again when, in 1871, Prussia defeated France in the Franco-Prussian War and the French people showed increasing displeasure with their ruler. Succumbing to the threat of insurrection from the Commune, a proto-socialist revolutionary movement, Napoleon gave greater powers to the French Chamber, which ended his rule, ushering in the establishment of the more liberal Third Republic.

Once again, press freedom opened the door to an outpouring of illustrated magazines advocating social justice and cultural openness. Satirical periodicals with such titles as *L'Eclipse*, *Psst ...*, *Gil Blas*, *La Sourire* and *Le Mot* were outlets for witty cartoonists commentating on everything from the military to the *boulevardiers*. These satiric periodicals, however, lost some avant-garde status when transformed into bona fide mass media serving a large population rather than the few aficionados. As a safety valve for social and cultural frustrations these publications were cautionary and curative, but as popular media they ultimately became soft and stylish. None the less, French periodicals represented the state of the graphic arts for the next two decades, until the German satiric weekly *Simplicissimus* was founded in 1896, which marked a shift to modern, Expressionistic, fluid graphics and the introduction of abstraction.

Clockwise from top left:
Petit Journal pour Rire, cover of no.251, 1878. This French magazine followed the design conventions of its day as a neutral frame for ribald cartoons.

Puck, no.14, 20 December 1882. This American magazine (which also published separate editions in German and English) introduced a new phase of satiric journal. Published by Joseph Keppler and Adolph Schwarzmann, and edited by Leopold Schenck, covers and spreads were printed in rich chromolithographic colours. This cover illustration is by Friedrich Graetz.

Judge, vol.52 no.1328, 30 March 1907, cover art by Emil Flohri. *Judge*, founded by *Puck* artist James Wales, supported the Republican Party and used its stable of cartoonists to attack the Democratic candidates. Its format and graphic style were similar to *Puck*.

Le Mot, no.5, 9 January 1915, 'After the execution' issue cover by Paul Iribe. *Le Mot* was published by Paul Iribe and edited by Iribe and Jean Cocteau. A French, World War I-era satiric journal with an anti-German bias, it had a modern appearance with its lower-case logo and the airy design of the cover and interior pages.

Actually, not one but two revolutionary periodicals were introduced that year in Kaiser Wilhelm's Imperial Germany. Munich-based *Jugend* (Youth) published by Dr Georg Hirth, gave a voice – and its name – to the distinctly contemporary graphic sensibility of Jugendstil, and *Simplicissimus*, published by Albert Langen and Thomas Theodor Heine, translated the new style into a lethal form of social commentary. Both signalled a rebellion of youth against state-sanctioned Romanticism and academicism with a style that was at once decorative and polemic.

Jugendstil was the German version of a short-lived, but exuberant, pan-European cultural episode that began in the late nineteenth century and ended before the outbreak of World War I. In Paris it was known as Art Nouveau, in England as the Arts and Crafts movement, in Scotland as the Glasgow School, in Italy as Stile Liberty, in Austria as the Secession, and in Czechoslovakia as the Bohemian Secession. Each nation imbued the ostensibly decorative style with its own socio-political characteristics, but there was also a shared visual language rooted in a rejection of all things sentimental. Art Nouveau inveighed against parochial nationalistic movements while promoting the international exchange of ideas. It refused to acknowledge any distinction between the 'fine and lesser arts' and was thus both ornamental and expressive.

Art Nouveau was influenced by the simplicity of traditional Japanese design. Its practitioners swore allegiance to the natural object and cultivated a new symbolism based on ancient icons and contemporary meanings. It was a lexicon of sinuous, naturalistic, curvilinear forms and German Jugendstil combined these organic impulses with a geometric edginess. Pervasive in Jugendstil was a fantastical melancholy communicated through Teutonic wit and folkloric symbolism. Jugendstil took nourishment from William Morris's Arts and Crafts movement in England yet did not reject all industrial production outright, though it was circumspect about its immediate virtues. Jugendstil artists rejected most traditional mannerisms, especially classical typography, choosing instead to render quirky, ornamental typefaces that were harmoniously intertwined with images. One-of-a-kind brush letter forms were used on posters and advertisements, while a few mass-produced, eccentric typefaces became emblems of the era when used in publications and on posters. The professional response was mixed. Classicists objected to the quirky letter forms but commercial printers welcomed it as a means to enliven the printed page.

Exponents of Jugendstil staunchly believed that good design could change the world – a modern, idealistic view. But while it may have exerted an impact on some aspects of society, this unrealized goal was abruptly halted by World

Below from left: **Jugend**, covers of vol.4 no.2, 7 January 1899; vol.4 no.17, 22 April 1899, by Barlady; vol.4 no.20, 13 May 1899, by I R W. *Jugend* covers were unprecedented. Unlike earlier satiric and cultural journals that retained the same basic format for every issue, *Jugend*'s cover and logo designs were routinely altered to suit the style of each artist. The logos were alternately curvaceous and spiky with a wide variety of unique letter forms. Most cover illustrations, including those here, had Jugendstil mannerisms and colours; some were rendered as representational scenes and others as allegorical vignettes.

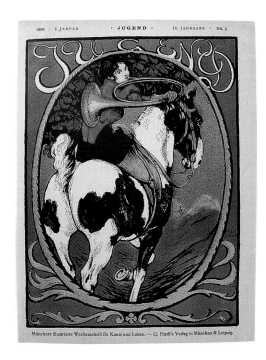

War I. Today, Jugendstil is both a stylistic reminder of rebellion against the status quo and a *passé* artefact of its times.

The principal outlet for the weekly dissemination of Jugendstil art and literature was the weekly magazine *Jugend*, published from 1896 to 1926. *Jugend*'s fanciful cover illustrations and mutating logotypes represented a stylistic rejection of the sentimental 'trash' of Wilhelmine Germany and a rebellion against entrenched, stolid artistic conventions. It replaced academic realism with fluid expression, and swapped rococo for naturalistic decoration. *Jugend* had a French influence but injected a German accent through hard-edged linearity and adherence, at least in body text, to traditional Black Letter typography (which was the standard in the Teutonic world as opposed to the Roman letter in other European countries). Page layout was dictated by the extravagance of the decorative illustrations that quite literally covered whole pages with meandering vines. While this style resulted in untold headaches for printers, whose job was to contour the type to fit the curvilinear patterns, the goal was to achieve an effect that distinguished *Jugend* from the magazines that preceded it while creating a new standard for others to follow.

Jugend was avant-garde in a broad sense but that did not prevent the magazine from having a comparatively large circulation. Georg Hirth believed that widespread acceptance of the magazine would help to purge the antiquated methods and styles from contemporary art and literature, so the cover price was held at a mere 30 pfenning (a few pence). Surprisingly, it boasted 30,000 subscribers in the first year alone, rising to over 100,000 within five more. It was, therefore, truly a mass-market publication that toed the line between the popular and the progressive. However, by the 1910s the former overcame the latter. After more than a decade of pushing back boundaries *Jugend* became an institution – and during that time Jugendstil had become outmoded as well.

Simplicissimus had a slightly longer life-span within the avant-garde because it did not base its visual content exclusively on the vicissitudes of style. Acute satire was the fuel that fired the mordant *Der Simpl* (as it was commonly known). The magazine's iconic mascot, a red bulldog with menacingly stone-cold white eyes and a broken chain hanging from its neck, eagerly waited to maul unsuspecting fools, nitwits and government buffoons with its sharp spiky teeth. As the charged graphic emblem of Germany's most trenchant satirical journal, it represented an editorial policy that enabled a cadre of artists and writers to relentlessly bite away at the ruling classes.

Der Simpl was rabidly anti-bourgeois and unrepentantly populist in its rejection of materialism and modernization.

Below from left: **Jugend**, no.35, 1896, inside page illustration by Otto Eckman; no.48, 1896, inside spread illustrations by Bruno Paul and Franken Weber. Interior page design was characterized by ornate rendering of sinuous vines and idealized beauties. The drawing was ostensibly linear, and lines curved and swayed around the page. Texts were often set in traditional Black Letter typefaces but text columns varied in width to conform to the layouts designed by the illustrators.

Right: **Jugend**, vol.4 no.18, 29 April 1899, cover art by Halmi. Covers in the Jugendstil style often extolled the virtues of ideal beauty.

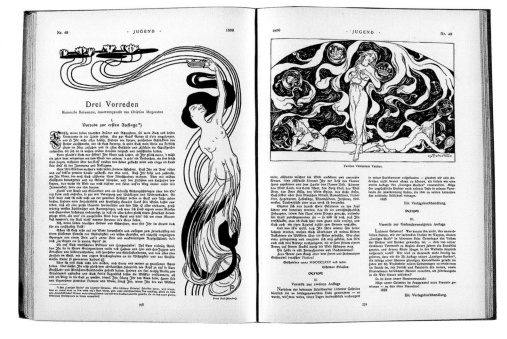

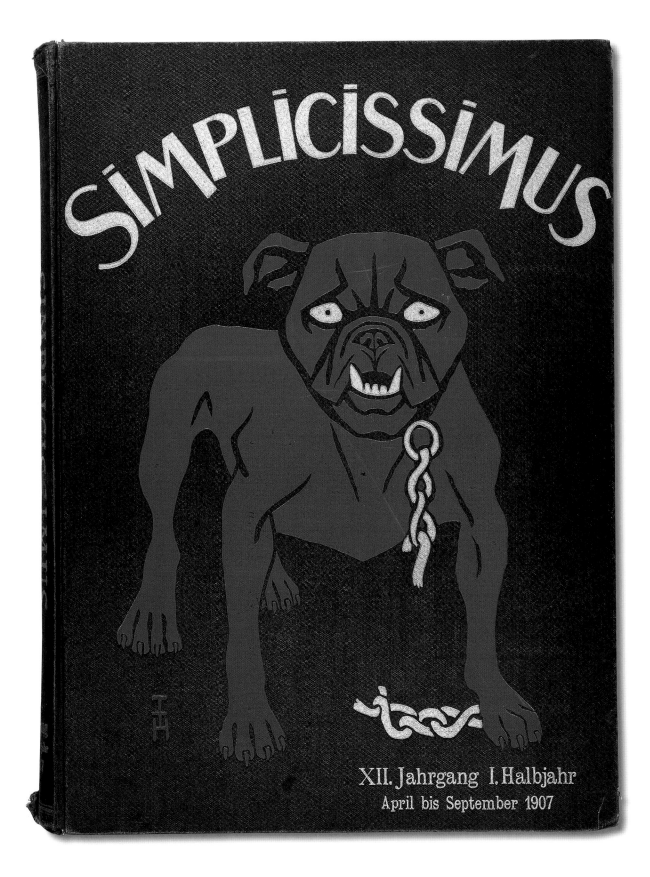

SIMPLICISSIMUS

XII. Jahrgang I. Halbjahr
April bis September 1907

It vilified the German Kaiser Wilhelm II and his ministers, as well as the Protestant clergy, military officers, government bureaucracy, urbanization and industrialization, and it lionized the peasant farmer and worker who were portrayed in the magazine's cartoons and caricatures as feisty opponents to the ruling powers, even if in reality this was an exaggerated view.

The authorities instituted stern measures to muzzle the dog, but despite attempts at censorship and frequent arrests for blasphemy against the royal court, the illustrated tabloid rarely missed a scheduled appearance. When it was confiscated by the police, a black, red and white poster, designed in 1897 by Thomas Theodor Heine, on which the bulldog was poised, warned friend and foe alike that *Der Simpl* could not be chained up for long. In fact, while bans lasted only a week or two at the most, rows of these posters hung for months at a time and undoubtedly attracted new readers to the magazine.

The power of *Der Simpl* to get under the skin and influence public opinion is implicit in its very name. This was borrowed from a fifteenth-century literary character, the puckish Simplicus Simplicissimus who acted the fool around aristocrats but, through subterfuge, tricked them into exposing their own folly. Likewise, *Der Simpl* served as an unforgiving mirror reflecting the greed, incompetence and corruption of the German monarchy, church and military.

During *Der Simpl*'s golden age, from 1896 to 1914, it published hundreds of strident political and social caricatures and cartoons attacking anything that suggested social and political malfeasance. Few other journals had such a profound influence, not only on public opinion but also on graphic style. Noted not only for its Jugendstil applications but for allowing its artists the freedom to work in any style, *Der Simpl* had an impact on everything from Plakatstil (German graphic poster style) to Expressionism. The magazine was, more importantly, one of the unrecognized forerunners of early modernism and the red bulldog exemplifies modern simplicity. Drawn in the manner of a woodcut, Heine used black paint to pick out the basic lines, leaving only the most descriptive features and a penetrating expression. The bulldog appeared in most issues of *Der Simpl*, if not on the cover then inside, making it the prototypical reductive logo, which in later incarnations was simplified even further and was as demonstrative in its day as the Nazi's swastika later in the century.

Although *Der Simpl*'s covers were not as stylistically varied as those of *Jugend* (the latter's masthead continually changed), the magazine none the less pioneered a unique, minimalist graphic sensibility – in contrast with the conventional, overly rendered cartoon images of the period – which had a quantifiable influence on other pictorial satire

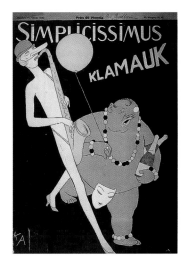

journals throughout Europe. Since artists were the main contributors to *Der Simpl*, cartoons and caricatures formed its primary content and most were given full-page display accompanied by only a caption and headline. *Der Simpl*'s stable of contributors included cartoonist Bruno Paul (1874–1968), whose woodcut-like, brutish brush-and-ink drawings were said to have influenced the later German Expressionists, and Eduard Thöny (1866–1950), who used exaggerated realism to lampoon the Junker (military aristocracy) with such beguiling subtlety that even his victims admired the work. The Norwegian émigré Olaf Gulbransson (1873–1958) was a master of eloquent, though biting, linearity that captured the most buffoonish expressions and Rudolph Wilke (1873–1909) managed to convey the humorous character of both Junker and common man in sardonic situations.

Der Simpl vehemently criticized the status quo until the advent of World War I when it was conscripted as a tool of patriotic propaganda, which demanded unquestioning loyalty to the Kaiser. Although somewhat neutered in its nationalist incarnation, *Der Simpl* directed its scorn towards the enemy, proving that humour could be effectively used for nefarious purposes. But its role as vanguard was surely gone for ever. During the Twenties and early Thirties, *Der Simpl* resumed a critical stance, attacking Italian Fascism and the emergence of first German paramilitary right-wing militias, the Freikorps, and later Nazism, but it was crippled from its wartime experience. One significant change was that the *Volk* were no longer portrayed as heroes – peasant-class romanticism was replaced by a cynicism that would lead some of its younger contributors to Dadaism. The Kaiser had abdicated prior to German surrender to the Allies, and the monarch was replaced by that doomed democratic experiment, the Weimar Republic, but the magazine's contributors failed to find a focus during this uncertain time. *Der Simpl* relinquished its avant-garde status to the Expressionist and Dada periodicals of the Twenties but remained a cautious social watchdog until 1933 when the Nazis came to power and made it their lapdog. It ultimately ceased publication in 1944 and then briefly appeared, in name only, many years later.

Given the great legacy of French satiric periodicals during the nineteenth century it is not surprising that France entered the twentieth century with a pioneering journal that both borrowed from, and built on, the tradition established by *Der Simpl*. Because France's transition into an industrial society, and its economic situation, was similar to that of Germany and England at this time, the distinction between the haves and have-nots was equally pronounced. France, however, had long trailed these other nations in finding solutions for poverty. The governmental infrastructure was

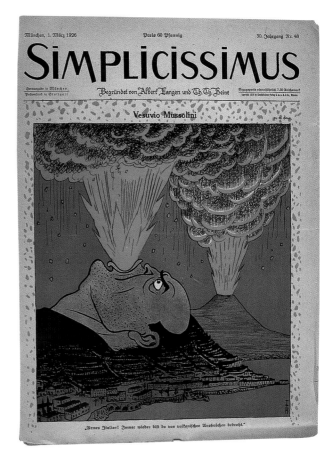

Right: **Simplicissimus**, no.48, 1 March 1926, cover art by Thomas Theodor Heine; inside page illustration by Wilhelm Schulz. *Simplicissimus*'s interior typography was not radical, but the layouts broke with tradition. Images were framed by generous amounts of white space, and covers, such as Heine's attack on Benito Mussolini, were free of intrusive headlines.

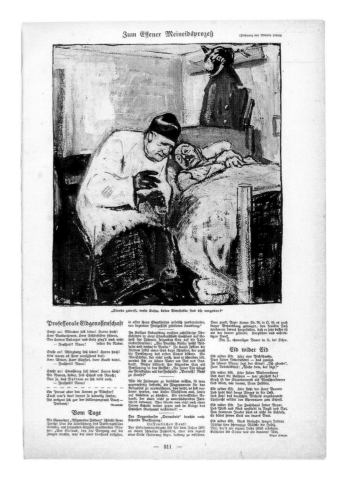

shockingly primitive, hampered by ineptitude and corruption. Logically, this state of affairs had become a recurring critical theme in popular graphics – a stark reminder of capitalism's inherent paradox. As Ralph Shikes comments in his book *The Indignant Eye*, 'Daumier's dream of a democratic France, responsive to the will and the needs of the people, was still far from fulfilment.'[1] On another front, the national crisis generated by the Dreyfus Affair, which pitted right-wing nationalists against left-wing republicans, seemed to excerbate the threat to the Republic by yet another coalition of military-Church-aristocracy and clericalism and militarism were under attack. Moreover the state apparatus, instead of being an instrument of the people, was a huge bureaucratic machine dominated by '*l'assiette au beurre*' – the butter dish – the nice, fat job-holders with the prerogative of dispensing favours for a price.

At this time Paris was also emerging as the art capital of the world. The *belle époque* was in full swing. Artists were streaming into the city from Europe and membership of ad hoc Salons des Indépendants, unofficial gatherings of artists in bars, cafés and galleries, was growing rapidly. Many of the socially conscious artists turned to anarchism as a way of transcending the insularity of bohemianism and through which to work off their political frustrations. They

often used cartoons as a weapon in their struggle and, therefore, sought outlets that extended their influence beyond the hermetic salons and ateliers. It was thus propitious (particularly since there were more starving artists in Paris than sources of publication) that in 1901 Samuel Schwarz founded a satirical weekly, aptly titled *L'Assiette au Beurre*, expressly to attack those bureaucrats and functionaries who lived off the fat of the population.

The journal provided a matchless opportunity for international artists of talent and passion to demonstrate their unique styles and viewpoints. It was a virulent, highly innovative, artistic publication whose professed mission as the overseer of social foible and immoral excess was successfully carried out over the next twelve years. *L'Assiette* not only served as a political weapon; it also helped to shoot many artists to prominence.

L'Assiette au Beurre was loosely based on *Der Simpl* and *Jugend*, with full-page drawings – mini posters, actually – as the main content. Text was minimal, if used at all. Art Nouveau was the predominant graphic style although the more decorative aspects were subservient to the caustic polemical ideas. And Art Nouveau was not the only style that was featured. In addition, representational rendering, devoid of stylistic flourishes, was also effectively employed as a

Below: **L'Assiette au Beurre**, no.42, 18 January 1902, cover by Wieluc; no.254, 10 February 1906, inside spread illustration by Gabriele Galantara. *L'Assiette*, which was published and edited by Samuel Schwarz, conformed to the *Jugend* model of changing its cover format and logo on every issue. Sometimes the logo, which traditionally was placed at the top of the cover, would appear in the middle or bottom of the page. Like *Simplicissimus*, *L'Assiette*'s artists took every opportunity to address current issues, such as the dangers of automobile racing and the failure of government bureaucracy.

LE RÉVEIL

polemical method. Paradoxically, Henri de Toulouse-Lautrec (1864–1901), whose poster style inspired considerable mimicry among many of the artists, was refused admittance to the ranks of *L'Assiette*'s contributors because his art was deemed too superficial. *L'Assiette* exemplified a holy marriage between draughtsmanship and the conception of ideas, and its editors believed that the cartoon medium was too volatile to be entrusted to mere illuminators or second-rate stylists.

The mastery of line, expert use of lights and darks, and subtle composition were all components of the socio-political message. Since, like *Der Simpl*, the main content of *L'Assiette* was visual, full-page drawings were accompanied by witty titles and pithy captions. The small tabloid format

(31 x 24 cm, 12 $^1/_4$ x 9 $^1/_2$ in.) offered artists room to breathe while experimenting with various media, including woodcut, pen and ink, and lithographic crayon. *L'Assiette* was published weekly; its issues were based on single themes that scrutinized specific events or international personalities, such as František Kupka's (1871–1957) satiric trilogy devoted to 'Money', 'Peace' and 'Religion'. Usually a single artist was responsible for all the artwork in any one issue – approximately sixteen large-scale drawings (some reproduced in two or three colours). At various times groups of contributors were invited to tackle a particular *bête noire*, including the faulty judicial system, the hypocritical hierarchy of the Catholic Church or the inept medical

profession. The most memorable single issues of *L'Assiette* are those executed by artists with fervent biases, such as Miklos Vadasz on homosexuality, Juan Gris on suicide, and René-George-Hermann Paul on Lourdes, the religious retreat which he believed exploited atavistic superstitions.

Some graphic commentaries nibbled rather than took deep bites, such as those aimed at snobs, cafés, sports, high fashion, automobiles and technology. A curiously provocative issue entitled 'Le Lit' (the bed) was devoted to the sleeping habits of various social groups – from rich to poor, as well as married couples, prostitutes and prisoners. Similarly, new phenomena came under scrutiny: another issue, entitled 'A Noulespace!', took a satiric look at a new invention called the

flying machine. In a similar vein, 'Predications' was a futuristic view of the human condition by Auguste Jean-Baptiste Roubille. Another special issue was devoted to the second coming of Jesus Christ, this time resurrected into the 'modern' *fin de siècle* world: it speculates on how the Son of God was repulsed by many deeds (i.e., those of organized religion) performed in his name. The pre-Cubist contributions of Juan Gris (1887–1927) revealed his fascination with geometric formulations, predating his later experimental canvases. Félix-Edouard Vallotton's (1865–1925) special issue of original lithographs, entitled *Crimes et Châtiments* (Crimes and Punishments), printed on heavy paper, in which each original stone lithograph is given an

Below: **L'Assiette au Beurre**, no.46, 1 March 1902, cover and inside page illustration by Félix-Edouard Vallotton. Vallotton's graphics are simplified forms that defy a general stylistic categorization, but they are strident in their primitive simplicity.

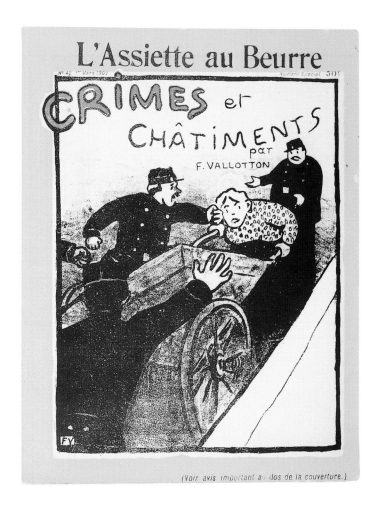

unprecedented single side of the page, aptly represents the cruelty of France's criminal system as well as documenting the punishments meted out by clergy and parents on children and adults.

L'Assiette's contributors refused to accept sacred cows in their editorial pasture. No official was so far above the fray that he could not be pilloried. Thomaz Leal Da Camara's issue entitled 'Les Souverains' (The Sovereigns) was complete with caricatures of the world's leading monarchs – a masterpiece of physical mockery. And no friendly or belligerent nation was beyond range of satiric ordinance either: England, France's historic enemy, was periodically attacked through caricatures of its leaders and farcical tableaux for what the editors of L'Assiette described as heinous foreign policies. The most notable of these was an issue illustrated by Jean Veber devoted to the establishment of the first concentration camps for the imprisonment of Dutch South African civilians and combatants during the Boer War. L'Assiette's few central European artists kept a watchful eye on the machinations of the Austro-Hungarian emperor and condemned his thirst for European dominance, while closer to home, the abusive treatment of black Africans in French colonies was also abhorred.

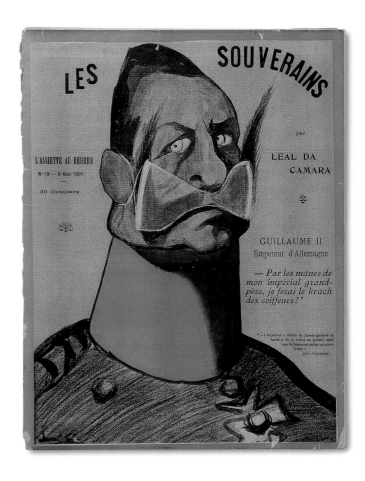

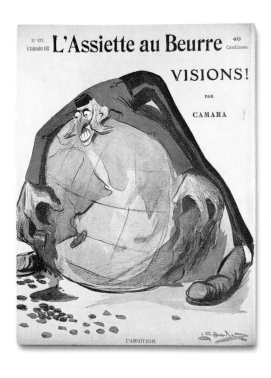

Particular rancour was reserved for la Belle France herself. For one special issue a group of *L'Assiette*'s contributors brought their journalistic fervour and critical zeal to bear on a tragic 'accidental' explosion at a gunpowder factory in Issy-les-Moulineaux where hundreds of workers were killed owing to inadequate safety measures. Another exposé targeted a scandal involving a dairy company that knowingly distributed sour milk throughout Paris, resulting in fatalities among young children. Some of *L'Assiette*'s sharpest barbs and venomous graphic commentaries were reserved for French Papists.

Not only was *L'Assiette* a hive of anti-establishment activity; it was also a venue where artists could graphically experiment before moving on to more avant-garde realms. In fact, many of its leading contributors eventually stopped producing satirical work in order to become painters in the modern movements of the day, including Cubists such as Juan Gris, Nabis such as Félix-Edouard Vallotton, Impressionists such as Kees Van Dongen and Jacques Villon, the Fauvist Louis Marcoussis, and the Orphist František Kupka. Other contributors pursued more profitable commercial art, such as poster and book illustration; these included Leonetto Cappiello, whose posters were highly prized collectables, and Charles-Lucien Léandre and Léon-

Adolphe Willette whose poster styles captured the excitement of Parisian night life. Still other distinguished contributors, Théophile Alexandre Steinlen, Caran D'Ache (Emmanuel Poiré) and Albert Robida, were admired for their political cartoons and social commentaries.

Inevitably, *L'Assiette* suffered censorship and confiscation at the hands of the authorities, often acting arbitrarily and without legal warrant. One issue, entitled 'Les Cafés Concerts', was subjected to the scrutiny of an ethics committee that stamped each acceptable drawing with 'Vise par Le Censor' (Passed by the Censor). A frequent *L'Assiette* contributor, Aristide Delannoy, was arrested, sentenced to a year in jail and fined 3,000 francs for depicting General d'Amade, the military occupier of Morocco, as a butcher with bloodstained apron. The same artist was later threatened with imprisonment when he visually attacked the French leaders Briande and Clemenceau. Minor witch-hunts were practised with *L'Assiette* as the target and yet the efforts at restraint often backfired, resulting in greater publicity and sales.

While *L'Assiette* supported the downtrodden, it courted the middle class as its primary readership and was priced accordingly. None the less, this did not undercut its success as a vanguard of anti-establishment opposition. It was

defiantly polemical and served as a rallying point for the anti-bourgeoisie and anti-reactionaries.

Europe at the turn of the century – before the ravages of modern world war forever altered the political and cultural landscape – was the place where the practice of art was most extreme. Here the superficiality of the *belle époque* was pitted against great compassion for mankind and outrage towards inhumanity, as expressed through painting and graphic commentary. *L'Assiette au Beurre* made an impact on a whole generation and, after it ceased publication in 1911, its spirit lived on in such satiric journals as *Le Mot*, edited by Jean Cocteau, and *Le Témoin*, edited by Paul Iribe.

Simplicissimus and *L'Assiette au Beurre* were the inspirations for Vienna's leading satirical journal, *Die Muskete*, which was founded in 1906, some years after these seminal magazines had made their respective impacts on art and politics. While *Die Muskete* provided an outlet for Austrian youth, it did not vociferously oppose Austro-Hungarian Emperor Franz Josef and only attacked the military in what one critic called the 'friendliest possible way'. Since humour was a vent for loyalists, the periodical was generally acceptable. But Austria did indeed have one *fin de siècle* periodical that challenged accepted cultural norms and used Jugendstil as its graphic language of opposition. *Ver Sacrum: Organ der Vereinigung Bildender Künstler Österreichs* (Sacred Spring: Organ of the Visual Artists of Austria) was the voice of the Vienna Secession movement (the name 'Secession' was coined by Georg Hirth) of artists who, in 1894, under the leadership of painter and graphic artist Gustav Klimt (1862–1918) withdrew from the venerable Künstlerhaus, the established arts institute, in protest over its biased selection criteria.

Ver Sacrum was more akin to *Jugend* than to *Simplicissimus*, though its very opposition to convention imbued it with political undertones. But whereas *Jugend* aspired to a large circulation, *Ver Sacrum*'s ambitions were decidedly more modest. In fact, it modelled itself to some extent on Germany's then leading art journal, *Pan*, a quarterly published between 1895 and 1900 whose circulation barely rose above 1,500. *Pan* was the voice of *demi-monde* Berlin, notably the patrons of a wine shop called Zum schwarzen Ferkel (The Black Piglet), which included August Strindberg (1849–1912) and Edvard Munch (1863–1944), and yet, oddly, it was more conservative than *Jugend* or *Ver Sacrum* and in fact regarded the avant-garde as undesirable. An editorial declared that the aim of this arts review was not to radically disrupt cultural politics but rather to cultivate art as an organic concept embracing the whole realm of artistic beauty.

Ver Sacrum also fervently promoted an Austrian national art. The magazine's editors did not seek out a large audience, yet none the less wanted to play a significant role on the world stage. The journal's title was taken from a poem of the same

Below: **Pan**, no.5, 1896, with cover art by Franz Stuck. *Pan*'s artists were moderate radicals proffering progress in the arts while retaining links to tradition. *Pan* was published by Paul Cassirer and edited by O J Bierbaum and Julius Meier-Graefe.

Opposite, clockwise from top left: **Ver Sacrum**, covers of vol.2 no.3, 1899, artist unknown; vol.2 no.5, 1899, by Alfred Roller; vol.1 no.3, 1898, by Gustav Klimt; vol.2 no.4, 1899, by Koloman Moser. Published by Verlag Von E A Seemann, *Ver Sacrum* was not a satiric journal like *Simplicissimus* or *L'Assiette*, and it was more arcane in its artistic leanings than *Jugend*, but it was the voice and visual manifestation of the Vienna Secession. This square-format magazine introduced the most radical typefaces and graphics of the era, as shown in these covers.

name that celebrates the 'sacred springtime' of Roman civilization, the last verse of which proclaims, 'You are the seed of a new world / that is the sacred springtime that God wills.'[2] This was the mantra of the young artists of the Secession as they revolted against Austrian culture and Vienna's city fathers by establishing a new standard of art outside the framework of academic institutions in its own Secession Gallery and through its publications. The charge for a new art was made in the magazine's first editorial in 1898: 'We intend to declare war on inactive muddling, Byzantine rigidity, and all lack of taste ... Our aim is to awaken, encourage and propagate the artistic perception of our time. We want an art that knows no servility to foreigners, but no fear or hatred of them either ... We know no difference between "great art" and "intimate art", between art for the rich and art for the poor. Art is the property of all ... [We] have dedicated ourselves, with our whole power and future hopes, with everything that we are, to the SACRED SPRINGTIME.'[3]

Before the appearance of *Ver Sacrum* in 1898 Austrian artists had no magazine to call their own because the *fin de siècle* 'art wars' took place in Munich, London, Paris and St Petersburg rather than in Vienna. Later the same year an unprecedented building was constructed with an emblematic golden dome that shone like the sun over the Viennese

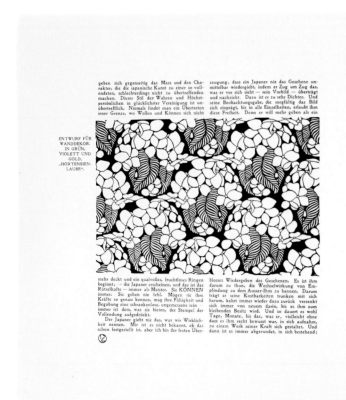

streets. This gallery became the icon and wellspring of new painting and sculpture, not the least of which was the controversial work of the Secession movement's leader, Gustav Klimt, whose very presence made the critical establishment apoplectic. The magazine, which represented the aims of a new movement, was produced without funding from patrons, although for the second year of its existence a legitimate publishing firm, E A Seemann in Leipzig, footed the bill.

The first issue of *Ver Sacrum* challenged convention with its unconventional, square format that allowed enough image space for the artists to strut their wares. One of the journal's leading contributors, Ludwig Hevesi (1842–1910), wrote of the launch number: 'Take a look at the first born of this new art periodical, and even before you see inside you will notice that this time the artist knows what he wants. You can see it from the very format. The linen paper of the cover, the light ochre of the background with its powerful, yet compatible red print, the colours alone, and in addition the mastery with which the picture and type, empty and full surfaces are combined.'[4]

Subsequent issues, including 'Founder's editions' (during the first and second years) and supplements to these editions, were equally stunning, some covers printed in iridescent metallic colours and with interior slipsheets on transparent paper. The covers by the Secession's leading stylists, Klimt, Alfred Roller (1864–1935), Rudolf von Ottenfeld (1856–1913), and Koloman Moser (1868–1918), may be prosaic by today's standards but their expressive naturalism was unique in its day and *Ver Sacrum* thus established a standard for the avant-garde graphic language. While categorized under the broad heading of Jugendstil, the magazine distinguished itself from *Jugend* with pages that were cleaner, less decorative and more rationally composed on a grid.

Ver Sacrum was published from an office in the Secession building. It was jointly edited by a constantly changing group of Austrian artists, designers and architects, notably Josef Hoffmann, Koloman Moser, Alfred Roller, J M Olbrich and Gustav Klimt. Although it published writing by Rainer Maria Rilke and Hugo von Hofmannsthal, among the leading Austrian poets and critics, it was always in need of a skilled literary editor. Yet those intimately involved were less interested in the literary than in the art side of the publication. *Ver Sacrum* was a proving ground for visual experimentation often before it reached the walls of the Secession Gallery, which separated it even further from *Der Simpl* and *Jugend* because these two journals were not affiliated with an organized art movement. Moser, for example, apparently felt more comfortable testing the boundaries of his graphic work in the magazine than

exhibiting the same work in public, perhaps fearing the harsh, derisive critical response that Klimt received for his purposeful eroticism on so many occasions. While the first two years were more or less devoted to promoting its experiments, from 1900 the magazine concentrated on publicizing Secession exhibitions and the remaining issues contained a large number of documentary photographs of these exhibitions.

With the notable exception of the English artist Aubrey Beardsley (1872–1898), whom the magazine's principals celebrated as an early inspiration, *Ver Sacrum* included few foreign artists in its pages. Its first duty was to help native artists and, while the magazine was not oblivious to those of other European nations who expressed the spirit of the new art, its job was to break the hold on culture of traditionalists, conservatives and reactionaries in its midst. During the six years that it continued to publish, *Ver Sacrum* did not reach anywhere near as large an audience as *Jugend* or *Der Simpl* but within its own orbit it successfully exposed the work of young Austrian artists and new ideas. Unlike the other two magazines, which ostensibly published cartoons and caricatures, *Ver Sacrum* vociferously pushed the relationship between 'high' art and industrial design, a marriage that became known as the *Gesamtkunstwerk* (total work of art). This certainly dominated the theory and practice of twentieth-century modernism and is frequently addressed in subsequent periodicals.

Ver Sacrum was none the less criticized for its idealism. In 1899 it was parodied in a faux issue entitled *Quer Sacrum: Organ der Vereinigung Bildender Künstler Irrlands* (Sacred Perversity: Organ of the Visual Artists of Crazyland) for its cultist adherence to an aesthetic that was viewed by critics as an orgy of nymphets and satyrs. Indeed, such obsessions with erotic naturalism gave the Sacred Springtime theme a dubious overlay, yet because the magazine was ahead of its time it was vulnerable to the vicissitudes of fashion. In 1903, as Jugendstil lost its anti-establishment lustre, and the Vienna Secession had achieved its desired effect on Viennese culture, *Ver Sacrum* ceased publication.

The magazines that formed this pre-modern vanguard each left an imprint on the nature of periodical publishing. But, most importantly, they paved the way for a long line of upstart titles to express opposition views through the print medium. While Gutenberg's printing technology of the fifteenth century made it possible for avant-garde expression to exist, the publications of the late nineteenth and early twentieth centuries inspired the increased stockpiling of newsprint and type as weapons in the war against complacency.

Opposite: **Ver Sacrum**, vol.2 no.4, 1899, inside page and spread illustrations by Koloman Moser. Pages for *Ver Sacrum* were designed with maximum ornament and yet maximum economy as well. Every piece was in its place and nothing was superfluous. Its artists applied the most modern principles of page design and ornament (or anti-ornament) of the day.

2

Futurism and its Malcontents:
A Revolution in Print

Italian Futurism was the perfect vehicle for a movement that advanced cultural renewal through technology and social purification through war. The name had a better cadence than other tongue-twisting terms like Dynamism and Electricism and greater resonance as an anti-bourgeois, forward-thinking ideology. Futurism radically altered art's traditional form and function and, true to its goal of transforming artistic activity, sent the old European art establishment into a tailspin. Futurists argued that art could no longer remain aloof from the social and political forces that forged it, and as civilization marched towards world war, this new movement refused to hide behind the romantic stereotypes of halcyon times. Art was a weapon in the war against stasis, and Futurism, and the disruptive army that promoted it, unhinged the tranquil traditionalism of an obstinate bourgeoisie.

Futurism, Futurista, Futurismus – repeated over and over as a battle cry – was the foe of nostalgia, the enemy of reason and the opponent of heritage. Futurism was the high-octane fuel that propelled a new aesthetic order. Futurism venerated technology and its offspring, speed. Filippo T Marinetti's (1876–1944) 'First Futurist Manifesto', published in 1909 in, paradoxically, the most respected Parisian newspaper, *Le Figaro*, was a paean to progress and a cry for vehemence – the first of many calls to arms that recruited art and artists into the service of cultural politics.

Futurist manifestos were written in heated prose, set in bombastic type that exploded on the printed page, and published as incendiary broadsides and periodicals throughout the first half of the twentieth century. Marinetti, a rebellious young poet, playwright and founder of the movement, accused a somnambulant culture mired in antiquated classicism of stultifying progress. At the age of thirty-three he was a rabble-rousing missionary poised to lead with bravado and hyperbole. His 'First Futurist Manifesto' was a declaration of independence *and* war, as the following extract from the original eleven-point proclamation attests:

- *Courage, audacity and revolt will be essential elements of our poetry.*
- *We affirm that the world's magnificence has been enriched by a new beauty: the beauty of speed. A racing car whose hood is adorned with great pipes, like serpents of explosive breath – a roaring car that seems to ride on grapeshot is more beautiful than the Victory of Samothrace.*
- *We will glorify war – the world's only hygiene – militarism, patriotism, the destructive gesture of freedom-bringers, beautiful ideas worth dying for and scorn for woman.*
- *We will destroy the museums, libraries, academies of every kind, will fight moralism, feminism, every opportunistic or utilitarian cowardice.*[1]

The 'First Futurist Manifesto' was typographically lacklustre compared to later proclamations but none the less prefigured the anti-bourgeois revolution of Italian Fascism and its leader Benito Mussolini. Its creator Marinetti became a fervent supporter of Mussolini who embraced him in return as a valued propagandist. After its release in *Le Figaro*, the manifesto was published in Italy as a four-page pamphlet, the first of hundreds of such manifestos and periodicals.

However, the first proto-Futurist periodical pre-dates Marinetti's seminal call to arms. *Poesia*, founded by Marinetti and published in ten numbers from 1905 to 1909, had its headquarters in his expansive apartment in Milan, which during these years became a cultural epicentre for new ideas permeating Italian literature. From the outset, however, the publication did not have a particularly Futurist appearance. Its cover was illustrated by Alberto Martini (1876–1954) in a Novocento or symbolist style. An ornate metaphorical illustration appeared on every issue so that, except for the change in background colour, each number looked the same inside and out. *Poesia*'s masthead was rendered in a late-nineteenth-century Art Nouveau (or Stile Liberty) style of lettering rather than given a twentieth-century Futurist typographic treatment. The 1909 edition of *Poesia*, in which the 'First Futurist Manifesto'

was republished, was also subject to the graphic styles of the past with its morose cover design and conservative interior typography.

Poesia's editorial focus was limited to literature: new poetry and prose from France, with some offerings from Europe and the United States, as well as Marinetti's prolific musings. Eventually Marinetti's emphasis shifted from free-verse poetics to turbulent Futuristic word-play which reflected his intoxication with speed and automobiles. In publishing this, *Poesia* was certainly in the vanguard, but was quickly overtaken by a frenetic spate of documents and periodicals mostly edited by Marinetti and devoted to Futurist action, aesthetics and intervention.

One of the few periodicals that Marinetti did not directly influence or dictate – at least in the beginning – was another Futurist journal, *Lacerba*. It was published in Florence from 1913 to 1915 and edited by Giovanni Papini (1881–1956) and Ardengo Soffici (1879–1964). 'The birth of *Lacerba* was an act of liberation,'[2] according to Soffici. And *Lacerba* was, certainly from the tone of its first editorial, conceived to be every bit as aggressive as Marinetti's missives in attacking and destabilizing the cultural elite, but followed its own path towards this goal. Soffici, for instance, embraced Cubism and the Parisian avant-garde while initially opposing Futurist painting. His eventual

Below from left: **Lacerba**, covers of vol.1 no.1, 1 January 1913; vol.2 no.1, 1 January 1914. When *Lacerba*, published and edited by Giovanni Papini and Ardengo Soffici, began publishing in 1913 it had not yet established the look of a radical Futurist periodical. Even a year later when its designer, Soffici, changed the logo to a bold slab-serif typeface it retained the traditional appearance of a conventional magazine.

rapprochement with the Futurists served to give *Lacerba* a louder voice in an Italian art world that was on the verge of being released from slavish ties to its classical past.

Lacerba's mission was cultural disruption and every artistic weapon was employed to this end. 'Since their aim was to shock, to awaken, and invigorate the minds and sense of their readers,' states historian Christine Poggi, '*Lacerba*'s writers adopted the technique of the *stroncatura* or savage critique.'[3] In a spirit of rebellion and absurdity, the review was replete with sarcastic essays that condemned humanitarianism and defended criminals, as well as other outrages against civility. Yet the appearance of the periodical was ironically deceptive. Soffici chose a classical Etruscan typeface for the masthead of the first year's issues, presumably to be irritatingly ambiguous to prospective readers, but also because it symbolized his Tuscan roots. Indeed the title itself, which suggests the sourness of unripe fruit (acerba or L'acerba translates as 'unripe'), indicates the bad taste that its editors hoped to leave behind; it also translates as the equally antagonistic terms, 'laceration' and 'rupture'.

Like a naughty child, Papini relished publishing scatological humour and was sued by the government for offending public morals. The Church forbade supplicants to read the magazine. But, owing to this sacrilegiously confrontational attitude, *Lacerba* reaped considerable financial reward from an avid following – even those not enmeshed in the avant-garde bought the publication on a regular basis. Its popularity made it a valuable channel for Futurist aims, which proved beneficial to Soffici and Papini. Without relinquishing complete editorial control, they allowed *Lacerba* to become the principal Florentine outlet for Futurist manifestos, combative articles and diatribes written for public demonstrations. In the second year, the typographic scheme changed as well; the Etruscan letters gave way to a bolder slab-serif, poster-like wood type that had found currency in the emerging Futurist typographic lexicon.

The forum which *Lacerba*'s editors created to promote their aesthetic and political ideals stimulated a new Italian culture through support of modern art while advocating nationalist, militarist and proto-Fascist social policy. Papini and Soffici stood for a generation of young intellectuals and artists who were angry over Italy's lack of power and a viable economy, as well as the government's inability to promise social advancement to the most gifted Italians. *Lacerba* further embodied a so-called 'interventionism' current in Italian, and later in European, politics: it advocated that Italy intervene in the war on the side of France and England against Austria because that country held Italian territory. So, from 1914 to 1915, the period of

Italy's neutrality, *Lacerba* devoted pages to a combination of patriotic and anti-Austrian agitation. It ultimately ceased publication when Italy entered the conflict and its interventionist role was finally fulfilled.

Before its demise, however, many of *Lacerba*'s pages were dedicated for a brief period to Marinetti's vision. This opportunistic alliance only lasted a little over a year owing to both personal and philosophical disagreements about the process and function of art – as well as differences of opinion between Soffici and Marinetti. None the less Soffici formally integrated Futurism's dynamism into his own Cubist-inspired collages. After ceasing publication in 1915, *Lacerba* was supplanted by other tabloid and newspaper-sized Futurist publications throughout Italy, and in Florence by *L'Italia Futurista*, which did not have the same visual bravado as many other published material in its genre.

If Futurism had accomplished nothing else but a profound shift away from an antiquated emphasis on central-axis composition to dynamic asymmetrical and otherwise sculptural typographic images, it would have made a lasting contribution to written and verbal language. Marinetti was the force behind an innovative typographical scheme that sought to overcome anachronistic vocabularies through the introduction of onomatopoeic word-play and typographic distortion. On 11 May 1912 he published the 'Technical Manifesto of Futurist Literature' (and three months later a supplement) in which he outlined the visual principles of Futurist poetry – as well as voicing his disgust with accepted notions of intelligence. The goal was to recast written and spoken language by eliminating conventional grammar and syntax, and this was manifest in the invention of his most emblematic visual/verbal poetic form, *Parole in Libertà* (Words in Freedom), which he created specifically to express notions of speed through a compositional economy of means. Non-essential verbiage such as adjectives and adverbs was rejected as well as punctuation. Verbs and nouns were exaggerated, repeated and forced to collide through madcap typographical compositions that quite literally flew around the page. The combination of onomatopoeic phrases and expressive typography effectively simulated the sounds of both street and machine, underscoring the cacophonous confluence of industrial sensations in the material world.

With the rejection of traditional alignment and standard juxtaposition of words and phonemes, Marinetti and other Futurists, notably Francesco Cangiullo (1884–1977), Paolo Buzzi (1874–1956) and Giacomo Balla (1871–1958), published typographical manifestations that reflected the sensations of mechanical progress and introduced sound to the written word. In 1914, the initially stolid pages of *Lacerba* were rattled by typographic bedlam

Opposite, from left: **Zang Tumb Tumb**, 1914, published by Edizioni Futuriste di 'Poesia', written by and with cover design by F T Marinetti. The book *Zang Tumb Tumb* is an account of the battle of Adrianopolis (Turkey) in 1912, in which Marinetti volunteered as a Futurist soldier. The sound of grenades and bullets is represented through onomatopoeias and shifts in typefaces of various sizes and styles.

Parole in Libertà, prospectus for *I paroliberi Futuristi*, 11 February 1915, cover typography and poetry by Paolo Buzzi, Francesco Cangiullo and Corrado Govoni; inside page illustration by Paolo Buzzi. Prior to *Parole in Libertà*, F T Marinetti published Futurist poetics in various publications. Published by Direzione del Movimento Futurista and edited by Marinetti, this publication embodies his Futurist language in the theory of simultaneity, where type is used to represent numerous sensations, such as motion and sound, at once. Given the scarcity of paper at this time the publication was printed on different sized sheets at different printers. The pages shown are from two different copies of the same issue.

when Marinetti's manifestos on poetry appeared in the journal. The same year he published a milestone book, *Zang Tumb Tumb*, which further illustrated the concept of 'words in freedom'. Issued by *Poesia*'s publishing arm, the book was an account of the battle of Adrianopolis (Turkey) of 1912 for which the author volunteered as a 'Futurist-soldier'. Poetic and literary simulations of grenade blasts and machine gun fire are graphically depicted through typographic 'illustrations' accomplished by setting different typefaces, some hand-lettered, in various sizes and in jarring juxtapositions. The text also featured a surfeit of onomatopoeias in order to express the variety of battle noises. A seminal document in terms of Futurism's formal attributes, the book further underscored one of the movement's key guiding principles: glorification of war as a cleansing apparatus.

Yet the most significant of Futurist documents for its overwhelming audacity as a visual/textual undermining of convention was released a year later, on 11 February 1915. *Parole in Libertà*, published by Direzione del Movimento Futurista in Milan, was a mini-tabloid-sized 'advertisement' for *I paroliberi Futuristi*, a series of Futurist manifestos that were being issued on a regular basis. Although it is not a periodical *per se*, its newspaper format is indicative of the Futurist interest in mass communication. The contents are examples of

'words in freedom' by four Futurist writers including Marinetti, whose explosive work 'Montagne + Vallate + Strade + Joffre' was based on Marshal Joffre's 1915 visit to the front lines after the bloody battle of the Marne. Also included was a poem by Francesco Cangiullo, a typographic simulation of an underwater scene by Corrado Govoni, and a typographic image of an aerial bombardment complete with airship by Paolo Buzzi.

Not all Marinetti's manifestos were typeset with such exuberance, but his 'words in freedom' were the most impressive of all Futurist disruptions. Marinetti's writings were anarchic rather than reasoned, often impenetrably theoretical and usually impractical (an appropriate characteristic for the avant-garde). He relentlessly dismantled any semblance of typographic (or literary) tradition by using words like 'torpedoes'. Communication no longer depended entirely on the meaning of a word but on its mutable position within an overall composition and on symbols that evoked a subtext. And as Marinetti suggested in the 1914 manifesto, 'La Splendeur Géométric et Mécanique et la Sensibilité', sensation, and facial expression when reading these works aloud, was endemic to the act of understanding them. But Marinetti's publications were by no means the sole exemplars of Futurist typographical expression.

Noi: Rivista d'Arte Futurista was published in Rome in two series – the first from 1917 to 1920, the second from 1923

Clockwise from top left:
Noi, covers of vol.1
no.1, June 1917; vol.3
no.1, January 1920; vol.6
no.10–12, 1925; vol.4 no.1,
April 1923. *Noi: Rivista
d'Arte Futurista*, edited
by Enrico Prampolini with
Bina Sanminiatelli and
Vittorio Orazi, linked the
revolutionary experiences
of the initial phase of
the Futurist movement
with other cadres of the
European avant-garde.
Prampolini designed
the early issues with
conventional formats but
by 1923 the radical Futurist
style of flamboyant type
began to emerge.

Opposite, from top: **Il
Futurismo**, cover of
no.1, 11 January 1922.
F T Marinetti, who edited
Il Futurismo, did not rely
entirely on his typographic
style 'words in freedom'.
Some of his publications
were composed in a
traditional typographic
manner.

Gioventu Fascista,
cover of no.33, 1 November
1932. The graphics for
this weekly magazine for
fascist teenagers, edited by
Carlo Scorza and Cesare
Marroni, popularized the
dynamic elements of
Futurist typography.

to 1925 – as a review of the international avant-garde. Edited and designed by the Futurist painter and graphic designer Enrico Prampolini (1894–1956), it was devoted to reviewing the intersecting developments in avant-garde circles. While *Noi*'s initial series was rather catholic in its interest in Cubism, Dada and Futurism, and was designed without an over-arching Futurist affinity, the second series was the best and most lavishly illustrated review of Futurism's second, post-war phase. Its typography was in perfect step with the avant-garde, and the cover design that ran on every issue (with only colour changes), designed by Prampolini, was a paradigm of machine aesthetic graphic design. Although Prampolini contributed to many other avant-garde journals, he saved his passion and innovation for this one.

Sometimes it seems as though there were as many different periodicals as there were leaders of the Futurist movement. While retaining loyalty to the overall movement, different members were affiliated with different periodicals and many of these reviews were tabloid or broadsheet newspapers that bore the Futurist name-plate and served as both record and demonstration of Futurist exuberance. As we have seen, Marinetti was closely involved, either as editor or contributor, in the vast majority of them. Among his editorships were *Le Futurisme: Revue Synthétique Illustrée*, published in Milan from 1923 to 1924, which featured the manifesto 'L'Art Mécanique' by Prampolini, Pannaggi and Paladini. Another of Marinetti's organs, *Stile Futurista*, was published in Turin around 1935 and was lavishly devoted to the aesthetics of the machine and its interaction with life.

Then there was *Il Futurismo: Rivista Sintetica Bimensile*, published in Milan from 1922 to 1931, a four-page tabloid that provided news of Futurist exhibitions and congresses and was designed with a bold typographic masthead and red overprints and surprints – some with Mussolini's trademark likeness emblazoned over the type. The alliance with Fascism was inextricable and profound. While not all Futurist periodicals used Mussolini as a veritable logo, either his appearance or the sign of the fasces was commonplace. The Futurists also directly influenced the look of party publications. Dynamic, speed-inspired mastheads, such as those at the top of *Gioventu Fascista*, the monthly of the Young Fascist Movement, were clearly inspired by the Futurist style.

If Marinetti was not the primary editor he was often the main theme: *Marinetti*, a one-off broadsheet newspaper edited in 1924 by Mino Somenzi in Milan, shows his heroic face glowering off the front page and he is accorded the status of modern god. Somenzi also edited the *Futurismo* (as distinct from *Il Futurismo*), which marked the highpoint of Futurism's second phase before it slid deep into Fascism.

As Arthur Cohen noted in *Constructivism and Futurism: Russian and Other*, '*Futurismo* was never equalled by other Futurist publications for the elegance of its layout or catholicism of its contents.'[4]

When Marinetti was not being worshipped by other editors he was frequently a principal collaborator. Yet during the mid to late Thirties, his agitation was often in support of the Fascist regime that kept a stranglehold on Italy. Such was his role in *Artecrazia*, edited from 1933 to 1939 by Mino Somenzi, a disturbing publication so imbued with Fascism as to seem almost an official organ of the political movement. Here Marinetti contributed a bombastic text in which the struggle for the artistic soul of Italy assumes the proportions of open warfare. Similarly, in *Mediterraneo Futurista*, edited in 1941 in Rome by Gaetano Pattarozzi, Marinetti underscores the movement's acquiescence to Fascist rhetoric; this was a vehement propaganda vehicle for Mussolini.

As the Fascist Party's power increased, it adopted as its graphic style a curious amalgam of Futurism and Roman classicism, an eclectic intertwining of new and old, in which the old usually held sway. Trying to maintain the integrity of Futurism's exuberance was the job of a member of the movement's so-called second phase, Fortunato Depero (1892–1960), the master of Futurist advertising art and design, and possibly the greatest contributor of the Futurist spirit to the mass market. Before Futurism fell victim to a war that demanded unambiguous graphic propaganda, Depero's distinctive rectilinear, vibrantly Mediterranean style was accepted by commerce and industry alike, and established a Futurist presence throughout Italian popular culture.

He produced numerous decorative covers for general and lifestyle magazines (*Vogue*, *Emporium* and *La Rivista*) and businesses, such as Campari, for whom he created a prodigious number of advertisements and trademarks. In 1932 he co-authored the 'Futurist Manifesto of Advertising Art', and celebrated the future of Futurist publicity in *Numero unico futurista Campari* (1931) and *Depero Futurista* (1927). The latter was also known as the 'bolted book' because this collection of typographic experiments and free-word-type poems was bound together with two industrial-strength bolts.

Depero developed theories of art and design and coined Futurist terms such as 'the plastic-architectonic use of writing', 'typographic architecture' and 'advertising architecture'. He brought the latter notion to life in his Book Pavilion at the Second International Biennale of Decorative Art in Monza, which had three-dimensional words sculpted on the face of the structure. As proprietor of his own art factory, the Casa d'Arte Futurista, in both Roverto in Italy

Opposite, clockwise from top left: **Marinetti**, no.1 (only issue), 1924, cover photograph by Caminada. **Futurismo Aerovita**, cover of vol.3 no.66, 1 May 1934. **Mediterraneo Futurista**, cover by Biazzi; no.14, 1941, cover of 'Trust in Mussolini' issue by Ernesto Thayaht. **Artecrazia**, no.118, 11 January 1939, cover art by Enrico Prampolini.

Futurists were prolific publishers of all kinds of ephemera. Large format (or broadsheet) newspapers were frequently published under various names and mastheads; *Futurismo Aerovita*, *Artecrazia* and *Marinetti*, edited by Mino Somenzi, are a few. Tightly packed, stolid columns of type announced Futurist events with little room for the stunning graphics that defined the movement. Benito Mussolini was featured on the cover of many Futurist periodicals. The cult of the leader was perpetuated through graphics like the covers of *Mediterraneo Futurista*, edited by Gaetano Pattarozzi, that portray him as a modernistic god with images that often dominated the covers and front pages of these otherwise progressive magazines. Marinetti's iconic portrait was also frequently used on Futurist periodical covers, such as Enrico Prampolini's illustrations for *Artecrazia* and *Futurismo*.

Right: **Futurismo**, vol.1 no.8, 28 October 1933, cover art by Enrico Prampolini. Edited by Marinetti and Somenzi, this broadsheet newspaper represented the intersection between the Futurist movement and the Fascist Party. Its design reflected the pragmatics of the former and the ideals of the latter.

esce ogni domenica   (settimanale)   **28 Ottobre XI**

FUTURISMO

a. 1° n. 8   cent. 50

DUCE DUCE DUCE DUCE DUCE DUCE

Evviva il genio futurista di BENITO MUSSOLINI

Piazza Belgioioso

La "Casa Rossa"

DVCE!

F. T. MARINETTI

EVVIVA MARINETTI

il Trionfo della Rivoluzione Fascista

W il Fascismo

and in New York, Depero enthusiastically propagated the Futurist sensibility through diverse media. In 1932 he published his own magazine *Dinamo Futurista* (the logo on a few covers were line drawings of a dynamo engine) in which he incorporated many of the Futurist ideas of type and image that can be found in his manifestos and catalogues. The journal was both an advertisement for his work (notably for Campari) and a model for new methods of graphic design. Of all the Futurists, Depero was doubtless the most fervently committed to making publicity through frenetic word compositions and he truly defined the Italian Futurist commercial style of graphic design, which ended in the early Forties when the Fascist government was overthrown.

Futurism was not, however, limited to Italy. The Russians were influenced by Marinetti's ideas, and his 'First Futurist Manifesto' was dutifully published in St Petersburg a month after it appeared in Paris. But it was not blindly embraced. In 1912 David Burlyuk (1882–1967), poet and painter from Kharkov, is said to have coined the term 'Cubo Futurism' to distinguish himself (and his group) from other Futurists. In fact, many artists involved in the Futurist/Hylaea group (Gileja or Hylaea was the region that gave birth to Russian Futurism) refused to recognize the primacy of the Italian Futurists. Instead, they embraced

Right: **La Rivista**, no.2, February 1932. Edited by Arnoldo Mussolini, *La Rivista* was the illustrated magazine supplement of his newspaper *Popolo d'Italia*. For a magazine that did not profess to be avant-garde, it published work by a generous number of Futurist artists, like this cover by Fortunato Depero.

Below: **Dinamo Futurista**, cover and inside spread of no.2, March 1933. Fortunato Depero edited and designed his own magazine, *Dinamo Futurista*, as much to extol the virtues of Futurism as to showcase his own graphic experimentation. The dynamo was one of the many symbols of the new age that Futurism espoused.

French Cubism as a unifying influence and a means of intervening with antiquated language. Yet Burlyuk and his colleagues did not simply mimic Picasso.

Russian Futurism was something of a composite of the Western world's avant-garde: the fragmentation of plastic forms (from Cubism), the focus on kinetics (from Italian Futurism), the bold colours and lines (from Neo-Primitivism), and a departure from objectivity (prevalent in various quarters). The Russians developed a unique style that involved the marriage of painting and poetry. Periodicals were not the main thrust of Russian Futurist publishing; rather, artists created limited-edition books comprised of prints, paintings and calligraphy. Kasimir Malevich (1878–1935), Natalia Goncharova (1881–1962), Lyubov' Sergeyevna Popova (1889–1924), Ilia Zdanevich (1894–1975), and Olga Vladimirovna Rozanova (1886–1918) were the prime contributors to this Russian variant. The Russians also developed a distinct typographic language called *zaoum*, whereby type-play underscored sounds rather than traditional words.

Although Cubo Futurism was a fully-fledged movement, its many declarations and manifestos were not imparted through serial periodicals but rather via books, pamphlets and posters. In fact, *Dokhlaia Luna* (The Crooked Moon), edited by Burlyuk during the spring of 1914, was the movement's first and only attempt at uniting the Russian Futurists under a single cover. Various members of the movement continued to issue one-off and occasional periodicals. In 1914 Burlyuk was co-editor of the *Gazeta Futuristov*, and in the same year A Kruchenykh edited *41 Degrees*, which included a manifesto declaring that *zaoum* was the supreme expression of its time.

Vorticism was another Futurist offshoot and originated as an English alternative to Cubism and Expressionism. The term Vorticism, from vortex or core of energy, was coined in 1914 by the American ex-patriot poet Ezra Pound (1885–1972) and literally represents the concept of greatest mechanical efficiency. Indeed, the kinship with Futurism's machine veneration is no accident. In 1912 Marinetti mounted an exhibition of Italian Futurism at the Sackville Gallery in London and drew a large crowd of soon-to-be Vorticists who were in sympathy with Futurism yet objected to Marinetti's active proselytizing for his own movement. The English sought equanimity within an integral group that represented British concerns. The stubborn individualists Ezra Pound and Wyndham Lewis (1882–1957), the principal forces behind the burgeoning movement, also objected to the relentless boisterousness of Italian Futurism. Lewis defined the vortex

Below from left: **Dokhlaia Luna**, no.1, 1914. **Gazeta Futuristov**, no.1, 1914. **41 Degrees**, 1923, 'Lidantiu as a Beacon' cover design by Naum Granovskii, with composition by Ilia Zdanevich.

The Cubo Futurists published few periodicals, such as these two edited by David Burlyuk, preferring to experiment with type and image in books, pamphlets and posters, such as the book *41 Degrees*.

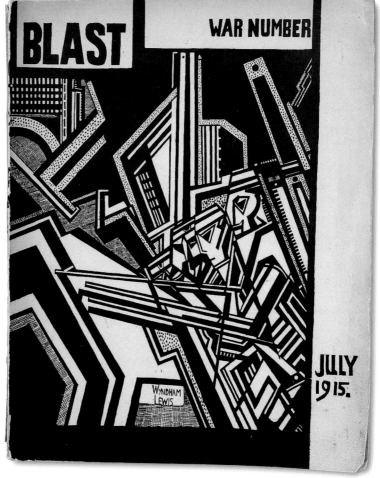

as a whirlpool, at the heart of which is a silent place where energy is concentrated (like the eye of a storm). At this point, he noted, is the Vorticist.

But in essence the Vorticist motives and ideals were barely distinguishable from the Italian Futurists. The first magazine of Vorticism was *Blast: Review of the Great English Vortex*, three issues of which were edited in London by Lewis from 1914 to 1915. In *Blast* no.1, Lewis wrote in 'The Melodrama of Modernity': 'Of all the tags going, "futurist", for general applications, serves as well as any for the active painters of today.'[5] The active Vorticist painting was indeed explosive – like the Futurist canvas – but Lewis insisted that it did not mindlessly embrace rapid motion as its only reason for existence. Vorticists did not entirely accept Marinetti's romanticized view of the machine, considering that the machine produced impersonal results that dehumanized the world.

Blast was aggressive, belligerent and sarcastic and quite literally blasted the complacency of English propriety and its stodgy history. Vorticism waged war on the antiquated and stagnant Victorian legacy and *Blast* zealously believed that England had more of a right than other European nations to define the twentieth century through its art. Factories, bridges and other accoutrements

of modernity were symbols in English painting, and Lewis chose this imagery as a subtle critique of the Italians whose 'automobilist pictures' were, he determined, too picturesque and romantic. The illustrations in the three issues of *Blast* reveal Cubistic influences – anti-representational yet not wholly abstract. The drawings and woodcuts in *Blast* no.2, 'The War Number', are linear and schematic – complex compositions using the most elementary geometric forms to represent skyscrapers, machines and modern soldiers. *Blast* proclaimed that machinery 'sweeps away the doctrines of a narrow and pedantic realism at one stroke'.[6]

War also cleansed the cultural palette with similar speed and efficiency. In the second *Blast*, Lewis described the movement's total support of war against Germany as a means of eradicating an unacceptable past. This was not simply a dispute of nations over economic, geographical and material power; it was a fundamental conflict of old and new cultures. 'Germany has stood for the old Poetry, for Romance, more stedfastly [sic] and profoundly than any other people in Europe. German nationalism is less realistic, is more saturated with mechanical obsession of history, than the nationalism of England or France.' He continued to assert that *Blast* stood staunchly opposed, 'from start to finish, to every form that Poetry of a former condition of life,

Opposite, from left: **Blast**, covers of no.1, 1914; no.2, July 1915, both edited and designed by Wyndham Lewis. The cover of *Blast* no.1 was in its own way a noise poem. The simple word against the puce background was a veritable explosion in print. The 'War Number' featured Lewis's linear abstraction symbolizing the hardware of armed conflict.

Below: **Blast**, no.1, 1914. For interior pages of *Blast* Lewis used gothic type, akin to the style used for wartime public notices, as a means of giving his poetics a resonant voice.

CURSE
the flabby sky that can manufacture no snow, but can only drop the sea on us in a drizzle like a poem by Mr. Robert Bridges.

CURSE
the lazy air that cannot stiffen the back of the **SERPENTINE**, or put Aquatic steel half way down the **MANCHESTER CANAL.**

But ten years ago we saw distinctly both snow and ice here.
May some vulgarly inventive, but useful person, arise, and restore to us the necessary **BLIZZARDS.**

LET US ONCE MORE WEAR THE ERMINE OF THE NORTH.

WE BELIEVE IN THE EXISTENCE OF THIS **USEFUL LITTLE CHEMIST** IN OUR MIDST!

12

 2
OH BLAST FRANCE
pig plagiarism
BELLY
SLIPPERS
POODLE TEMPER
BAD MUSIC

SENTIMENTAL GALLIC GUSH
SENSATIONALISM
FUSSINESS.

PARISIAN PAROCHIALISM. Complacent young man, so much respect for Papa and his son!—Oh!—Papa <u>is</u> wonderful: but <u>all</u> papas are !

BLAST
APERITIFS (Pernots, Amers picon)
Bad change
Naively seductive Houri salon-picture Cocottes
Slouching blue porters (can carry a pantechnicon)
Stupidly rapacious people at every step
Economy maniacs
Bouillon Kub (for being a bad pun)

13

no longer existing, has foisted upon us'.[7] With this battle cry, *Blast* published a series of poetic volleys and graphic bombs against the traditions of the enemy.

The cover of *Blast*'s first issue underscored its antagonism towards tradition. Designed by Lewis, it was not only a total rejection of Victorian ornament; its diagonal gothic type across a field of luminescent puce – Blast – expressed the immediacy of its purpose. Inside, the typography was just as confrontational. For the leading 'Manifesto' Lewis used alternating gothic capitals and lower-case letters as a graphic equivalent to a machine gun's report. Similar to Marinetti's 'words in freedom', differing weights shot throughout the page, but Lewis's composition was more disciplined – and legible. For most poems and prose, gothic news headlines sat atop the pages as though a call to arms. The body text was set in a bold, Latinate serif typeface that aggressively grabbed the reader's eye. Larger words and bolder letters and words were used, akin to Italian Futurist typographics, to emphasize phrases and ideas. It was reported that the Constructivist artist El Lissitzky (1890–1941) took a copy of *Blast* – one of the most inventive English typographical specimens of the period – back to Russia and included it in one of his earliest essays on the New Typography.

Blast's second issue coincided with the outbreak of war and its third was published during the early months of the conflagration. By 1916 most of the Vorticists were fighting in France and unable to produce plastic art, although guns and armaments were artistic materials of a different kind. When they returned from the battlefields, Vorticism could not be jump-started to regain its pre-war momentum in an altered world. By 1920 the movement had fizzled out, its individual members having dispersed into other art and political movements, including Fascism. From 1921 to 1922 Lewis edited a comparatively insignificant magazine, *The Tyrol*, before turning his attention to a more vital publication free from the orthodox Vorticist overlay.

The Enemy: A Review of Art and Literature was Lewis's journal of longest duration, from 1927 to 1929. It was also Lewis's magazine in every sense of the word, for he contributed most of the prose and included reproductions of his own graphic work. He further designed and rendered all its covers in full colour. In the opening editorial Lewis announced: 'By name this paper is an enemy, though over against what particular individuals or groups it occupies that position is not revealed in the general title, nor whether a solitary antagonist or an aggressive communion is concealed within its covers.' He went on to say that *The Enemy* is not the gatehouse of a movement and seems to have moved outside the confines of obligation to a party or individual. But the title, he claimed, 'publicly repudiates any

of those treacherous or unreal claims to "impartiality ...".' He also stated that, if asked his politics, he would truly answer: 'I have none.'[8] Indeed, within *The Enemy* his code of conduct was his own.

The Enemy was more traditionally designed than *Blast*, with a conventional, justified column composition, perhaps an expression of 45-year-old Lewis's maturity or sagacity. But the covers were very striking in form and content, especially issue no.2 with its orgy of hand-drawn letter forms and colourful, linear doodles that combined both Cubist and Futurist sensibilities. It is the most timeless of Lewis's compositions and even today is a precursor of the Neo-Expressionist renderings of the digital age. With over a hundred pages, *The Enemy* was more like a book than a review. The first issue contained Lewis's lengthy essay on the cultural Zeitgeist as he interpreted it. The magazine also received more notice in press and periodicals than any other 'little magazine' (a magazine with a small circulation), but as a little magazine it was doomed to extinction when the funds ran out.

The publications produced during the Futurist/ Vorticist period lead to one conclusion: the importance of graphic design as a tool (and weapon) of the avant-garde. Typography was unalterably transformed by Futurism's 'words in freedom' and the rejection of antiquated rules and standards continued to have an impact throughout the twentieth century. The next stage of avant-garde publishing (Dada, to be discussed in the following chapter) and design experimentation in general, owes an incalculable debt to this initial revolution in print.

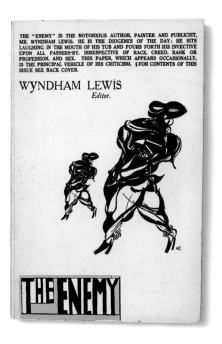

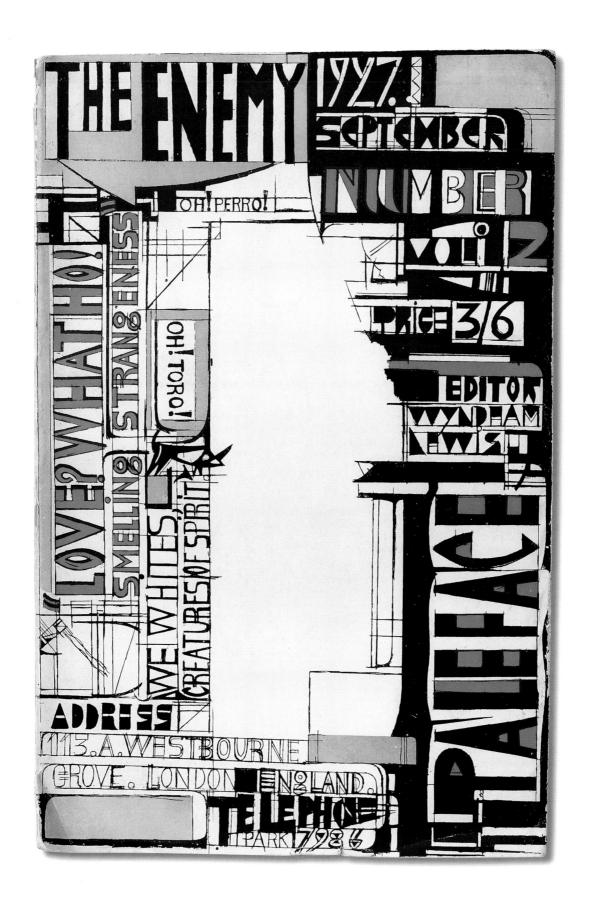

291

No. 1   10 cts.   March 1915

back its forelock.

3

The Art of Anti-Art:
The Magazine as Clarion
of Protest

M. de Zayas

Dada was unrepentantly confounding. The proverbial question 'What is Dada?' was as much of a recurring, albeit ironic, mantra within the movement as it was a real quandary to the world outside. Written in typical Dadaese by Dadas themselves, the official definitions were mockingly vexing: 'Dada is a tomato.' 'Dada is a spook.' 'Dada is never right.' 'Dada is soft-boiled happiness.' 'Dada is idiotic.' 'Dada is nothing, nothing, nothing,' and then again, 'Everything is Dada.'[1]

'Dada' was a nonsense word on which a no-nonsense anti-art/art movement, which lasted from 1916 to 1924, was predicated. 'Dada' may have been arbitrarily selected (then again, maybe not); it may have started as an 'empty shell' but it definitely became the linguistic signifier used to distinguish what is not, as well as what might be, Dada. Dada was an amalgam of ideas embraced and rejected and embraced again by a group of people who waged war against other groups, structures and conventions. In physical terms, Dada was cabaret, exhibition, demonstration and publication – synthetic, plastic and sometimes ethereal. However, the propagation of Dada – indeed, the acceleration of Dada's anti-art/anti-everything, ironic self-destruct message throughout Europe and the United States – was communicated through periodicals. Indeed, print was the deadliest weapon of Dada.

When coined in 1915 (or 1916 because historians disagree), the word 'Dada' was affixed to acts of cultural disruption that fused into a revolution of young intellectuals brought together in Zurich from across war-torn Europe. Each adherent swore allegiance to the nebulous Dada. And yet what exactly did the Dadas actually worship? Was Dada mystical, rational or vegetable?

André Breton (1896–1966) whose review *Littérature* prefigured the Dada journals, wrote that there is no Dada truth – Dada is one thing and the other. Tristan Tzara (1896–1963), the titular founder of the Zurich movement, said that Dada was born of not only a need for independence but of a distrust of unity. Dada definitions differed from place to place, from person to person, from minute to minute. To analyse Dada, historian Michel Sanouillet wrote, one needs 'a Dada metalanguage, which only Dada can use and understand'.[2] And yet Dada had a mission that spread beyond its most intimate members, defined by purpose and rooted in a creed that resisted both modishness and, therefore, out-modishness. Dada aspired to everything and nothing, to madness and sanity, yet ultimately its aim was to alter the world.

The prime word – and the lasting utterance – that adorned most of its periodicals and manifestos, and which became both logo and trademark, is a baby's sound of affirmation – nonsense in search of sense. 'Dada' literally

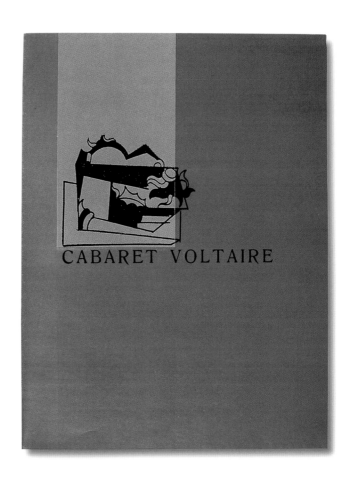

PABLO PICASSO:
DESSIN

ARBRE

Tu chantes avec-les autres tandis que les phonographes galopent
Où sont les aveugles où s'en sont-ils allés
La seule feuille que j'ai cueillie s'est changée en plusieurs mirages
Ne m'abandonnez pas parmi cette foule de femmes au marché
Ispahan s'est fait un ciel de carreaux émaillés de bleu
Et je remonte avec vous une route aux environs de Lyon

Je n'ai pas oublié le son d'une clochette d'un marchand de coco autrefois
J'entends déjà le son aigre de cette voix à venir
Du camarade qui se promènera avec toi en Europe tout en restant
En Amérique
Un enfant
Un veau dépouillé pendu à l'étal
Un enfant
Et cette banlieue de sable autour d'une pauvre ville au fond de l'Est
Un douanier se tenait là comme un ange
A la porte d'un misérable paradis
Et ce voyageur épileptique écumait dans la salle d'attente des premières
Engoulevent Grondin Blaireau
Et la Taupe-Ariane
Nous avions loué deux coupés dans le transsibérien
Tour à tour nous dormions le voyageur en bijouterie et moi
Mais celui qui veillait ne cachait point un revolver aimé

Tu t'es promené à Leipzig avec une femme mince déguisée en homme
Intelligence car voilà ce que c'est qu'une femme intelligente
Et il ne faudrait pas oublier les légendes
Dame-Abonde dans un tramway la nuit au fond d'un quartier désert
Je voyais une chasse tandis que je montais
Et l'ascenseur s'arrêtait à chaque étage
Entre les pierres
Entre les vêtements multicolores de la vitrine
Entre les charbons ardents du marchand de marrons
Entre deux vaisseaux norvégiens amarrés à Rouen
Il y a ton image
Elle pousse entre les bouleaux de la Finlande

Ce beau nègre en acier

La plus grande tristesse
C'est quand tu reçus une carte postale de La Corogne

Le vent vient du couchant
Le métal des caroubiers
Tout est plus triste qu'autrefois
Tous les dieux terrestres vieillissent
L'univers se plaint par ta voix
Et des êtres nouveaux surgissent
Trois par trois
GUILLAUME APOLLINAIRE

11

IL FAIT SOIR

Traduit du roumain 1913

Les pêcheurs reviennent avec les étoiles des eaux
ils partagent du pain aux pauvres
enfilent des colliers aux aveugles
les empereurs sortent dans les parcs à cette heure
                qui ressemble à l'amertume des gravures

les domestiques baignent les chiens de chasse
la lumière met des gants
ferme-toi fenêtre par conséquant
sors lumière de la chambre comme le noyau de l'abricot
                comme le prêtre de l'église

bon dieu: fais la laine tendre aux amoureux dolents
peins les petits oiseaux à l'encre et renouvelle l'ima-
                ge sur la lune

— allons attraper des scarabées
pour les enfermer dans la boîte
— allons au ruisseau
faire des cruches en terre cuite
— allons nous embrasser
à la fontaine
allons au parc communal
jusqu'à ce que le coq chantera
et la ville se scandalisera

où au grenier
le foin picote on entend les vaches mugir
puis elles se souviennent des petits
allons Mamie partir partir

TRISTAN TZARA.

16

M. JANCO:
AFFICHE POUR LE „CHANT NÈGRE" DU
31IÈME MARS 1916

has different meanings in different languages; in French, as was discovered by chance in the *Petit Larousse Illustré*, it is a hobby-horse. Some argue that Hugo Ball (1886–1927) found it (and he certainly takes the credit); others, notably Jean Arp (aka Hans Arp, 1887–1966), insist that it was Tristan Tzara; and still others say that it was Richard Huelsenbeck (1892–1974) – in fact, the latter has claimed that he and Ball together snatched the word from obscurity. Huelsenbeck noted in *En Avant Dada: A History of Dadaism* (1920) that, whatever its origins, 'it is impressive in its brevity and suggestiveness.'[3] Soon after its adoption, 'Dada' became the mnemonic for all that was performed at the vanguard Cabaret Voltaire, Zurich's Dada epicentre and namesake for the first official Dada review.

Hugo Ball opened Cabaret Voltaire in 1916 as a stage for the artists and writers – performers all – who flocked to Zurich. Spontaneous combustion occurred within the tight quarters of the Meierei Café where Cabaret Voltaire was housed. Along with the star performers – Tzara, Marcel Janco (1895–1984), Huelsenbeck and Arp – the cabaret became a playground of intoxication for those liberated from the horrors of war by music, poetry, performance and plastic art. Janco wrote in his essay 'Dada à deux vitesses': 'At the Cabaret Voltaire we began by shocking the bourgeois, demolishing his idea of art, attacking common sense, public opinion, education, institutions, museums, good taste, in short, the whole prevailing order.'[4]

In addition to the homegrown art of its *habitués*, the indecorous words and pictures by, among the leading literary avant-garde troublemakers, Blaise Cendrars (1887–1961), Guillaume Apollinaire (1880–1918), Alfred Jarry (1873–1907) and Arthur Rimbaud (1854–91) were also seen and heard. Although their combined creative energies did not fuse into a unique Dada style at that time, it marked the early contractions of Dada's official birth. But the influence of the Cabaret Voltaire was transitory and proscribed, so an international review, one that would presumably have circulation beyond the small cabaret audience, was conceived to publish the words and pictures that ultimately spread (and documented) the Dada gospel.

Ball proposed the name 'Dada' for the review's masthead and suggested that his colleagues take turns in editing individual issues. When the magazine finally appeared, however, it was called *Cabaret Voltaire*, perhaps because the cabaret's name was more recognizable than the nonsense syllables. None the less, Ball believed that 'Voltaire' was an apt name for the cabaret because he saw the nightly review of avant-gardisms as a kind of *Candide* of its time. Voltaire's sly hero was something of a proto-Dada who accepted that conventional morals and mores were being desecrated by modern life and believed that a new order was imperative.

Drawing upon the eclectic essence of the cabaret, the new periodical was a boisterous display of Expressionism, Futurism and Cubism, experimental poetry, imagery and confrontational manifestos. In thirty-two pages, *Cabaret Voltaire* was a synthesis of literary modernism but its graphic design was fairly conventional, created by a jobbing printer using established templates rather than by the Dada artists whose ignorance of convention would later define a new typography. The periodical had yet to assume a Dadaesque appearance, except for two examples of Italian Futurist poetry that it published, F T Marinetti's and Francesco Cangiullo's dynamic *parole in libertà*, which prefigured and influenced the outrageous typographical assemblages that would define Dada's visual persona. Like some of its precursors, *Cabaret Voltaire*'s format began cautiously despite the precedence of earlier radical periodicals. But eventually it made an indelible mark on the culture of its time.

The *memento mori* of Dada includes books, pamphlets, manifestos, ready-mades, montages and collages, yet the over-arching character of Dada is forged through its typography. The most distinctive effect of the cultural disruption and social havoc ignited by Dada was that of forcing the eye to see differently. It changed the common perception of the written word in unimaginable ways, or, in the words of the historian Arthur Cohen, enabled the eye 'to discover meanings sequestered in hidden places, slogans printed upside-down or obliquely, or in circles – language biting its tail.'[5] What Dada did was attack the rectilinear conventions of the printed page and break apart the sequential order of typeset lines. This, in turn, undermined the classical order, balance and equilibrium of a rationally composed page. Italics were thrown in helter skelter, capitals and lower-case letters were seemingly applied at random – all for maximum disruptive jolt. Dada crusaded against the sanctioned conveyance of meaning by shouting and screaming and thus imitating sound through printed words.

But Dada's invention was not entirely its own. Decades earlier, the advertising industry, which propagated twentieth-century commercial culture, discovered that loud, flashy and vulgar typography could attract consumers. As tools for moving goods, different styles of grotesque wood-block typefaces were frequently jumbled discordantly together in ads and posters to draw the eye away from complacent reading patterns. In addition, garish colours, sensational pictorial images and purposefully misplaced diacritic marks and exclamation points were used in frenzied compositions that attracted attention and stimulated a response to sales messages. Demonstrative typography was, in fact, in increasing demand as the accelerated pace of city life gave passers-by less time to casually ponder the barrage of advertising messages.

Advertising is, however, but one inspiration for Dada. Experimental poetry that disrupted the rules of writing is another. Stéphane Mallarmé's (1842–98) poem, 'Un coup de dés jamais n'aborlira le hasard' (A Throw of the Dice Will Never Abolish Chance), published in the British magazine *Cosmopolis* in 1897, an early example of what later became 'words in freedom', was composed on the printer's stone to evoke both auditory and emotional sensation. Rather than following the classical format for short verse, the words in this poem are spaced apart within generous areas of white, positioned in such a way as to deliberately emphasize words and, thus, expressions. Mallarmé's composition had antecedents in the Middle Ages and, closer in time, to Lewis Carroll whose description of the mouse's tail in *Alice's Adventures in Wonderland* (1895) was purposefully written and typeset so that it curled off the end of a paragraph to appear like the tail described in the text. But Mallarmé's poem was the first to transform the classical page into a modern page. It also made possible Apollinaire's calligrammatic poem, 'Il Pleut' (It Rains), which streamed down the page like a rivulet of water when it appeared in the journal *SIC*. These typographic transgressions both inspired and gave licence to Dada's precursors, discussed in Chapter 2.

Since type was used to represent noise, towards this aim it was necessary to increase and decrease the size of type numerous times on the same page – and often within the

Below: **Cosmopolis**, inside spread of vol.6, April–June 1897. The composition of Stéphane Mallarmé's 1897 poem 'Un coup de dés jamais n'aborlira le hasard' was a precursor to the dynamic poetics that became the common design language in Dada publications.

420

SOIT
     que

          l'abime

blanchi
     étale
          furieux
               sous une inclinaison
                    plane désespérément

                              d'aile

     la sienne

par avance retombée d'un mal à dresser le vol
          et couvrant les jaillissements
                    coupant au ras les bonds

          très à l'intérieur résume

l'ombre enfouie dans la transparence par cette voile alternative

               jusqu'adapter
                    à l'envergure

     sa béante profondeur en tant que la coque

          d'un bâtiment

     penché de l'un ou l'autre bord

421

LE MAÎTRE
                    hors d'anciens calculs
               où la manœuvre avec l'âge oubliée
surgi
     inférant

                    jadis il empoignait la barre

          de cette conflagration
                    à ses pieds
                         de l'horizon unanime

               que se prépare
                    s'agite et mêle
                         au poing qui l'étreindrait
          comme on menace un destin et les vents

le nombre unique qui ne peut pas en être un autre

     esprit
          pour le lancer
                    dans la tempête
               en reployer l'âpre division et passer fier

                    hésite
                         tout chenu
cadavre par le bras écarté du secret qu'il détient

     plutôt

                    que de jouer en maniaque la partie
          au nom des flots
                         un envahit le chef
                         coule en barbe soumise

     naufrage cela direct l'homme

               sans nef
                    n'importe
                         où vaine

same paragraph. The densely packed kinetic typography was meant to agitate, unnerve and confuse the public, which was Dada's mission. But so was its desire to outlive all earlier avant-gardes when their respective experimental lives were exhausted. So, while Dada shared some of the more emblematic typographic notions in its denial of ordinary writing and presentation, it was not a carbon copy of the earlier 'isms'. What's more, the typography in each of the Dada reviews, while adhering to the idea that type must squirm so that the reader would do likewise, was different for each one, according to the proclivities of the typographer. While some pages were carved up texts, others were skewed ideograms. For Dadaists there could be no uniformity, and yet there was consensus that conventional art and language represented the bourgeois elite.

Dada certainly hijacked gaudy mass-market typography as a means to convey ideas. It borrowed from advertising, was influenced by Futurism, and went even further in its symbolic and conceptual application of Cubist typographic fragmentation. Rejecting sanctimonious concerns over what is high and low art, Dada employed a vernacular visual language to underscore its own rebellion. The periodicals were the prime examples of this typographical revolution.

Cabaret Voltaire, in both French and German editions (appealing to its Swiss audience),[6] prefigured a string of Dada magazines. But the initial four issues of the Zurich-based magazine, *Dada*, published between July 1917 and May 1919, concretized the movement's core principles. The first two numbers were typographically tame, indeed *Dada* nos. 1 and 2 were 'literary and artistic reviews'. The basic print-run of *Cabaret Voltaire* and *Dada* was cheaply produced because of rationing, which limited access to paper and printing ink. To garner additional operating funds, each number was also printed in a more expensive, deluxe edition (sold at six francs as opposed to two) with original prints appearing on thin, different-coloured papers, which may have been the result of availability rather than deliberate design.

By the time issue no.3 was in preparation, Tzara had named himself the chief editor responsible for soliciting manuscripts. Once he had assumed sole editorship, *Dada* degenerated into unruly visual pandemonium. In addition to the typographic noise, red was added to the masthead, and brightly coloured words and sentences were used to stimulate the reader's eye. In the editorial/manifesto of issue no.3, 'Manifeste Dada 1918', Tzara extols 'Dada disgust' for the status quo. To underscore this, many of the poems and texts were printed sideways, while advertisements for

Below: **Dada**, no.1, July 1917, cover art by Marcel Janco; no.2, December 1917, cover art by Mille H de Rebay.

Opposite: **Dada**, no.3, December 1918, cover art by Marcel Janco; and inside page with Paul Dermée's poem 'Bâton' and woodcut by Arthur Segal. Tristan Tzara published, edited and designed seven issues of *Dada*, which showed the evolution from a movement without a defining graphic style (in the first two issues), to the raw homemade Dada look with its cacophonous typography in subsequent numbers. When the *Dada* series was first published, radical page design had not yet been codified; white space was a luxury and sideways typography was taboo.

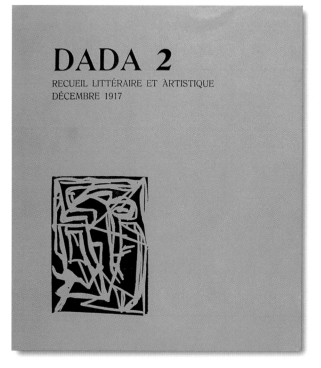

other publications and reviews were thrown as if at random into the editorial content. *Dada* no.3 was the first issue to introduce the signature Dada typography with skewed and angular lines of text. Set diagonally in gothic lower-case type, cutting into the masthead, is Descartes's phrase 'Je ne veux même pas savoir s'il y a eu des hommes avant moi' (I do not even want to know if there have been men before me). Inside, embedded in Tzara's editorial/manifesto, the word 'Dada' is set in a variety of serif, sans-serif and even medieval-looking typefaces; a poem by Paul Dermée was composed in a craggy typewriter font. *Dada* no.4–5 included orange, blue and pink pages on which drawings by Francis Picabia, woodcuts by Augusto Giacometti and Hans Arp, poems by Jean Cocteau and Pierre Reverdy and a manifesto by Tzara appear.

Among the advertisements, announcements of new reviews, including those published by Mouvement Dada, gave the appearance of an intellectually charged movement. One of them, a single issue of *Der Zeltweg*, published in 1919, was what Hans Richter (1888–1976) referred to as the afterbirth of Dada.[7] It contained works by most of the Zurich Dadas as well as Huelsenbeck and Kurt Schwitters (1887–1948) who formed his own Dada group in Hanover. *Der Zeltweg*, edited by Otto Flake (1880–1963), Walter Serner (1889–*c*.1942), and Tzara, was named after the street in which Hans Arp had his studio. When compared to the later issues of *Dada*, the format of *Der Zeltweg* was decidedly neutral, but it none the less marked the first Dada periodical whose distribution and accessibility was no longer proscribed by the horrific war.

When the war was over, Dada immediately bifurcated. Tzara and the Zurich/Paris axis turned more to matters of art, while Huelsenbeck, who founded Dada in Berlin, became increasingly more political and driven by revolutionary zeal. On the artistic side, abstract art came to the fore, and Dada's Zurich/Paris group fought against what they argued was 'overblown' painting endemic to certain German Expressionists, such as the work of Franz Marc's Der Blaue Reiter group founded in 1911. On the political side, expressive art of all kinds, notably abstraction, was considered bankrupt.

In the midst of the turmoil, after meeting Francis Picabia (1879–1953) – a regular contributor to Paris and New York based Dada periodicals who had become something of a maverick even within Dada – Tzara left Zurich for Paris in 1920. Among Picabia's avant-garde pursuits was the sole editorship of *391*, his own iconoclastic Dada publication which ran from 1917 to 1924 (the longest-running Dada review) in New York, Barcelona and Paris. *391* and Picabia's other self-published magazines, notably *Cannibale*, confounded and angered even the Dadas with its attacks –

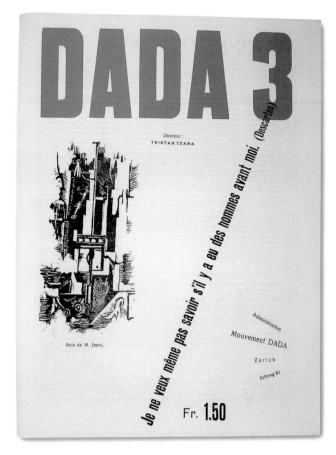

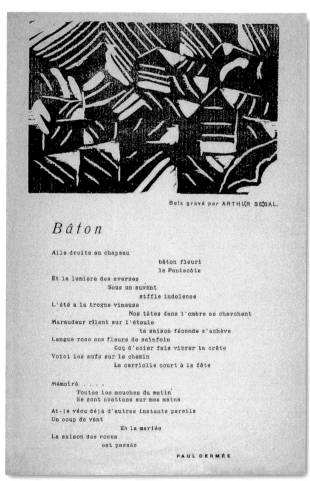

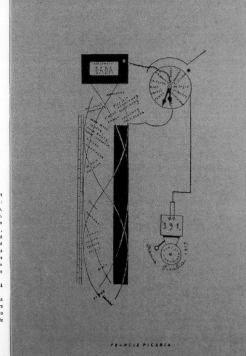

both real and satirical – on other Dadas. None the less, from *Dada* no.3 onwards, Tzara published Picabia's revolutionary (proto-Pop Art) machine drawings. He proclaimed 'Long live Picabia the anti-painter ...' and gave pride of place on the front cover of *Dada* no.4–5 to Picabia's *Réveil matin*, a rough-hewn mechanical drawing of a disassembled watch that contrasted markedly with the abstract woodcuts of the other Zurich Dadas – and owed a debt to the scandalous ready-mades of Marcel Duchamp (1887–1968).

Picabia's influence on the appearance of Dada publications was significant. He had become fanatical about expressive typography, using typefaces to mirror his mercurial moods and to illuminate commentaries presented in his own magazine. Picabia enjoyed using illegible typefaces as well as fashionable advertising fonts. He scoured the stylish catalogues of the Parisian Deberny and Peignot type foundry for the most frou-frou 'perfume types' used in fashion advertising and mixed these with diametrically contrasting styles. This approach lent *391* its untutored yet distinctive look and gave Tzara ideas of his own. While living in Paris, Tzara worked on *Dada* nos. 6 and 7 in Picabia's apartment. Both issues were even more loosely designed than the Zurich ones. Issue no.6 was called *Bulletin Dada*, with a huge red slab-serif wood type for the Dada masthead, and issue no.7 was titled *Dadaphone* – its

masthead typeset in a bold gothic typeface that towered over a line drawing by Picabia. Owing to Picabia's influence, both publications solidly resembled *391*.

Zurich, and later Berlin and Paris, were not the only capitals of Dada. During the early years of World War I, New York had become a mecca for European artists, including Picabia and Duchamp. This migration brought with it a need to proliferate ideas and ideologies of art through periodicals. An awareness of modern art was already being stimulated by the exhibitions of controversial new work which Alfred Stieglitz (1864–1946) had been showing at the 291 Gallery (located at 291 Fifth Avenue in Manhattan) since 1908. Stieglitz's periodical *291* was dedicated to modern art and visual satire, and it was based almost entirely on the activity surging from his gallery. Prior to this, Dada was regarded as a European phenomenon and did not resonate with American artists in the same revolutionary manner.

The over-arching principle of *291* was that the art of Europe was dead and America was now the epicentre of the new. The review was planned to appear for a limited period only, 1915–16, and Stieglitz's long-running periodical, *Camera Work*, was suspended for a year while his energies were redirected into *291*. Marius de Zayas (1889–1961), known as a caricaturist of celebrities and literati, contributed both text and illustrations to *291*. De Zayas had told Tzara in a letter

Opposite, clockwise from top: **Dada**, no.4–5, January 1919, cover art by Francis Picabia; and inside spread with poem by Tristan Tzara and drawing by Picabia.

Der Zeltweg, no.1 (only issue), November 1919, inside spread with poem by Richard Huelsenbeck and art by Kurt Schwitters; and cover with art by Hans Arp. The page in *Der Zeltweg* was a stage on which Dadas exhibited and performed their work. It was edited by Otto Flake, Walter Serner and Tzara.

Below left: **Cannibale**, no.1, March 1920. This cover belied the Dada sensibility but showed that in Picabia's hands type could be expressively quiet or boisterously ostentatious. Picabia edited and designed *Cannibale*.

Below centre and right: **391**, no.12, March 1920, cover art by Marcel Duchamp; cover of no.19, October 1924. *391* was Picabia's proprietary journal. It was a repository for his own theories, and those of other artists.

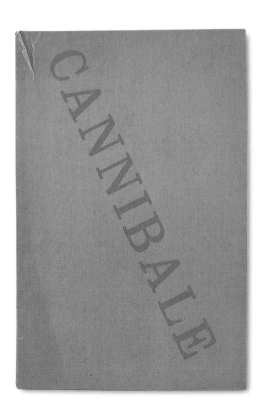

that the publication was to have a short life and that it was also a rather extravagant venture, with its premium paper stock, good ink and fine printing. The contents were experimental in addressing issues of aesthetics and science within the realm of contemporary art and photography, which consequently gave it a somewhat esoteric air.

Typographically influenced by Apollinaire and Marinetti, *291* extended the boundaries of what its editors dubbed 'psychotype' – the artistic manipulation of type to reveal inner expression and meaning. Instead of being concrete signifiers, random letters embodied covert ideas and were manifested as symbols on an expressive canvas. Each psychotype was designed specifically for printing and so was more exact and rigid than if done in the form of a painting. The magazine's commixture of the serious, the satiric and the esoteric made it a forerunner of later Dada reviews. Although the term it coined for the new typography never caught on, the method had resonance throughout the Dada world.

In the end, *291* ran to only twelve issues, in part because its circulation hovered at a paltry one hundred copies. It did, however, inspire Picabia, whose anti-drawings were published in its pages, to name his own slightly later periodical *391* as a homage to Stieglitz.

Marcel Duchamp was editor of the proto-Dada publication *The Blindman*, founded by Henri-Pierre Roche (1879–1959) and Beatrice Wood (1893–1998) in order to announce the first exhibition in New York of the New Society for Independent Artists, the Armory Show of 1913. Apart from Duchamp's *Nude Descending a Staircase* (1912), which received considerable attention, the most notable feature was the first ever reproduction – photographed by Stieglitz – of his infamous work, *Fountain* (1917), the porcelain urinal that he signed R Mutt to hide his true identity. This was rejected from the otherwise alternative Independents' exhibition, causing Duchamp to resign from the hanging committee. In protest, *The Blindman* no.2 (May 1917) published an account of 'The Richard Mutt Case' and confronted the philosophical question: what is art? The scandal was reduced to a Dadaesque circus of absurdity in which a piece of plumbing was put on trial for being immoral and vulgar. *The Blindman*, which certainly viewed contemporary art from a sight-impaired vantage point, published two issues in 1917 that married sophisticated amateurism with conventional publication design.

Between the two numbers of *The Blindman*, Duchamp edited a single edition of *Rongwrong* that was more akin to an improvised newsletter than a bona fide magazine. It published the results of a bizarre chess game that determined whether Picabia's *391* or *The Blindman* would be the organ of the Independents. Picabia won. So *391*

Right from top: **Bulletin Dada**, no.6, 5 February 1920, cover by Tristan Tzara. **Dadaphone**, no.7, 7 March 1920, cover art by Francis Picabia.

These two magazines were published, edited and designed by Tristan Tzara. Picabia's influence on Tzara produced some of the outrageous text and design that gave Dada its emblematic appearance.

Opposite, top row from left: **291**, no.1, March 1915, cover art by Marius de Zayas; and inside page with 'Ideogram' poem by Guillaume Apollinaire; July–August 1915, cover art by Picabia. Published and edited by Alfred Stieglitz, *291* was an offshoot of his 291 Fifth Avenue Gallery, a very early avant-garde venue in New York. It was designed with an eye towards the Italian Futurists.

Opposite, centre row from left: **The Blindman**, no.1, 10 April 1917, with cover art by Marcel Duchamp, and inside page with advertisement; no.2, May 1917, inside page with photograph by Alfred Stieglitz of Duchamp's infamous 'Fountain by R Mutt'. *The Blindman* was edited by Henri-Pierre Roche, Beatrice Wood and Marcel Duchamp.

Opposite, bottom row from left: **Rongwrong**, 1917 (only issue), cover and inside spread edited and designed by Marcel Duchamp. Duchamp's *Blindman* and *Rongwrong* were designed in an ad hoc manner without concern for the niceties of type.

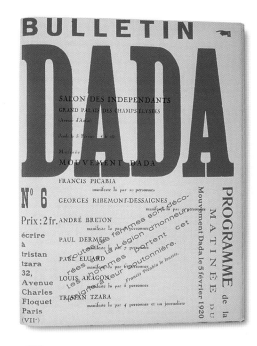

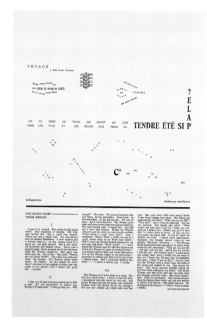

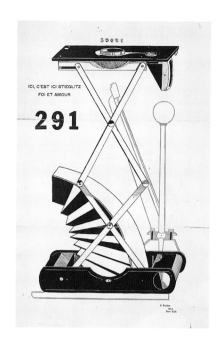

continued to be published in New York, eventually experimenting with various grades and sizes of paper. Picabia was more than an artistic independent; he was independently wealthy and could thus afford to indulge himself through his publication, which he moved from New York to Paris on a whim. And whim seems to have determined how *391* would look. The American numbers, in particular, exhibited Picabia's penchant for type as mutable and expressive. These early issues relied on classic typefaces but never used the same one throughout. Later, *391* introduced modern typefaces that were plentiful at type houses in New York; it was both a hothouse and a playground for typographic tomfoolery.

In 1921 Duchamp teamed up with Man Ray (1890–1976) to produce a single issue (four pages in all) of *New York Dada*, ostensibly the first time that the term Dada was officially used in America. The publication was a tenuous bridge between the US and European avant-gardes. *New York Dada* was influenced, but did not mimic, the later issues of Tzara's *Dada*. Each page was, however, like its counterpart, a distinct typographic and visual experience that appeared to mix art and advertising techniques into a *mélange* of eccentricity. The cover was a masterpiece of contorted typesetting – a page stuffed with hundreds of rows of the typewritten words 'New York Dada April 1921' cascading in red upside down and framing in its centre a bottle of Belle Haleine perfume. Inside, the layouts were typically skewed but no more raucous than in other journals. Tzara's own testament to (and authorization of) *New York Dada*, entitled 'Eye-Cover, Art-Cover Authorization, Corset-Cover', appears in blue ink on the second page and is laid out in a rather unexceptional manner. In fact, despite an attempt by some artists to capture the evanescence of the core movement, little of European Dada's unorthodox design sensibility really took hold in the United States.

Some of the typographic rules so flagrantly broken by European Dada (and Futurism) were followed in certain avant-garde periodicals in America but not with the same degree of enthusiasm or fervency for graphic design. *The Little Review*, founded in Chicago in 1914 by Margaret Andersen (*c*.1886–1973) and Jane Heap (*c*.1887–1964) as an independent literary journal, had a New York 'Dada phase', while the European-based *Broom*, founded in November 1921 by Harold Loeb (1891–1974), proselytized American Dada. These were among the periodicals with design formats that ventured into the netherworld between convention and experimentation, but the results were mediocre. Ultimately the American Surrealist magazines

Below: **New York Dada**, April 1921 (only issue), cover by Marcel Duchamp and inside spread. *New York Dada* was edited and designed by Marcel Duchamp and Man Ray. On the cover, the title of the journal is meticulously typeset in rows framing the bottle of Belle Haleine perfume. However, the interior typography is fairly conventional.

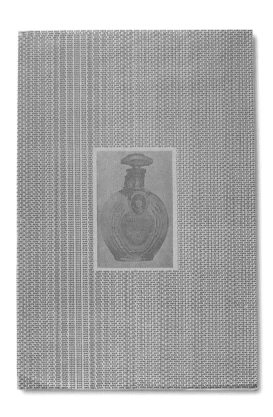

View and *VVV*, published after the earlier Dada movement had foundered, adopted the quirky graphic design that helped to define the later movement (see Chapter 7).

Back in post-war Europe, two later Dada-inspired periodicals, *Mécano*, founded in 1922 by De Stijl artist Theo van Doesburg (1883–1931), and *Merz*, founded in Hanover by Kurt Schwitters, were clarions of progressive art that also trumpeted their respective editors' unique creative visions. Neither artist was exclusively Dada, nor were their publications.

In 1917 Van Doesburg and Piet Mondrian founded *De Stijl*, the organ of the Dutch Neo-Plastic movement (see Chapter 5). *Mécano* began as a free-standing Dada supplement to *De Stijl* (its official publisher) to confront issues emanating from the 1922 Düsseldorf Congress of International Progressive Artists at which, in a spontaneous revival of Dada, members protested against the focus on business at the event. Van Doesburg, Hans Richter, and the Russian El Lissitzky organized an alternative Congress of Constructivists and Dadaists at Weimar, which reported on and supported the insurrection through the publication.

Mécano was a mixture of subversion and aversion. A manifesto which Van Doesburg had introduced in *De Stijl* appeared under the pseudonym I K Bonset, supporting Dada typography as the basis of a new poetic language while attacking the Russian Constructivist notion of utilitarian or productivist art. The Bauhaus also came under fire for its 'solemnities'. But *Mécano* was more than a vehicle for negative propaganda. Van Doesburg saw the power in graphic design. He experimented with type and layout in a fairly disciplined though free-form manner that commingled raucous Dada and rational Constructivist principles, resulting in a more structured, legible version of Dada ad hoc-ism. The first three numbers, which were not magazines *per se* but broadsheets printed on glossy white paper, were each folded into three sections then folded again into sixteen panels which, when unfolded, revealed discordant juxtapositions with texts positioned sometimes in reverse directions. The verso was printed in bright primary colours found in *De Stijl* – first blue, then yellow and then red. Van Doesburg further separated, ordered and underscored texts using heavy black rules – similar to Constructivist and Bauhaus typography. Arguably these page-like grids suggest the tenets of Neo-Plastic painting. The fourth and final issue of *Mécano* was printed on a broadsheet with a white verso, folded into quarters and bound more like a conventional journal.

Merz was a self-styled abstract art movement, the invention of Kurt Schwitters. Like 'Dada', 'Merz' was a

Below from left: **The Little Review**, covers of vol.12 no.2, May 1929; vol.11 no.1, Spring 1925. **Broom**, vol.1 no.3, January 1922.

The Little Review, edited by Margaret Andersen and Jane Heap, and *Broom*, edited by Harold Loeb, both sported different covers (with consistently changing logos) for each issue. The anonymously designed May 1929 cover (left) shows the influence of Constructivism and the Spring 1925 cover is a hypnotic drawing by Marcel Duchamp. The January 1922 issue of *Broom*, designed by Fernand Léger, is Constructivism incarnate.

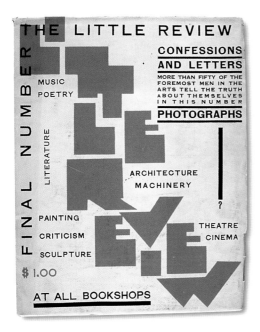

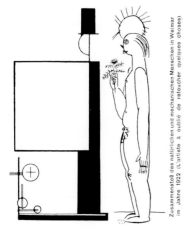

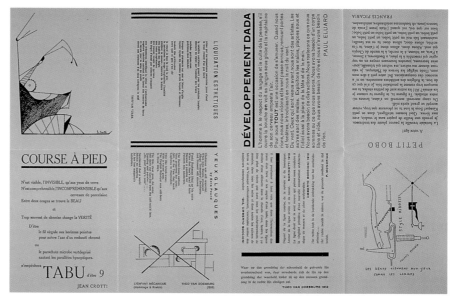

nonsense word selected at random, reportedly from a typographic fragment. Schwitters wrote: 'The word "Merz" had no meaning when I formed it. Now it has the meaning which I gave it. The meaning and concept "Merz" changes with the change in the insight of those who continue to work with it. The backbone of Merz was rhythmic design that embraces all branches of art in an artistic unit.'[18] Both Schwitters and Van Doesburg sympathized with aspects of Dada, but like Picabia they were ardent mavericks. Indeed, Schwitters was a one-man movement who proclaimed that 'antidada' was a like-minded alternative.

Schwitters was a feisty iconoclast with a penchant for commercial advertising and publicity. When the magazine *Merz* was founded he had already been consumed by his Merz art (including phonetic poems, abstract paintings and 'Merzbau' – an organic and monumental sculpture of found objects and common detritus that grew to huge proportions and enveloped the interior of his home). He had collaborated with Van Doesburg on a visit to Holland in 1923, in a series of performances promoted as a Dada tour. The early issues of *Merz* were advertisements for his ideas and the work of his kindred artists. The periodical was built on a geometric grid armature with a clear De Stijl influence and evolved into a model of what Jan Tschichold (1902–74), a visionary young German graphic designer, would celebrate in 1925

as 'Elementare Typographie' (Elementary Typography).

Schwitters used *Merz* to address pressing artistic/ideological themes, though the radical politics that consumed Berlin Dada were absent (see Chapter 4). The first issue was devoted to Holland Dada and included written and visual contributions by Van Doesburg, Schwitters and Tzara. The seven subsequent issues align with Zurich and Paris Dada and with De Stijl. Schwitters predictably flies a banner for an international and classless abstract art that is reflected in his Merz paintings and sculpture. But *Merz* did not adhere to a strict format for long.

From issue no.8 onwards, the publication's size varied considerably. The most significant number, from the standpoint of proffering a new typography, was issue no.8–9, titled 'Nasci', guest-edited and designed by El Lissitzky, which marries his Constructivist principles with a Dada panache. With Schwitters, Lissitzky also designed brand-new advertisements for the Pelikan ink company (including photogram experiments). *Merz* no.11, the 'TYpo REklame' issue, was a portfolio of Schwitters's geometrical compositions – a dynamic array of red and black surfaces and sans-serif type that boldly framed an anarchic array of words and images promoting the venerable office product. A hybrid *Merz* collaboration between Schwitters, Käthe Steinitz and Van Doesburg was devoted to fairy tales and

Opposite, clockwise from top left: **Mécano**, cover of no.1, 1922; inside spreads from nos.1, 2 and 3, all 1922. *Right:* cover and inside spread from no.4–5, 1923. Theo van Doesburg published and designed *Mécano* as a large single sheet printed on both sides and folded in quarters. Each number was distinguished by a different primary colour (blue, yellow, red) on one side and the random, anarchic typography. The cover particularly, with its letters separated by black bars, was consistent with the prevailing Dada aesthetic.

Above from left to right:
Merz, covers of no.8–9, April–July 1924, by El Lissitzky; no.11, 1924, by Kurt Schwitters; no.16–17, 1925, typography by Schwitters, drawings by Käthe Steinitz. *Left and opposite:* **Merz**, no.11, 1925, inside spreads designed by Schwitters. *Merz* was edited by Kurt Schwitters. He used the magazine as an experimental and promotional review, and invited various collaborators to help him with the design. The logo remained constant but the covers and interiors changed according to theme. *Merz* no.11 was a showcase for Schwitters's bold advertisements for Pelikan ink. Schwitters promoted his graphic design studio through this issue and presented the New Typography in all its discordance. *Merz* no.16–17 was devoted to his collaboration with Steinitz who co-edited this issue.

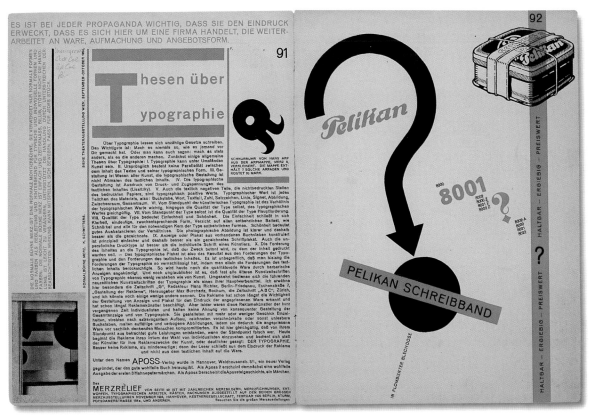

entitled 'Die Scheuche' (The Scarecrow). Though more of a book than a magazine, it was reminiscent of Lissitzky's Constructivist children's classic, *The Tale of Two Squares* (1922); the characters are people in the form of letters and the text typography expresses their thoughts, words and deeds. *Merz* continued in a tabloid format until issue no.18–19 but for its final three issues it became a smaller booklet, produced over the course of two years and devoted to new architecture. After *Merz* came to an end, Schwitters continued his unstoppable 'Merzbau' until an Allied bombing raid in 1943 destroyed the building in which it was housed.

Hanover was not the only Dada cell in Germany. Starting in 1919, Cologne had a movement with three indigenous reviews, *Der Ventilator*, *Bulletin D* and *Die Schammade*, and three influential proponents, Max Ernst (before leaving for Paris in 1921), Johannes Baargeld (1892–1927) and Hans Arp. Baargeld, whose father was a local banker, financed *Der Ventilator*, a weekly Dada paper with Marxist leanings, and served with Ernst as co-editor until banned by the British Army.[9] Akin to Berlin's political journals, *Der Ventilator* used satire to address social ills. Though it was not as graphically interesting as its counterparts in Berlin, it marked the beginning of a Dada presence in Cologne and was quickly followed in 1919 by *Bulletin D* (ostensibly a catalogue of Ernst's work) and *Die Schammade* (the more visually adventurous of the two).

Ernst (1891–1976) was less involved in political events than Baargeld and so took a more active role in *Die Schammade* which was produced to parallel the first Dada exhibition in Cologne (noteworthy for having its entrance through a men's cloakroom). Visitors were encouraged to vandalize anything in the exhibition that they did not like and some of the results were documented in the periodical.

Die Schammade's typographic display was fairly fluid. None the less, among the various typefaces that signified Dada, Ernst included, presumably ironically, Blackface (or Fraktur), the antiquated German style of lettering that was anathema to Dada (and to modernists in general) because of its imperial symbolism. Ernst's own penchant for manipulating nineteenth-century engravings and commercial art clichés developed at this time as a consequence of working with printers. He was also predisposed to collage as an expressive medium and ransacked volumes of type foundry sample books, textbooks and industrial catalogues for raw materials. Through their association with *Die Schammade*, Ernst et al. were part of the international Dada community that included the ubiquitous Picabia and Tzara. The review was terminated in 1921 when Baargeld forsook Dada entirely and Ernst left for Paris where he ultimately allied himself with the Surrealists.

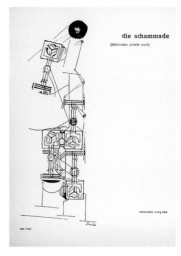

The Zurich/Paris/New York phase of Dada ended (although the date is unclear because different individuals left at various times) with an implosion of warring factionalism and petty feuds. Dada's demise involved a rash of periodicals and demonstrations and merits a history all its own. Picabia, who arguably found the most freedom in Dada and to whom Dada gave celebrity as a poet and artist, was one of its leading assassins. Dada was built on destructive tendencies: enmity among the members developed overnight, and intrigue rooted in philosophical and programmatic disagreement, as well as rivalry over who claimed the invention of Dada, consumed one and all. Picabia, for one, turned on his former friend Tzara, who turned on others as they, in turn, decried him. The last issue of *Dada*, published in 1921 and entitled *Dada In Tirol* (also known as *Dada Au Grand Air*) was an orgy of riotous typography in what historian Georges Hugnet calls 'this last free and spontaneous expression of Dada on the brink of the abyss'.[10]

With Dada sliding towards irrelevance, the 'Congress of Paris' was planned by André Breton to address the need for realignment but failed to materialize owing to increasingly embittered relations. Picabia aired his feelings in his book *Pomme de Pins* (Pine Cone) 1922, which showered violent abuse on his enemies (and, in characteristic fashion, on himself as well). But perhaps the most significant historical document, both for its content and design, was Tzara's single issue of *Le Cœur à Barbe* (The Bearded Heart): *Journal Transparent* in 1922, a response to *Pomme de Pins* and a counter-attack on Breton and the Paris Congress. This publication contained the last series of manifestos of this phase of the Dada movement; its cover, through a witty application of random nineteenth-century typefaces and printer's clichés, symbolizes the marriage of Dada and Surrealism. Dadaesque publications continued to appear after 1922 (including Picabia's *391*). But *Le Cœur à Barbe* serves as a headstone for the air of nonsense, incoherence and contradiction inherent in Dada. Its cover unwittingly entombed the graphic style of the artistic phase of Dada (the political one developed its own vocabularies) and signalled the launch of a Surrealist graphic language as well.

Right: **Dada In Tirol**, cover of no.1, September 1921. *Dada In Tirol* was so named because editor Tristan Tzara and contributors Max Ernst and Hans Arp spent time in the town of Tirol.

Far right: **Le Cœur à Barbe**, no.1 (only issue), April 1922. Ilia Zdanevich and Tristan Tzara designed the cover of *Le Cœur à Barbe* using old-fashioned printer's cuts in an ironic manner to form a visual rebus that has no rational meaning but served to reinforce the absurdity for which Tzara, the magazine's editor, was known.

Die Aktion

IX. JAHR. HERAUSGEGEBEN VON FRANZ PFEMF[ERT]

VERLAG · DIE AKTION · BERLIN · WILME

HEFT EINE MARK

4

Protest and Resistance:
Berlin from World War I to the
Third Reich

In post-World War I Berlin small-circulation, alternative – often contraband – magazines and newspapers were the chief media of political and cultural dissent. The radical left-wing polemical periodicals published in Germany until the advent of the Third Reich, were not only among the most caustic but exemplary for their marriage of polemics, art and design. Although international Dada inspired some of these, Berlin's Dada movement was distinct from the movements of Zurich, Paris, New York and even Hanover in the intensity and focus of its political fervency. The mission of Berlin Dada's leaders and the goal of its publications was to obliterate the remnants of Germany's imperial regime. They then sought to challenge the legitimacy of the fatally flawed Weimar Republic and ultimately to promote a Communist ideology.

That these publications failed to prevent the rise of Nazism is endemic to the limited potency of any small-scale press facing the immense apparatus of government, totalitarian or otherwise. An alternative press will predictably succumb to the greater censorial force. None the less, marshalling the talents of committed writers, artists and designers, the German left-wing press attacked political foes with all the intellectual and satirical weaponry at its disposal. Such was its vehemence that it became the model for anti-establishment publishing many decades afterwards – its main influence being on the Sixties Underground press.

The Berlin Dadaists, including Richard Huelsenbeck (the German member of Zurich Dada who brought the movement to the city in 1917), Johannes Baader, George Grosz (Georg Grosz), Raoul Hausmann, Hannah Höch and John Heartfield (Helmuth Herzfelde), saw themselves as Soviet-style agents of the proletariat. They were primed for political revolt and insurrection, using poetry and art as armaments in their struggle. Their aim was to disrupt the status quo, which meant the political, cultural and social systems and their demigods, through as many media as possible – exhibitions, demonstrations, cabaret and periodicals.

Germany had a number of venal demigods, from Bismarck and Kaiser Wilhelm to Hitler, all prime targets for satire that was routinely dispensed through magazines and newspapers, such as *Simplicissimus* (see Chapter 1). Although *Der Simpl*'s artists used acerbic caricature and cartoon to lash out against the burgeoning Nazi Party and Italian Fascism, the magazine did not overtly support the socialist or Communist policies that were wielding influence against the radical nationalists at the time. *Der Simpl* was also feeling its age. The illustrations and typography were rooted in an earlier period and, editorially, it had become more acceptable to the bourgeois rather than the *Volk*, which in pre-war days was its avowed constituency. Change was necessary to keep it vital. But, more importantly, there was impetus among radicals to create new publications addressing the growing polarization between political, economic and ideological groups warring for ultimate power in Germany.

The Left launched periodicals that supported the radical art of Expressionism and introduced unorthodox lettering and typography as a symbol of its anti-bourgeois stance. Two of the left-wing journals that combined art and politics, *Die Aktion* edited by Franz Pfemfert (1879–1954), and *Der Sturm* edited by Herwarth Walden (1878–1941), published raw-edged woodcuts and bold brush-and-line drawings that rejected the decorative and figurative illustration of mass-market magazines. When *Die Aktion* (The Action) appeared in 1911 it was the clarion call of Expressionism in the service of the Communist Party and

Previous page: **Die Aktion**, detail of no.49–50, 1919, cover by Oskar Birckenbach.

Below from left: **Die Aktion**, covers of vol.5 no.33–4, 1915, by Ottheinrich Strohmeyer; vol.6 no.11–12, 1916, by Hans Richter; vol.7 no.1–2, 1917, by Hans Richter; vol.7, no.22–3, 1917, by A H Pellegrini. Published and edited by Franz Pfemfert, *Die Aktion* adhered to a consistent format with a Black Letter logo placed above an Expressionist woodcut or ink drawing. The hard-edged graphics became a symbol and a clarion call for alternative and radical politics attacking the Weimar Republic.

used art initially as a means to fight the monarchy and, later, both right-wing and centrist elements of the Weimar Republic. By the time it had ceased publication in 1932 it was already overshadowed by other artistic developments. Paradoxically, the Nazis had seriously considered adopting Expressionism as their 'national' art but opted instead for heroic, National Socialist realism owing to ideological divisions within the Party. This suggests that by the late Twenties, at the latest, Expressionism was a neutered art.

Der Sturm (The Storm) was a key outlet for the work of leading German and European modernist writers and painters before World War I and introduced the work of the Italian Futurists and French Cubists to Germany. It generated a storm of controversy in academic art circles with its advocacy of modernism as well as of topical issues, including birth control and women's rights. Like *Die Aktion*, its newspaper format – a graphic cover with an interior layout of two to three columns of type per page – gave the magazine's written content a credible appearance that lent authority to its polemical stance in contemporary social and political debates. Walden's own editorials were mostly satirical attacks on *bêtes noires* similar to those of Berlin Dada, including cultural nationalism and the narrow prejudices of the German bourgeoisie. *Der Sturm* was also a pivotal outlet for art criticism. But by the time it ceased publishing in 1932, Berlin Dada's resolute anti-art militancy took over as the gold standard of radical, polemical thinking about art and politics.

'The revolutionary effervescence and social distress of Berlin amid the decline of a rotting imperialism, the filthy lesson taught by the leaders of society and by the great disillusionment of the war, automatically set spontaneously revolutionary Dada on a positive, realistic plane,' wrote Georges Hugnet in a brief personal history of Dada. 'A concrete and immediate task was open to those who, through outward and inner experience, had developed an instinctive revolt and come to recognize the need for political intervention and planning.'[1]

Towards this end, a new periodical, *Club Dada*, which published under the auspices of the newspaper *Die Freie Strasse* in 1918, was the first of the key Berlin Dada publications. Its typography, characterized by disparate typefaces from a variety of type families set in both symmetrical and asymmetrical compositions, was influenced by Zurich Dada publications, and so was the writing: the contents included eccentric poetry, which read more like noise music than verse. However, the attitude was different from the more apolitical Swiss in that *Club Dada* was anarchistic and nihilistic; it overtly attacked the Weimar Republic and Germany's bourgeois revolution for not being radical enough to truly change society into a workers' paradise. As Georges Hugnet commented: 'Behind its trimmings of typographical disorder, gratuitous foolery and

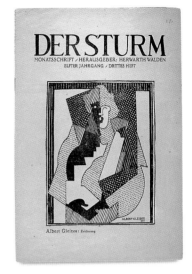

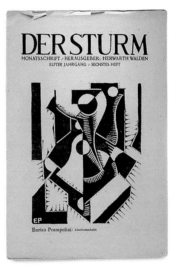

Clockwise from top left: **Der Sturm**, covers of vol.7 no.8, November 1916, by Oskar Kokoschka; vol.11 no.3, 1920, by Albert Gleizes; vol.11 no.9–10, 1920, by Johannes Molzahn; vol.20 no.7, May 1930, designer unknown; vol.11 no.6, 1920, by Enrico Prampolini. *Der Sturm*, published and edited by Herwarth Walden, went through a few graphic changes on its covers but, like *Die Aktion*, for the majority of its tenure woodcuts and drawings were regular fare. Towards the end, in the early Thirties, it adopted a cover motif influenced by Constructivism and the Bauhaus.

subversiveness, we discern, in big red letters, this statement among others: "The disappointed hopes of the German Revolution."[2] This quotation emphasizes the fact that, although in appearance *Club Dada* projected the benign mischief of Dada, it was unquestionably meant to be a thorn in the side of a new establishment that had made too many compromises with the old order. But *Club Dada* was also the embodiment of Dada itself, which Richard Huelsenbeck described in an editorial as 'chaos from which thousands of systems arise and are entangled again in Dada Chaos'.[3]

Berlin Dada's commitment to pragmatic politics – the direct intervention in, or disruption of, government – is debatable. Even though Huelsenbeck was Commissar of Fine Arts during the abortive revolution in 1917, he was arguably not as involved in the struggle as some other Berlin artists. He and a colleague, Raoul Hausmann, focused their attacks on antiquated or misguided art forms, notably Expressionism. Berlin Dadaists objected to the fact that Expressionism began to enjoy a popular vogue. According to the Dadaists, Expressionists had become a generation in search of a respectful place in history, and such introspection made it impossible to be a radical force in its own time. Mounting hunger and growing rage was now rampant in Berlin and in the essay 'En Avant Dada' (A History of Dada, 1920) Huelsenbeck wrote, 'Here we would have to proceed with entirely different methods if we wanted to say something to the people. Here we would have to discard our patent leather pumps and tie our Byronic cravats to the doorpost.'[4] Like Dadas elsewhere, Berlin Dada rejected new art as a substitute for old, tired arts, but even more fervently because the dogs of war unleashed by Germany had for five years devoured itself and Europe as well.

Berlin Dada, therefore, argued that most art – and Expressionism in particular – was a fraudulent moral safety valve, a means of confronting social ills from a safe distance. Hausmann and Huelsenbeck, who comprised the Dadaist revolutionary central council of the German Group, offered through their manifesto, 'What is Dadaism and what does it want in Germany?', a dictum that tied art to harsh political realities, and made the following demands:

• *The international revolutionary union of all creative and intellectual men and women on the basis of radical communism;*

• *The introduction of progressive unemployment through comprehensive mechanization of every field of activity. Only by unemployment does it become possible for the individual to achieve certainty as to the truth of life and finally become accustomed to experience;*

• *The immediate expropriation of property (socialization) and the communal feeding of all; further, the construction of cities of light, and gardens which will belong to society as a whole and prepare man for a state of freedom.*[5]

Below: **Club Dada**, cover of no.1, 1918. *Club Dada*, which was edited by Richard Huelsenbeck, Raoul Hausmann and Franz Jung, was one of many periodicals serving as an outlet for the Berlin Dada group. The typographic jumble on this cover, a woodcut by Raoul Hausmann, symbolized Dada's rabid displeasure with entrenched design traditions.

Opposite top: **Der Dada**, cover of no.1, June 1919. The covers and interior layouts of *Der Dada*, conceived, edited and designed by Raoul Hausmann, exhibit the sarcastic and anarchic sides of design in the Dada movement. His cover design for no.1 uses words as illustration.

Opposite bottom: **Der Dada**, cover of no.2, December 1919 and inside spread with illustrations by Johannes Baader and George Grosz. In Raoul Hausmann's cover of no.2, a collage by Hannah Höch appears. In *Der Dada* gross variations in type size and style direct the reader to key words and slogans.

Berlin Dada was called 'German Bolshevism' but in reality it was an attack on all archaic 'isms', with special vehemence reserved for the art of bourgeois culture. Huelsenbeck declared that art deserved a sound thrashing and that Dada would deliver the punishment. This took the form of satire, irony, bluff and occasionally violence. Primarily, however, Berlin Dada's ire was expressed not with guns and bombs, but ostensibly through print.

Hausmann, Baader and Huelsenbeck (as editor) also collaborated on the review *Der Dada*, which published the first of three issues in 1919. Consistent with the overall Dada ethos, *Der Dada*'s nonsense motto read, 'He who eats of Dada dies if he is not Dada'. *Der Dada*'s intentionally disordered type and image was the archetype of Berlin Dada's visual form and content. Letters of all types and sizes were placed, helter-skelter, around the cover and interior pages, and Hebrew characters printed in every direction were mingled with sentences in French and vignettes borrowed from the illustrations in dictionaries. Rather than an organized scheme with typographic heirarchies, this was an expressive collage in the Cubist sense. *Der Dada* also included an Expressionist-style woodcut by Hausmann, along with old-fashioned printer's dingbats, fleurons and clichés, amid an array of deliberately retained, and otherwise arcane, proof-reading marks used to frame and amplify sound poems and tracts. *Der Dada* differed slightly from the Zurich journals that tended to be

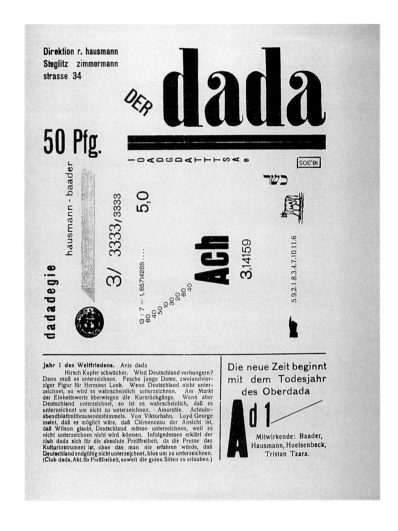

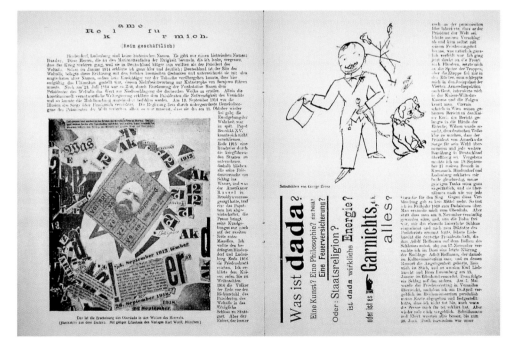

even more crammed with jumbled material, suggestive of a simultaneous poem. On first sight, *Der Dada* may appear resolutely anarchic but, in fact, it is simpler and relies more heavily on the contrast between a page of type and a single word emblazoned across it like a slogan.

Subsequent issues of *Der Dada* included contributions by what Huelsenbeck hyperbolically referred to as a company that soon became the terror of the population, including Francis Picabia, John Heartfield (1891–1968) and George Grosz (1893–1959). The latter two worked in concert to produce ironic collages composed of strips of newspaper and press photographs fused into surreal, though acerbic, vignettes. The collages were symbolic of the de-individualization underscoring the artefacts of the new movement that disavowed the individual brain in favour of communal activity. Indeed, each member of the movement was given a facetious honorific that expressed their loyalty to the cause. These included Hausmann's Dadasoph and in the second issue Baader (aka Superdada) was anointed the Oberdada, the figurehead that anti-Weimar Dadaists planned to proclaim as the President of the Earth. Then there were Grosz's Field-Marshal Dada and John Heartfield's Monteurdada (*Monteuranzüge* are overalls symbolizing the worker).

The third, and final, issue of *Der Dada*, in April 1920, was edited by 'groszfield, hearthaus, and georgemann' and was something of a high-water mark of Dada's influence in Berlin. It was released two months before the International Dada Fair (Dadamesse) held in June 1920, which brought together both sides of Berlin Dada in one sacrilegious event designed to challenge the authorities with an exhibit of Dada contraband, including Grosz drawings, radical periodicals, puppets of capitalists and an effigy of a military officer with a pig's head hanging from the ceiling. The most effective visual instrument was photomontage that fused type and image in an anti-government visual rhetoric. Grosz, Wieland Herzfelde (Heartfield's brother and outspoken poet) and Baader were prosecuted for libel against the state. Although Baader was acquitted, the other two were fined for their offence. Moreover, although the banner that flew over the entrance to the fair read 'Dada fights on the side of the revolutionary proletariat!', many of the group did not accept these radicals as comrades.

In 1920 Grosz, Heartfield and Hausmann further collaborated on *Dadaco*, designed as an anthology of Berlin Dada tracts and visuals. Although *Dadaco* was never published, a prospectus for the anthology titled *Was Ist Dada?* was produced. Within this collection of colourful printed pages appear some of Heartfield's most emblematic early collages, including the headless Dada man and his own screaming self-portrait, and also newspaper-clipping collages by Hausmann and typographic noise poems by Hugo Ball. The anarchic page layout was not entirely lacking in deliberate formal hierarchies. Pages were composed with traditional typographic materials yet the reading pattern, or flow, was interrupted by arbitrary printer's marks and a cacophony of surprints and overprints in flat colour and illustrative images.

While Berlin Dada was forged in the crucible of artistic revolution, and was enmeshed in the fractious politics of the ailing Weimar Republic, in Germany Dada was a brief phenomenon. The political tinder-box that was Weimar necessitated quick and radical shifts in thought and deed. The majority of German Communists who were not involved with Dada accepted that Dada could be useful to the cause, but realized that pictures and demonstrations alone were not going to defeat the state. So there was often as much dissension within the Left as there was throughout the nation.

Rising from Berlin's polarized political environment, the Communist Party tried to win the hearts and minds of workers and other sympathizers. The Party's leading artist-propagandists joined together to spread the gospel through demonstrations and printed missives, often in the face of official censorship and police resistance. In the 1925 pamphlet *Die Kunst ist in Gefahr* (Art is in Danger) Wieland Herzfelde and George Grosz declared that the revolutionary relationship between art and the political struggle was a moral imperative. 'Today's artist, if he does not want to run down and become an antiquated dud, has the choice between technology and class warfare propaganda. In both cases he must give up "pure art". Either he enrols as an architect, engineer or commercial artist in the army ... which develops industrial powers and exploits the world; or, as a reporter and critic reflecting the face of our times, a propagandist and defender of the revolutionary idea and its partisans, he finds a place in the army of the suppressed who fight for their just share of the world, for a significant social organization of life.'[6]

The pamphlet in which this call to arms was published was one of many produced by the Malik Verlag, a Berlin-based, radical publishing house founded in 1917 by Herzfelde, Heartfield and Grosz. The Malik was the framework that allowed these artists to print attacks on the status quo. For back in 1916, when opposition to German involvement in the lost war was mounting at a fast pace, there was greater need for protest outlets apart from the lone voice in the wilderness, *Die Aktion*, which was monitored by the censors. Herzfelde assumed editorship of the anti-war arts periodical *Neue Jugend* (New Youth) to publish the work of those who had encountered opposition to their political ideas and lack of understanding by the public. Although its format was an unexceptionally

Opposite: **Der Dada**, cover and inside page of no.3, April 1920. Edited by Raoul Hausmann, John Heartfield and George Grosz. The cover montage by John Heartfield for *Der Dada* no.3 is an explosion of quotidian images and words. Heartfield and Grosz collaborated on the witty 'capitalist puppet' on the inside page.

traditional quarto with a staid typographic cover and justified columns of unadorned text inside, it was a wellspring of leading progressive German authors and so-called enemy foreigners, such as Walt Whitman. After a few issues it was officially banned for its seditious editorial policy; a few months later it defiantly resumed publication and was banned again. None the less Herzfelde opened up the publication to sympathizers by announcing that all lovers of freedom would have a voice in *Neue Jugend*.

During World War I the government issued licences for periodicals and publishing houses based on a principle of 'pressing need'. Infuriated by the forced closure of the original *Neue Jugend*, John Heartfield concocted a publishing strategy whereby a new Malik Verlag was established on 1 March 1917 as a ploy to legally revive the magazine. In his application for the publishing licence it was stated that a novella entitled *Der Malik* by Else Lasker-Schüler had earlier appeared in instalments in the first editions of *Neue Jugend*. To complete the publication of this book, there was a 'pressing need' for the creation of a publishing house. Although the logic was shaky, the licence was granted. However, instead of completing the novella, the Malik Verlag illegally published two Grosz portfolios of incendiary anti-military cartoons and the first of two more weekly edition issues of *Neue Jugend* in a large, four-page, broadsheet-size format. In June, a three-colour issue, mockingly called 'Pamphlet for a Little Grosz Portfolio', was published in which the only mention of the portfolio was a small advertisement; the rest of the periodical included articles by Grosz. The first issue was comparatively staid, but the second, dated June 1917, was designed by Heartfield (Malik's art director). According to Herzfelde, '"Dadaism" was its layout.' It was admittedly Heartfield's art directorial debut and arguably sparked a typographic revolution. 'The sovereign, fascinating way in which he conjured up something unprecedented from old type, plates, lead bars and rings reveals the artist who – almost overnight – had found his own unmistakable style,'[7] wrote Herzfelde admiringly.

Heartfield's cover typography was a rejection of conventional design tenets. It involved the playful use of variegated typefaces, composed in an asymmetrical manner, with numerous cliché images taken from the jobbing printer's type-case. Inside, type-case 'furniture' was also used as a graphic element, prefiguring the symbolic Constructivist typographics of El Lissitzky and Aleksandr Rodchenko. Visually, *Neue Jugend* was true to its name. It was not a typical, staid political manifesto nor was it decorous commercial art. Rather, the typography summoned the reader to action. *Neue Jugend* took its mission to end the war seriously. Heartfield planned a third large, broadsheet-sized issue to be printed in white ink on black mourning

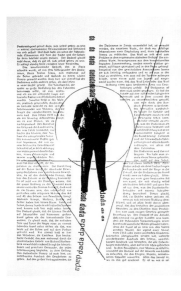

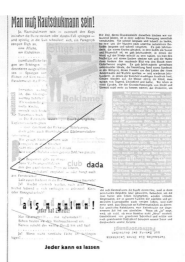

Left: **Neue Jugend**, cover and interior pages from no.1, May 1917. *Opposite top:* cover of no.2, June 1917. The two broadsheet versions of *Neue Jugend*, both edited by Wieland Herzfelde, John Heartfield and George Grosz, and designed by John Heartfield, were as different as day and night. The first (May 1917, *left*) was comparatively conservative in an effort to subvert the censors. The second (June 1917, *opposite*) unleashed the typographic exuberance that typified Berlin Dada while still maintaining the appearance of a newspaper.

Opposite bottom: **Jedermann sein eigner Fussball**, cover and inside spread from no.1 (only issue), February 1919. With this cover John Heartfield published his first political photomontage, a parody of a political beauty pageant for which he uses a fan showing the heads of Weimar's leaders. The mascot in the 'ear' of the cover illustrates the title, 'Everyman His Own Football'. Inside George Grosz contributed cartoons, including his scabrous anti-war satire about validating a rotting corpse for active duty. This publication, like *Neue Jugend*, was published by the Malik Verlag and edited by Wieland Herzfelde, John Heartfield and George Grosz.

crape, yet this never came to pass because the Malik Verlag was curtailed by restrictive wartime edicts. Following Germany's defeat and the rise of the Weimar Republic, political parties and paramilitary groups violently battled for power across the ideological divide. Nazis were pitted against Communists and both were at odds with the Social Democrats leading the fragile new Republic. The Malik Verlag was poised to influence public debate and agitate followers, so, to revive the imprint that had been dormant for two years, in 1919 Heartfield and Herzfelde created a satiric, tabloid-sized newspaper entitled *Jedermann sein eigner Fussball* (Every Man His Own Football), which became one of the central documents of Berlin protest and Dada. The front page was designed by Heartfield in a stark yet playful manner. In what is known in newspaper argot as the 'ear', the space to the left of the masthead contains a collage of a man whose torso is a football. The main illustration – which was the first time a montage was used as political satire – is of a fan with the silhouetted heads of the leaders of the Ebert–Noske–Scheidemann administration superimposed upon it. This image carried the facetious title: 'Sweepstake! Who is the Most Beautiful?' Inside, a banner headline read: 'Revolutions are the Locomotives of World History'; and the articles lent support to Communist aspirations to power. In addition, a Grosz cartoon attacked the Church, a Salomon Friedlaender essay

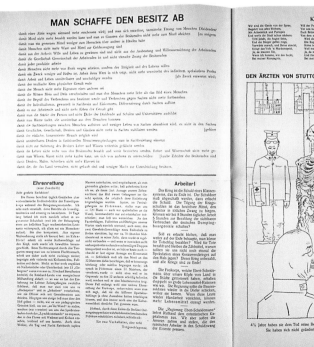

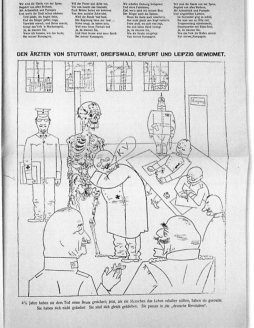

attacked the military, and Walter Mehring's poem 'Coitus in "Drei Mädelhaus"' was proposed as a new national hymn.

Despite the freedoms assured by the constitution of the Weimar Republic, *Jedermann* challenged decrees that enforced confiscation of the publication. As a decoy, the editors hired a brass band to play patriotic songs while Dadaists and others marched through the working-class districts of Berlin selling every last copy of the initial 7,500 printing. After the spectacle was over the editors were indeed arrested and tried, yet eventually released without being sentenced. However, *Jedermann* only published one issue.

Later that same year, while the trial was still in progress, Herzfelde, Heartfield and Grosz brazenly published another confrontational journal, *Die Pleite* (Bankrupt), an organ of the Spartacist faction of the Communist Party. 'It was *Jedermann* ... but with a clearer political alliance,' comments historian James Fraser.[8] It was also visually more refined. Its hand-scrawled masthead sat atop a satirical Grosz drawing rendered in an expressive pen-and-ink line. These cartoons routinely attacked the unholy alliance between the Republican (Social Democratic) leaders and the army, police and Freikorps (nationalist mercenaries). Heartfield also published photographs with political texts, including those of soldiers fallen in battle with the caption 'Hindenburg Breakfast', referring to the famed general who

later became President of the Republic. *Die Pleite*'s typography was more restrained than most other Dada printed matter, but more modern than the official Nazi or Communist periodicals.

Between the first and third issues of *Die Pleite*, Heartfield produced a sixteen-page pamphlet with a cover illustrated by Grosz, entitled *Schutzhaft*, which included an account of being held in protective custody, accused of being a potential enemy of the state, during the *Jedermann* incident. Subsequent issues of *Die Pleite* followed the same format as the first and were published irregularly – despite further confiscations – from 1919 to 1920. In 1920 *Die Pleite* became a supplement of the monthly *Der Gegner* (The Opponent), another strident political journal originally edited by 21-year-old Julian Gumperz (1899–1972) and published by the Malik Verlag with Herzfelde as co-editor. Both publications were issued in tandem until 1922 when financial woes felled *Der Gegner*, although the Malik continued to publish books and pamphlets on leftist themes and issues.

Less than a year later, the publication void was filled by *Der Knüppel* (The Club, lasting from 1923 to 1927), a dedicated Communist tabloid which was illustrated with Grosz's less artful polemical brush drawings. The spare design formats of *Die Pleite* and *Der Gegner* had already signalled a formal break with raucous Dada as the language

Below from left: **Die Pleite**, covers of no.4, 1 May 1919; no.5, 15 December 1919; no.6, January 1920. Each cover for *Die Pleite*, the Malik Verlag's staunchly polemical journal edited by Wieland Herzfelde, John Heartfield and George Grosz, was drawn by Grosz (with some interior illustrations by Heartfield). Such illustrations attacked the Weimar government's arrest of political opponents and reliance on right-wing Friekorps troops as police.

of opposition. *Der Knüppel* was even less Dadaesque in its rather stiff format that signified no-nonsense polemics against the rising tide of Weimar censorship and the crackdown against left-wing opponents. *Der Knüppel* was one of many periodicals, pamphlets and posters that filled the streets as political violence between left, right and centre was played out in Berlin.

In addition to stark drawings and bold paintings, photomontage played a crucial part in the arsenal of Communist graphic weaponry, but photography as both information and propaganda medium was equally significant. Throughout Europe, and especially in Germany, the picture magazine was used to win the hearts and minds of certain constituencies. Among the most influential of these was the Socialist/Communist-inspired *Arbeiter-Illustrierte Zeitung* (Workers' Illustrated News) which began in 1921 as an offshoot of *Sowjet Russland im Bild* (Soviet Russia in Pictures), designed to propagate a positive image of the Bolshevik workers' paradise. Although it was not initially radical in format, indeed it looked like any mainstream or even Nazi publication, it evolved into a striking document of dissent.

AIZ was edited by Willi Münzenberg (1889–1940), a fervent supporter of the Russian Revolution, who saw the picture magazine as a vehicle for aiding German workers in their struggle against capitalism. When *AIZ* began, it was proving difficult to obtain photographs that addressed workers' concerns from the leading picture agencies. Münzenberg therefore developed a strategy to encourage societies of amateur photographers who would, in turn, become photo correspondents. In Hamburg, in 1926, he established the first Worker Photographer group, which grew into a network of viable cameramen throughout Germany and the Soviet Union. He also founded a magazine called *Der Arbeiter Fotograf* (The Worker Photographer), which offered technical and ideological assistance.

Bertolt Brecht, the German playwright, once wrote in a letter to Münzenberg that the camera could lie just as easily as the typesetting machine, so the task of *AIZ* was to serve up the truth and reproduce real facts. In fact, while many of the photographs in *AIZ* were objective accounts of workers' triumphs, the layouts often served to heroicize (and therefore politicize) the activities that were recorded in its pages. Except for its ideological orientation, the *AIZ* was formally no different from its Nazi counterpart the *Illustrierte Beobachter* (Illustrated Observer, founded in 1926), which employed similar photojournalistic conventions. In fact, the design formats of both were also similar. Both magazines were printed on rotogravure presses in inks that gave the pages a velvet aura. The interior text and headline type echoed the apolitical mainstream photo magazines, featuring bold gothic typefaces and hand-rendered scripts.

Below from left: **Der Gegner**, vol.2 no.3, December–January 1920–1, cover by John Heartfield; vol.1 no.8–9, November–December 1919, cover by Raoul Hausmann; **Der Knüppel**, cover of vol.4 no.6, June 1926.

Der Gegner, which was published by the Malik Verlag, and edited by Julian Gumperz and Wieland Herzfelde, published harsh written and visual criticism of the Weimar Republic. However, its small size (a quarto compared to *Die Pleite*'s tabloid) did not allow for ambitious design. *Der Knüppel*, a tabloid published by KPD (German Communist Party) and edited and designed by John Heartfield, was also designed in a more conservative manner.

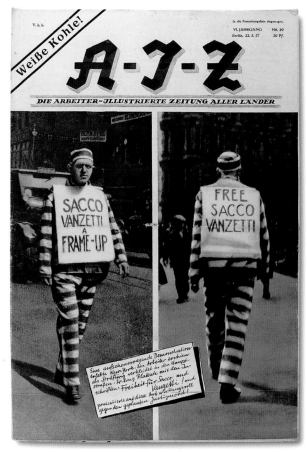

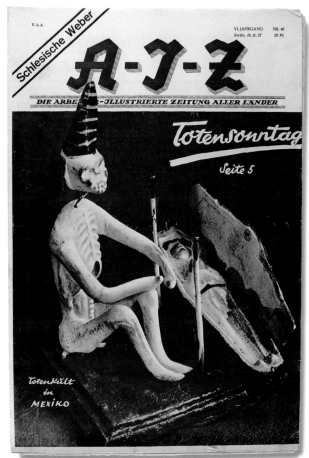

The main distinction between these two photojournals was the acerbic and brazen pictorial anti-Nazi content of *AIZ*. In 1930 John Heartfield started to produce satiric photomontages for *AIZ* that graphically ripped the facade off the Nazi leaders and their functionaries. Montage was all-important to *AIZ* in the years after the Nazi ascendancy because the Worker Photographer movement in Germany was officially crushed, with the result that usable, politically acceptable images of proletariat triumphs that supported the socialist agenda were unobtainable from mainstream photo agencies. Only through photomontage – the ironic juxtaposition of realities in the service of polemics – could the magazine continue to convey strong messages that served as credible propaganda.

When the Nazis assumed power in 1933, *AIZ* was decreed contraband and its editors were targeted as enemies of the state. After the last issue was published in Berlin on 5 March, Münzenberg moved the operation to Prague, where the circulation dropped from 500,000 copies to around 12,000. Attempts to circulate a miniature version that was smuggled into Germany were unsuccessful. In 1936 *AIZ* was renamed *Volks Illustrierte* and two years later, when German occupation of Czechoslovakia was imminent, the magazine was moved to France where it published only one issue. Most of the picture stories are now forgotten, but Heartfield's iconic and ironic photomontages are still celebrated as prime documents of agitation and protest.

Hitler's appointment by President Hindenburg as Reich Chancellor in 1933, and the consequent rise of a Nazi majority in the Reichstag, gave him the power to legally end these radical publishing activities in Germany. Seeing the writing on the wall, Herzfelde had already re-established the Malik Verlag in Prague in 1932 and it remained operational until 1938 when Gestapo activity made it impossible to continue. Then he and Heartfield moved to London. Later, Herzfelde moved to New York where he ran the Aurora Verlag from 1945 to 1947. Grosz had emigrated to New York in 1933 where he worked for a small satirical magazine, *Americana,* and taught watercolour painting at the Art Students' League.

The era of the left-wing German journal was over for the duration of the Third Reich, yet what remained was a legacy that influenced a future generation. During the Sixties, 'Underground' or alternative newspapers sprang up like weeds in major cities and college towns to protest against the Vietnam War. Although most of the young contributors had never heard of *Jedermann*, *Die Pleite* or *Der Gegner*, a few acknowledged the spiritual debt and the formal relationship. The times and issues had changed, but the fundamental means of address were the same.

RED

měsíčník pro moderní kulturu

10

LET

sově
kult
prác

1917·1927

listopa

listop

ODEON

5

Karel Teige

Rational Radicals:
Modernism and the New Typography

Twentieth-century modernism developed in the 1910s as a movement of kindred artists, designers, and writers from all over Europe who commonly believed that a wave of industrial mass production and technological progress had caused profound social repercussions in all realms of society. Art and design, the adherents argued, had to lead the culture aggressively into this new century so that outmoded styles were replaced with new formal languages in all media from painting and film to typography. Modernism was an ethical and aesthetic manifestation that viewed the world in black and white and sometimes in red: black and white because modernism was reductive – void of the past's superfluities, adhering to maximal economy; red because modernism was utopian with socialist affinities leaning towards Communism and proffering social and political revolution.

Modern movements with disparate traits were founded in Holland, Germany, Russia, Czechoslovakia, Yugoslavia, Poland, Romania and Hungary, incorporating design languages unique to their respective cultures yet consistent with pan-cultural concepts, notably the 'rightness of form'. Methodologies developed through such key movements and schools as Holland's De Stijl, Russia's Constructivists and Germany's Bauhaus and were exported via their respective reviews, newspapers, and magazines throughout Europe, the United States and Japan.

These periodicals comprised a virtual Internet of the era, a web of communication that informed, proselytized and critiqued. While different verbal tongues were potential obstacles in promoting the universal language of modernism, the moderns introduced signs, symbols, and images designed to reach broader publics. A few periodicals were bilingual and others such as *Veshch/Gegenstand/Objet*, produced by El Lissitzky (1890–1941) and Ilya Ehrenburg (1891–1967), were even trilingual. Cross-pollination between foreign artists was encouraged – so that ideas of the Dutch influenced the Germans, which in turn influenced the Russians, and so on. In 1917 Theo van Doesburg helped to found the De Stijl movement and its journal of the same name that influenced the content and look of certain Bauhaus and Bauhaus-inspired periodicals. By the mid-Twenties the Bauhaus was the most recognized of modern pedagogical institutions. It was not the sole magnet for international students but it was the most publicized, owing to its copious publication programme that inspired other periodicals throughout the network.

The history of avant-garde periodical publishing in western, central and eastern Europe is important in tracing the diaspora of progressive art and design between the wars. It also marks the development of what Jan Tschichold dubbed in 1925 'Elementare Typographie', known a few years

Previous page: **Red**, detail of vol.3 no.2, November 1927, cover design by Karel Teige.

Below: **Veshch/ Gegenstand/Objet**, no.1–2, April 1922. The same cover of *Veshch/ Gegenstand/Objet*, designed by El Lissitzky, was used from issue to issue and was typical of the Constructivist typographic style. The magazine was edited by Lissitzky and Ilya Ehrenburg.

later as the New Typography (see Chapter 6). This was a critical rejection of archaic central-axis type composition and ornamental design, and graphically symbolized the present and future.

Futurism and Dada advanced expressive (if also anarchic) typography as a tool of artistic revolution. Elementary typography incorporated radical thought into quotidian communications and was constructed on the armature of geometric grids with prescribed typefaces as an alternative to the status quo. Although there were some exceptions to the basic tenets, elementary typography was characterized by asymmetrical arrangements, sans-serif typefaces, bold horizontal and vertical bars arranged like a Mondrian painting, masses of geometric shapes and, often, the pervasive colour red.

While these are but the superficial manifestations that gave the phenomenon a graphic identity, the modern movement's vanguard typographic language is more importantly related to upheavals in twentieth-century painting, architecture and poetry. The first official break with conventional type composition was suggested in F T Marinetti's 'First Futurist Manifesto' of 1909. The rational stage of modernism emerged in 1917 with the advent of De Stijl, a reductive aesthetic language in which all plastic form derived directly from the rectangle and the three primary colours, plus black.

Van Doesburg and his co-founder of the journal *De Stijl*, Piet Mondrian, believed that the rectangle was the Holy Grail of modernity because it introduced natural order to art, in contrast to Art Nouveau and its variants which had devolved into ornamental randomness and excess. Under Van Doesburg's editorship, the journal's frequently changing format innovated modern graphic design as it evolved into a rational language. In the early issues of *De Stijl*, the logo was constructed from rectangular patterns arranged on a strict grid, contributing to its blocky appearance. The interior typography was less overtly geometric yet it was devoid of ornament of any kind. The layout was without flourish, allowing photographic illustrations of artwork to take centre stage.

In 1924 Van Doesburg moved to Paris and began working on paintings in which he introduced oblique rectangles for dynamic effect. This asymmetrical arrangement departed from orthodox De Stijl principles, which forced a split with Mondrian who vociferously argued that it unhinged the 'cosmic equilibrium' he had sought to achieve with his own art. Mondrian left the movement but Van Doesburg remained as the spiritual head of De Stijl and edited seventy-six issues (ninety numbers) of the journal over a period of fifteen years.

As an international review, with publishing outlets in Warsaw, Leiden, Hanover, Paris, Brno and Vienna (which followed the footprints of Van Doesburg as he spread the modern gospel), *De Stijl* served as a document of modern art. In issue no.9 (1924–5), Van Doesburg published his own historical critique on the doctrines of Futurism, Cubism, Expressionism, Dadaism, Purism and Constructivism. In 1926 he produced an extended, annotated listing of all the extant avant-garde periodicals as a means of binding together the diverse factions. Above all, modern innovators found an unprecedented outlet in *De Stijl* that validated their respective positions in twentieth-century art history. It was one of the longest continuously published journals but did not, however, survive the death of its editorial mentor in 1931.

Russian Constructivism further influenced rational typography in significant ways. Constructivists believed that a designed object should not have a discernible style but was a product of industrial creation. Constructivism was the technical mastery and organization of materials according to three principles: tectonic (act of creation), factura (manner of creation) and construction (building of creation). Constructivist artists were also engineers, embodying all that this philosophy implies: they oversaw the total creation and manufacture of a product and therefore were masters of production from start to finish.

In the early Twenties Berlin was a point of entry for Russian progressives who made pilgrimages to Weimar. At this time El Lissitzky, a teacher at the design school in Vitebsk where he produced non-objective, geometric paintings called 'Prouns', had developed an innovative graphic design language utilizing circles, squares and triangles in dynamic juxtapositions to heighten the impact of printed messages – both political and commercial. During an extended stay in Berlin, Lissitzky turned his attention to typography, prodigiously experimenting with metal type-case materials (rules, bars, leads) to construct typographic compositions in the manner of his Prouns, that had an architectonic quality and oriented the printed page in unprecedented ways. Despite severe bouts of pulmonary tuberculosis he was a ubiquitous presence in the capitals of modernity – Germany, Switzerland, Holland, France and Poland – which certainly helped to promote Constructivism as both design philosophy and method. Among other outlets, he used various avant-garde periodicals to express his views on typography.

While in Berlin, Lissitzky co-edited and designed the trilingual magazine *Veshch/Gegenstand/Objet*; in Hanover he collaborated on *Merz*; in Holland he contributed to *De Stijl*, as well as a number of central European journals. Between 1924 and 1928 he was a patient at a sanatorium in Switzerland, but this didn't stop him from being co-editor of the Basel-based architectural review *ABC*. He not only had a strong influence on its content and typographical style, he published material in it from the Soviet Union that was

MAANDBLAD VOOR DE MO-
DERNE BEELDENDE VAKKEN
REDACTIE THEO VAN DOES-
BURG MET MEDEWERKING
VAN VOORNAME BINNEN- EN
BUITENLANDSCHE KUNSTE-
NAARS. UITGAVE X. HARMS
TIEPEN TE DELFT IN 1917.

Above: **De Stijl**, no.1, 1917,
cover by Vilmos Huszár.
Right from top: covers
of no. 3–4, 1923; no.87–9,
1928. With its veritably
pixelated logo by Theo van
Doesburg and geometric
woodcut by Vilmos Huszár,
the first issue of *De Stijl*
underscored the dominance
of geometry in modern
art. In later issues Van
Doesburg, who edited and
designed the magazine,
replaced the original logo
with a simple sans-serif
type against a field of
empty, unadorned space.

new to western Europe. Along with articles by, and about, other modern exemplars, including Jan Tschichold, Willi Baumeister and László Moholy-Nagy, Lissitzky contributed an article to *ABC* (no.3) describing his Prouns as a universal language. He also created covers for other journals that promoted his approach; these included a 1923 American issue of the international magazine, *Broom* (vol.4, no.3) and a 1920 issue of the Dutch magazine *Wendingen* (vol.4, no.11). The former was a coloured woodcut and the latter a printed version of a Proun composition, each dramatic examples of geometric design in a Constructivist mode.

Ultimately, what was deemed rational was not absolute. Lissitzky's and Van Doesburg's rationalism was plagued with irrational tics. Variations on what constituted the fundamental rightness of form emerged in their different works and experiments at the time. The design of Van Doesburg's *De Stijl* between 1917 and 1931 was distinct from that for his Dadaist magazine *Mécano* of 1922–3 (see Chapter 3). Lissitzky's 1922 *Veshch/Gegenstand/Objet*, which was classically Constructivist in its approach, did not in any way resemble the more objective 1924 issue of *Merz* that he designed for Kurt Schwitters, which lacked graphic flourish and Constructivist-influenced geometry. Yet, overall, Constructivism and De Stijl rested on the foundation of asymmetrical design and the dynamic juxtaposition of type and image.

The adherents of modernism promoted the idea that graphic tension and drama could co-exist with clarity and accessibility. The manipulation of form in space, and the interplay of type and image were more rational than ad hoc, more constructed than haphazardly scattered over the page. None the less, improvisation gave Constructivism and De Stijl – and the various international journals that embodied these ideas – their defining visual identities. On the one hand, Lissitzky and Van Doesburg deliberately selected letter forms and printing materials that were conducive to their formal conceptions. On the other hand, when the typefaces were not available they constructed them out of metal 'furniture' found in printer's type-cases. So, making do and making new with available material ultimately defined the entire genre and inspired professional type designers to produce typefaces that echoed modernist concepts.

Another master was the Constructivist painter, stage designer, photographer, art director and typographer Aleksandr Rodchenko (1891–1956), who significantly contributed to the modern lexicon of printed visual form. He saw the page as an organic entity, and introduced extreme geometrical forms as a substitute for literal illustration as well as a symbolic hallmark of mass production. As a teacher at Moscow's avant-garde VKHUTEMAS art school in 1920, he introduced a course devoted to Productivism (or

Below from left: **ABC**, no.4, 1926. **Broom**, vol.4 no.3, February 1923. **Wendingen**, vol.4 no.11, 1921.

Like Van Doesburg, El Lissitzky, a ubiquitous presence as a periodical designer, worked in different styles. For the cover of *ABC* which he also edited, he applied minimalist typography while for his covers of *Broom* and *Wendingen*, edited by Harold Loeb and Hendrik Theodorus Wijdeveld respectively, he applied Constructivist composition.

production art) with the goal of creating a cadre of artist-engineers who designed functional, utilitarian, indeed commercial wares to boost the Soviet economy. In this new society, pure art was a luxury that the Revolution could ill afford. Rodchenko frequently worked with the poet Vladimir Mayakovsky (1893–1930) to create advertising for the GUM department store in Moscow, Mospoligraf, a government publishing house, and other commercial businesses, as well as propaganda (ROSTA) posters promoting literacy and attacking enemies of the Soviet Revolution. These missives were hung in post-office windows, painted on railway cars and served as the first significant popular art of the Revolution.

Constructivism was forged during the period when the theories of Marxism were turned into practical matters of state. Art and design were poised to play a major role after the 1917 Bolshevik October Revolution overthrew the Provisional Government of Russia and the Council of People's Commissars was established to map out how the 'dictatorship of the proletariat' would operate. LEF (*Levyi front iskusstv* – Left Front for the Arts) was an idealistic group of progressive artists in Moscow organized by Mayakovsky; its multilingual journal of the same name, which Mayakovsky co-edited with Rodchenko from 1923 to 1925, espoused an ideology of 'Communist Futurism'

propagated through poetry, prose and art. *Lef*'s contributors saw the Soviet ascendancy as an opportunity to free art and culture from the strictures of the imperial past and of capitalist culture in general. Students of VKHUTEMAS reproduced their applied arts projects in the magazine and designers explored the concepts of production art, Constructivism, agitprop and publicity (or what Mayakovsky called 'economic agitation'). *Lef* also published class analysis of culture, art, architecture and literature inspired by the new proletariat ideology.

The covers of the seven issues of *Lef* resemble basic advertising placards with blocky, gothic wood-types and bold rules, yet each is based on a systematic ordering of logo, issue number, and image or headlines. While the covers are bold, the interior design is somewhat lacklustre, reflecting both a certain ideological heavy-handedness in the text and fundamental difficulties in primitive production techniques. By the time of its final issue in 1925, *Lef*'s circulation had fallen to 1,500 from 5,000 in 1923 when it had first appeared. Mayakovsky blamed the slide on bureaucratic mismanagement but, in fact, *Lef* was not well received by the general public or by many intellectuals. Despite its avowed sympathy with the Soviet people, the newspaper *Pravda* (Truth) and other state-sanctioned publications harshly criticized the magazine for the so-called hidden agendas of

Constructivism and abstract art. In 1925 the publication was stopped by order of the State Publishing House (Gosizdat), which oversaw its production. None the less, Rodchenko experimented further with typography and photography during the later Twenties and fused these forms into a modernist idiom. In 1927, when *Lef* was revived by Mayakovsky as *Novyi Lef* (New Left Front for the Arts), produced by the State Publishing House for the edification of the proletariat, its content stressed the cultural advancements of the October Revolution. For twenty-four issues (most of which were edited by Mayakovsky) it published a diet of essays on political-cultural relations, Soviet film commentary and criticism, Mayakovsky's most rousing poems, Rodchenko's 1925 Paris diary, excerpts of the proceedings of conferences sponsored by *Novyi Lef*, and a series of covers (all of which were designed by Rodchenko) that established a standard for rational modern design.

Rodchenko incorporated photographs into his cover designs for *Novyi Lef* that revealed a new kind of objectivity. Modernists considered that photographs were the mechanical art for the mechanical age. In Rodchenko's hands, they were both documentary tool and dynamic representation. The covers of *Novyi Lef* were entirely composed around photographic images that served a narrative and iconic function. One cover (issue no.6), featuring a profile of a Red Army soldier, is a veritable recruitment poster that prefigures later socialist realism. Another cover (issue no.7) carries a photograph of a Caribbean or Pacific Island woman in an angular position and in silhouette (looking very contemporary by today's standards). The cover of a later number, featuring a dramatically lit overview of a movie camera (issue no.11–12), is a paean to new film technology. Still another (issue no.10), the most curiously abstract, offers a photographic side view of files and papers with the words 'Down With Bureaucracy' printed in script that climbs up one side of the page in an obvious critique of governmental red tape.

The new streamlined logo (in contrast to the blocky, old *Lef* logo) is placed at the top, bottom or middle of the covers, often in a coloured rectangle that signals its modernity as it mirrors the designs of other European avant-garde magazines. Yet, despite the high quality of the design and content, *Novyi Lef* was unable to make a substantive impact on either the Soviet people or the government, and thus ceased publication towards the end of 1928. That year Stalin introduced his first Five-Year Plan and initiated increased patronage of the arts. However, the days of an artist's interpretation of the Party's needs were over; the Communists now demanded an official aesthetic of socialist realism. Consequently, the Constructivists' work was condemned as too formalist. *Novyi Lef* would not have

Opposite, from left: **Lef**, no.1, March 1923; no.2, April–May 1923; no.3, June 1923. *Lef* covers, designed by Aleksandr Rodchenko, used the most common advertising typefaces to create uncommonly striking Constructivist designs. *Lef* was edited by Rodchenko and Vladimir Mayakovsky.

Below: **Novyi Lef**, cover of no.7, July 1928. *Novyi Lef* was designed by Rodchenko and edited by Vladimir Mayakovsky. It experimented with more rational design concepts than its predecessor, with its dynamic use of photography, the grid-based breakdown of space and streamlined type composition.

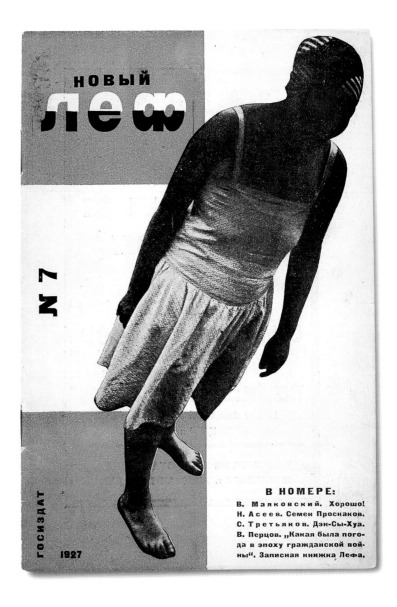

Left: **Novyi Lef**, vol.1 no.10, October 1929, cover design by Aleksandr Rodchenko.

Opposite, clockwise from top left: **Novyi Lef**, covers of vol.2 no.1, 1928; vol.2 no.2, 1928; vol.1 no.5, 1927; vol.2 no.10, 1928; vol.2 no.8, 1928; vol.2 no.3, 1928, all designed by Rodchenko.

Overleaf: **USSR in Construction**, cover, inside spreads and back cover from no.7, 1940. This issue, designed by Rodchenko as a celebration of Vladimir Mayakovsky, involved the dramatic use of photomontage and collage, as well as special printing techniques, such as slipsheets and gatefolds that added a cinematic dimension to the page-turning. Most of issue no.7, which was edited by Lev Kassíl and V Pértsev, is shown here.

stood a chance in this environment but it did influence the appearance of many other journals in Europe.

During the early Thirties Rodchenko found refuge as a reporter, designer and photographer for *USSR in Construction*, the multilingual picture magazine that propagated the virtues of Soviet life to the outside world. He also produced photomontages with acute angular cropping and dynamic framing that were documentary in scope and adhered to the new demands of art. The most significant issue (no.7, 1940) was that devoted to his colleague Mayakovsky, for which he created a symphony of photographic layouts and montages as a visual narrative. Rodchenko used radical shifts in scale between photos and reproductions of Mayakovsky's documents to approximate a cinematic presentation of his colleague's life as a leader of Soviet art and culture.

The widespread dissemination of otherwise arcane journals and periodicals, such as those discussed above, certainly hastened the proliferation of modernist design thinking throughout Europe. But the nexus of modernism was the Bauhaus, the progressive art and design school based first in Dessau, then in Weimar and later in Berlin. Here, new typographic and graphic design ideas coalesced through the work of László Moholy-Nagy (1895–1946), Herbert Bayer (1900–85), and Joost Schmidt (1893–1948), who were responsible for many of the most significant Bauhaus publications and periodicals.

In theory the Bauhaus and De Stijl sought to create a similar formal language that embraced a holistic or total work of art – from painting to consumables – but there were also points of disparity. The Bauhaus began, in the early years of the twentieth century, under the jurisdiction of the Grand Duke of Saxe-Weimar as the Weimar School of Arts and Crafts with an Art Nouveau bias and the aim of producing applied artists as contributors to a new German economy. In 1919, after World War I and the dissolution of ducal rule, the architect Walter Gropius (1883–1969) was appointed to head a confederation of two schools renamed Staatliches Bauhaus, and published a manifesto that outlined his goal to eliminate the barriers between artist, craftsman and industrial worker. In addition to the painting, furniture, textile and photography departments, master classes in graphic design and advertising were introduced to promote the New Typography.

During the first two years of the Bauhaus, Expressionism, which had been Germany's avant-garde prior to World War I, held sway and was manifest in its earliest publications, which eschewed aesthetic clarity for incongruent eclecticism. However, eventually Gropius pressed for a method that was more standardized and thereby more in sync with emerging industrial sensibilities. Although favouring systematic approaches, Gropius differed

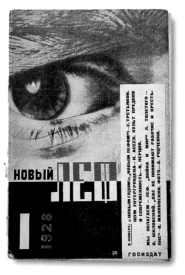

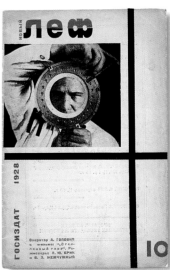

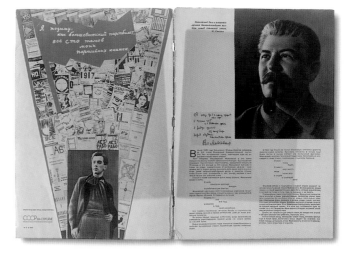

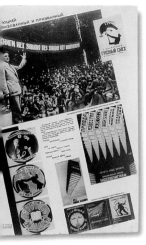

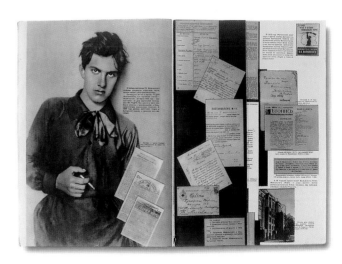

philosophically with Van Doesburg (who had ventured to Weimar in 1920 and set up home near the school) over the imposition of an impersonal style. While Gropius appreciated De Stijl's vanguard achievements, he rejected its dogmatic tenets and instead encouraged stylistic individuality among students and faculty. Yet, owing to his proximity to the school, Van Doesburg, who was not officially on the staff but made his presence at the Bauhaus known to student and teacher alike, influenced the manner in which graphic design was eventually taught and practised.

In 1923 László Moholy-Nagy, who had written about modernism as a determinant of new society in the Constructivist avant-garde magazine *MA* (from Hungary), was appointed first to lead the school's metal workshop and later to oversee the typography programme. Moholy-Nagy was a utopian who believed in the idea that the machine made every artist equal. He argued that Constructivism, which was neither 'proletarian nor capitalist', 'without class and without ancestor', expressed the pure form of nature, which was abstract. For Moholy-Nagy, Constructivism, which used machine aesthetics as a way of transcending static communication, led to new ideas about typography. He developed his own method, 'Typofoto', the seamless integration of type, photograph and montage, and he defined the new designer as equal parts aesthetician and technician. According to Moholy-Nagy, typofoto was 'the visually most exact rendering of communication'.[1]

Below from left: **Bauhaus**, vol.1 no.1, 1928, cover design by Herbert Bayer; cover of vol.3 no.3, 1929. The *Bauhaus* review, principally designed by Herbert Bayer and edited by Ernst Kallai, is the quintessence of functional design. Bayer's most inventive composition was the montage for the first issue that shows a cover within a cover, with the symbols (square, circle, cone) of the Bauhaus.

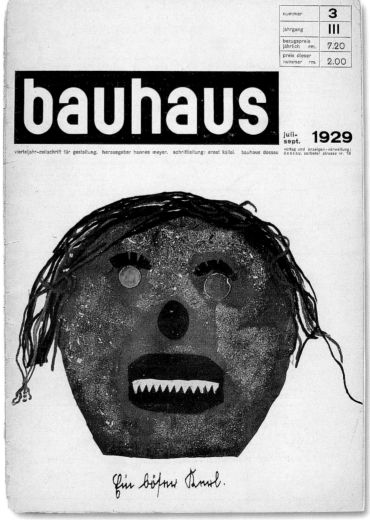

The epitome of a typofoto composition, and the embodiment of Dessau Bauhaus rationalism, was the cover for *Bauhaus: Zeitschrift für Gestaltung*, edited by Ernst Kallai and principally designed by Herbert Bayer in 1928. The cover is a photomontage/still life of a folded *Bauhaus* magazine cover with a cone, circle and square sitting on top – a cover within a cover.

Bayer had been working as a package and interior designer before enrolling at the Bauhaus in Weimar in 1921, where he studied under Paul Klee (1879–1940) and Moholy-Nagy. In 1925, when the Bauhaus was forced to move to a new location – the brand-new Gropius-designed building in Dessau – Bayer had taken charge of the typography workshop. There he proceeded to lobby for standardization of all design based on a single alphabet devoid of capital letters. His single-case 'alphabet universal' (designed in 1926) was a reaction to the illogic of using two characters of ostensibly unharmonious alphabets (i.e., upper and lower case) in the same word. Motivated by a desire to make the German language accessible throughout modern Europe, Moholy-Nagy and Bayer argued in favour of compositional coherence that used geometric forms as navigational aids for reading on a page. Reducing extraneous type was a further means of increasing legibility (and cutting production costs).

Under Moholy-Nagy and Bayer, print communication was a key part of the curriculum and experimentation was encouraged as long as it fell within the prescriptions of the school's methods. In 1929 *Bauhaus* magazine took these

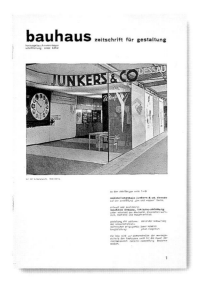

experiments into the market-place when it announced that the publicity workshop was accepting orders from outside clients for modern typographical treatments for everything from advertisements to trademarks. The *Bauhaus* magazine itself was an advertisement for the efficiency of the New Typography as a commercial tool.

A year before the Bauhaus officially sought clients from the outside world, a group of practitioner/educators had founded Ring Neuer Werbegestalter (Circle of New Advertising Designers or The Ring). Initially this loose-knit group was made up of advertising artists, including Kurt Schwitters (as president), Willi Baumeister, Max Burchartz, Walter Dexel, César Domela, Georg Trump, Johannes Molzahn, and Jan Tschichold, dedicated to the propagation of their mutual avant-garde aesthetics. In 1928–9 their work was individually exhibited in various cities throughout Germany and also in combination with the work of other avant-gardists, including Bayer, Moholy-Nagy, Van Doesburg and the Czech typographer and photographer Karel Teige. Eventually the group grew to over twenty-five and their collected work was catalogued in the publication *Gefesselter Blick* (The Captured Glance), which was a showcase for typofoto and the New Typography. Aside from the common stylistic manifestations – sans-serif type, bold rules and the emphatic use of red – the design content was totally the product of machines (indeed, only schematic drawings were used). The New Typography signalled contemporaneity, although within its parameters the aesthetic proclivities of the individual designer resulted in a range of distinct approaches to the theme of modernity.

In Holland, the birthplace of De Stijl, modernism took various routes that ran the aesthetic gamut from hybridized Art Nouveau to systematic rationalism. Somewhere between these poles was the magazine *Wendingen* (Upheaval), one of the principle sources for chronicling the history of twentieth-century design and architecture. Published between 1918 and 1931, virtually all of its 116 issues were edited and designed by Hendrik Theodorus Wijdeveld (1885–1989), a Dutch architect and graphic designer who trained under Gropius and Frank Lloyd Wright (1867–1959). Influenced by Nieuwe Kunst (Dutch Art Nouveau), *Wendingen* was resolutely eclectic in design and content and gave equal coverage to Expressionist, individualist and even mystical sensibilities. In contrast to Van Doesburg's *De Stijl* (which pre-empted *Wendingen* by three months), Wijdeveld's journal was superficially extravagant, unrepentantly decorative and devoutly geometric – yet totally avant-garde.

Wendingen was printed in an unprecedented square format (34.25 cm, 13^1/$_2$ in.) on high-grade paper; each page was one side of a sheet that was folded into two pages in a Japanese block-bookbinding process. Though it did not

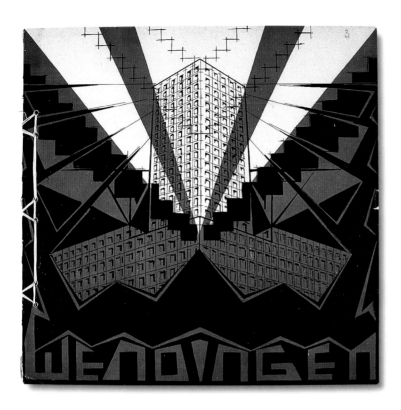

advance orthodox New Typography, *Wendingen* published covers by some the movement's principal designers – among them El Lissitzky, for an issue on Frank Lloyd Wright, and De Stijl artist Vilmos Huszár for one on Diego Rivera. In his own typographic concoctions Wijdeveld shared certain methods with Constructivists and Dadaists, using printer's materials to build quirky letter forms. His idiosyncratic evocation of expressive modernism was referred to as the 'Wendingen style' or Linear School, yet its influence barely went beyond the Netherlands.

Even though *Wendingen* spanned the watershed of European modernism, Wijdeveld's world vision placed it at odds with the more ideologically orthodox avant-garde groups. Wijdeveld's distinctive architectonic layout and rectilinear type design provided a forum for a wide range of the editor's concerns, from Art Deco to Javanese ornament, from architecture to political cartoon. While the interior format of *Wendingen* was more or less consistent, the cover design changed constantly. Architects and graphic artists alike were invited to design, illustrate and compose covers that expressed different schools and national or folk origins. However, Wijdeveld's own covers, whether for a series devoted to the architect Wright or to Erich Mendelsohn, were rendered in his blocky, emblematic, typographical style that often came under harsh criticism for its

illegibility. Despite (or perhaps because of) its excesses, *Wendingen* was 'one of the most progressive magazines of its time, a work of art', wrote historian Alston Purvis. 'It differed from other avant-garde publications such as *De Stijl* ... in that it was a vehicle for the message rather than the message itself.'[2] The magazine was a bridge between the disorder of the previous century and the new century's design. It advanced the grand notion of *Gesamtkunstwerk* – that all art fed a common functional purpose – but was none the less an alternative to the strict rationalism of the orthodox modernists.

Wijdeveld's style was difficult to copy and impossible to standardize. However, *Het Overzicht* (The Survey), a Flemish journal co-edited by Fernant Berckelaers (aka Michel Seuphor, 1901–99) and designer Jozef Peeters (1895–1960), published in Antwerp starting in 1921, exhibited a similar eclectic sensibility. The magazine covered modern painting, sculpture and typography, including Dutch, Belgian, Russian, Italian and German avant-gardes. Peeters designed some of his covers as typographic woodcuts in which letter forms of varying shapes and sizes cavorted on the page in a confluence of influences including Expressionism and Futurism. The review included contributions from an array of modernist artists and writers, including Adolf Behne, Moholy-Nagy,

Sonia Delaunay, Albert Gleizes, Vilmos Huszár, Tristan Tzara and the Italian Futurist advertising artist Fortunato Depero. Like *Wendingen*, *Het Overzicht* had a comparatively small print-run but was included on the reading list of international modernism. It ceased publication in 1925 when Peeters founded a less graphically compelling publication called *De Driehoek*.

The term 'experimental' is often as slippery as 'modern' and must be used with care. While *Wendingen* challenged the formal conventions, after a brief period it settled into a fairly predictable, unpredictable format. Similarly, *Het Overzicht* did not push form very far from its home moorings. On the other hand, the nine issues of *The Next Call*, a Dutch periodical edited and designed by a commercial printer in Gröningen, H N Werkman (1882–1945), was a sustained challenge to conventional design – a self-initiated experimental exercise that had an impact on the larger design culture.

Werkman fancied himself as a painter and exhibited with an arts group called De Ploeg that had a fairly conservative methodology. He had become aware of international avant-garde movements following visits to exhibitions of De Stijl, Constructivism and Expressionism in his home town and, in 1923, decided to found a publication that would underscore his penchant for abstraction and

his roots in commercial typography. Using an English title, *The Next Call*, Werkman drew on his wood-type printing experience to create typographic pictures that he later called 'druksels' (from *drukken*, to print) and 'tiksels' (from *tikken*, to type). Each issue's front and back cover was a semi-abstract design made from letters and type-case materials printed in black and various translucent inks. Some resembled Constructivist designs, others were even more abstractly free-form. Werkman wrote most of his own texts, which were boldly composed in sans-serif wood-types that were often purposely smashed together to effect a text block as pattern. Since he printed each number himself, he maintained complete control over the end product.

While working on *The Next Call* Werkman received avant-garde magazines from all over Europe and exchanged his own with those of Jozef Peeters in Belgium and the Zenit and Blok groups in Yugoslavia and Poland respectively. Yet because *The Next Call* was the product of an iconoclast who was not affiliated with any particular movement or school, his work was not codified as a style. Werkman wanted to communicate ideas about art and design that had relevance within the modern milieu but he never sought out rationalism as a method of doing so. *The Next Call* ceased publication with issue no.9 in 1929 but Werkman continued to produce prints and paintings. Between 1940 and 1945 he

Below: **The Next Call**, cover and inside spread from no.5, July 1924. H N Werkman's private periodical, *The Next Call*, which he edited and designed, was comprised of his typographic invention called 'druksels', works of art employing printer's type and type-case materials as his medium.

also published forty subversive broadsheet periodicals called *De blauwe Schuit* (The Blue Barge) – a reference to Hieronymous Bosch's painting *Ship of Fools* (1490–1500). But in April 1945, three days before the liberation of the Netherlands, he was executed by the Nazis for producing contraband.

The Next Call was an idiosyncratic experiment and a personal vision. In Holland, the road towards a universal design language took a separate route. More consistent with later periodicals from the Bauhaus was the Amsterdam-based journal, *Internationale Revue i10*, which published twenty-two numbers in nineteen issues between 1927 and 1928. Published by Arthur Müller Lehning (1899–2000), with cover concepts by César Domela and interior layouts by László Moholy-Nagy, its contributors included the architect J J P Oud, the musician Willem Pijper and the advertising artists Max Burchartz and Vilmos Huszár. *i10* was a multi-disciplinary modernist review of art, architecture, music, film, photography, typography and philosophy. It promoted De Stijl as one of its affinities and published the work of Dutch modernists, Mart Stam, Gerrit Rietveld, Bart Van Der Leck and Piet Mondrian. The De Stijl-inspired typographer and Ring member, Paul Schuitema, contributed an article entitled 'Advertising' as a paean to the New Typography. Articles by Wassily Kandinsky, Kurt Schwitters and Hans Arp covered modernism abroad, and essays about the Russian Revolution and its social philosophy were prominently featured. Also covered were such socially important issues as town planning and workers' housing. The design of *i10* was spare – a typographic cover was built upon a grid of rectangles that framed the logo and table of contents. The cover was similar in concept to that of *Bauhaus* magazine, except that each was distinguished by varying the colours in the headline type and logo.

Dutch rational periodical design should be considered in two categories: those that were sparsely typographical and others that were image-based, using typofoto. *De Stijl* became reductive to the point of transparency. But a short-lived quarterly, *Film: Serie Monografieen over Filmkunst* (A Series of Monographs on the Art of Flm), edited from 1931 to 1933 by C J Graadt van Roggen with covers designed by Piet Zwart (1885–1977), built on the modernist predilection for machine art, translucency and simultaneity. Zwart was actively interested in photography and film: he was the Dutch member of the Stuttgart film society. Although his photomontages reveal the influence of Rodchenko and Lissitzky, whose work he definitely knew, they uniquely integrated type and image into an iconic narrative. Each of the ten *Film* covers printed in blue and red was consistent in overall form yet conceptually different, telling distinct stories related to their respective content.

Top right: **i10**, no.13, 1928. *i10* was published by Arthur Müller Lehning, and edited by Lehning, J J P Oud and László Moholy-Nagy. The magazine was designed on a strict, architectonic grid as can be seen on this cover by César Domela. Its covers were unambiguous billboards for the contents of each issue

Bottom right and opposite: **Film**, cover of no.1, 1931; covers of nos. 2–10, 1931–3. Piet Zwart's covers for *Film*, a series of monographs edited by C J Graadt van Roggen, use montage to encapsulate the scope of each magazine. While the interior typography is economical and static, the covers, though using only two colours (red and blue), express the movement of film itself.

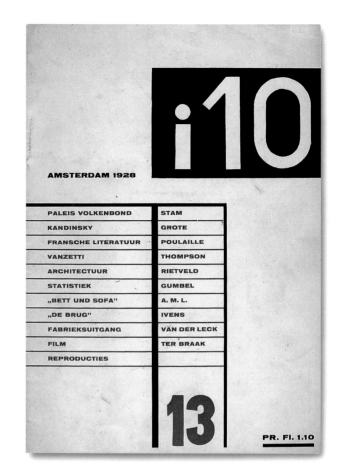

werkeloozen uit „Nieuwe Gronden" van Joris Ivens

Piet Zwart and Paul Schuitema (1897–1973) were the most influential Dutch graphic exponents of the commercial visual vocabulary fostered by De Stijl and influenced by the Bauhaus. Both employed dynamic typography as a means of attracting consumers to consumables. Zwart had initially mimicked Van Doesburg's typographics but then went beyond them. In creating the identity of the Dutch cable manufacturer, Nederlandsche Kabelfabriek Delft (NKD), he incorporated a range of typofoto techniques and revolutionized the presentation of an industrial catalogue. What better way to express modernism than through industrial imagery? Likewise, Schuitema applied the modernist typographic idiom to advertisements and brochures for Berkel, a manufacturer of scales, in what are now considered paradigms of modern layout. Around the same time that Zwart designed covers for *Film*, Schuitema produced a series of photomontage covers for *Filmliga* (Film League), the organ of the Dutch film society (Amsterdam and Rotterdam), as well as *Opbouwen*, a progressive journal featuring interiors and architecture. He used generous amounts of white space on the covers of these magazines and forced the viewer to see multiple images on one plane. This avant-garde method set a new standard for commercial design.

During the Twenties and Thirties when modernism held sway, it is sometimes difficult to pinpoint which individual or group, and what publication, was influenced by which designer. Clearly, many of the traits that are ascribed to modernism were adopted after they were pioneered or initiated by a vanguard school or group. In this sense *Das Neue Frankfurt* (The New Frankfurt), edited by Ernst May, Fritz Wichert and J Gantner and published in Frankfurt-am-Main between 1926 and 1933 (24 numbers in 21 issues), was a key interpreter of Bauhaus design in Germany with its own unique style. Profusely illustrated with architectural plans, drawings and photographs, the magazine was devoted to new architecture and urban culture as well as film, theatre, fashion and photography. The covers and interior design by Hans Lestikow, a *Bauhausler*, were based on Herbert Bayer's rationalist format for the *Staatliches Bauhaus* exhibition catalogue of 1923. Among the frequent contributors to the review were Walter Dexel, a painter and proponent of the New Typography, Charles-Edouard Jeanneret (Le Corbusier), Frank Lloyd Wright, Marcel Breuer and Oskar Schlemmer. The defining characteristic of *Das Neue Frankfurt* was its cover; this featured a grid that allowed for white space and an image area which divided the space in half. The bold sans-serif logo sat underneath the top panel, dwarfed by the issue number. The crisp typography enabled the most eclectic cover illustration to seem harmonious with the overall format.

The Berlin-based *G: Zeitschrift für Elemantäre Gestaltung* (G stands for *Gestaltung*, or Form) was another

Opposite: **Filmliga**, vol.7 no.1, January 1934, cover with film still from *Nieuwe Gronden* by Joris Ivens. *Filmliga* was edited by L J Jordaan and Henrik Scholte. Paul Schuitema's covers for the magazine attempt to recreate cinematic movement in static form by employing overprinting and transparency to establish layers of dimension.

Below from top: **Das Neue Frankfurt**, no.6, 1927, and no.23, 1930. *Das Neue Frankfurt*'s covers, designed by Hans Lestikow, were a confluence of rationalist principles, sans-serif type, photomontage and a strict grid that ensured consistency. The magazine was edited by Ernst May, Fritz Wichert and J Gantner.

magazine that showed the evolution of modernist design. This organ of the Constructivists in Europe, edited by Hans Richter (1888–1976), Werner Gräff (1901–78) and the ubiquitous El Lissitzky, began in 1923 in a broadsheet newspaper format. Although the review published one of Van Doesburg's manifestos entitled 'Elemental Formation', which called for 'the systematization of the means of expression', *G*'s typography was a dissonant blend of the rational and the ad hoc – both standardized and improvisational. By 1924 the periodical reduced in size to a magazine format and the cover of its June issue, designed by Mies van der Rohe (1886–1969), was a collage that included a huge 'G' printed in translucent colour over photographs of buildings. In the last year of publication (1926), *G*'s cover, designed by Kasimir Malevich (1878–1935), featured an aerial photograph of New York City skyscrapers alongside one of his Suprematist paintings with an overprinted G (Malevich was the founder of Suprematism). The covers of *G* have a similar look to those of Zwart's *Film* and show, once again, how visual ideas of this kind permeated vanguard practice.

In modernist culture, architecture was the epitome of progress. Although many of the plans for modern buildings failed to see the light of day, the paper architecture that appeared in many avant-garde periodicals anticipated a utopian future. The most important Soviet architectural review, *CA* (aka *SA*, Contemporary Architecture), was published in Russian and German from 1926 to 1930 and publicized new trends in Russian architecture while popularizing those of Western culture. It was the principal organ of the Union of Contemporary Architects, and was edited by Moisey Ginzburg (1892–1946) and Alexander Vesnin (1883–1959), an architect as well as a graphic and theatre designer. Although Vesnin had a graphic input, the magazine covers were designed by Aleksei Gan (1893–1942) who created a bold sans-serif logo within stark rule bars printed in black and a primary colour, along with extremely generous amounts of empty space in an apparent tip of the hat to the Bauhaus. The magazine was ardently enthusiastic about the new methods of technology found in the West and saw their potential in post-Revolutionary Russia. Although graphic design was not its primary concern, *CA* was none the less a vehicle for the development of rational typography.

Every nation with an avant-garde published periodicals that reflected its unique characteristics while promoting

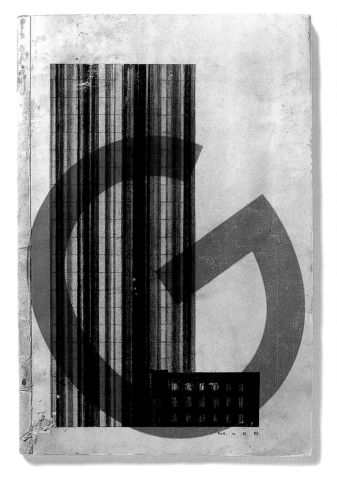

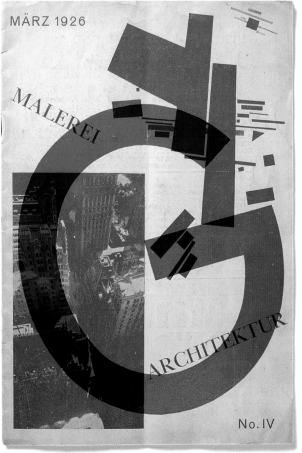

the worldwide vanguards. The Swiss avant-garde culture journal, *Information*, published in Zurich from 1932 to 1934, adhered to the same typographic principles and was sparsely geometric. Its chief designer, Max Bill (1908–94), a former *Bauhausler*, created a strict grid-based format that was mostly text yet included photomontage imagery from time to time. One of his most startling images was a cover montage of Hitler gnawing on a dagger, like a pirate; the magazine also included numerous texts decrying the emergence of Nazism.

Poland's avant-garde first emerged with Expressionism in 1917 and announced itself through a curiously tame magazine called *Zdroj* (Source). Futurism arrived in Poland the following year and the poet Anatol Stern founded a magazine called *Nowa Sztuka* (New Art), which expressed ideas through typography that enhanced the meaning, indeed nuance, of words. However, the New Typography did not come to fruition in Poland until 1922 when the Constructivist Henryk Berlewi (1894–1967) developed the theory called *Mechano-factura*. This proposed an abstract mechanical art devised from geometric textures simulating both musical and architectonic rhythms. Berlewi established

an advertising agency in Warsaw called Reklama Mecano where he created commercial publicity that used graphic forms similar to Lissitzky's Prouns. Berlewi avowedly rejected caprice and argued that art must break with the boudoir-type art of yesterday.

In 1924 Mieczyslaw Szczuka (1898–1927) began publishing *Blok* which was based on similar Constructivist design principles. Along with Berlewi, Szczuka contributed his own mechanical type experiments. Starting in the very first issue, *Blok*'s bold gothic masthead and cover grid divided by heavy rules of various weights was the epitome of architectonic design. To underscore this, the opening number included a statement by Mies van der Rohe on the philosophical underpinning of modern building. Other contributors from abroad included the usual cast of characters: Kasimir Malevich, Hans Arp, Theo van Doesburg and El Lissitzky. *Blok*'s editorials pushed for economy of means, utilitarian beauty and a programme of mechanization of art. In *Blok* no.5 an editorial advocated the New Typography as being richly economical and endemic to modernity. Szczuka further advanced his own method of photomontage – 'poetico-visuals' which symbolized the

Below from left: **CA**, no.2, 1929; no.5, 1929. **Information**, no.3, August–September 1932.

The covers of *CA*, which was edited by Moisey Ginzburg and Alexander Vesnin, were designed by Aleksei Gan. They were not always graphically exciting but were elegant in their simplicity. Conversely, this cover of *Information*, designed by Max Bill, a former *Bauhausler*, combines Bauhaus utility with acerbic satire for a montage of Adolf Hitler, who in 1933 became the German Chancellor and effectively stamped out the avant-garde in Germany.

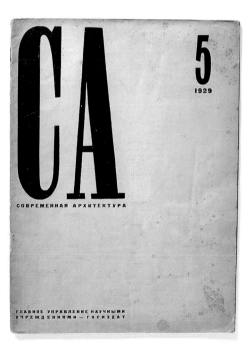

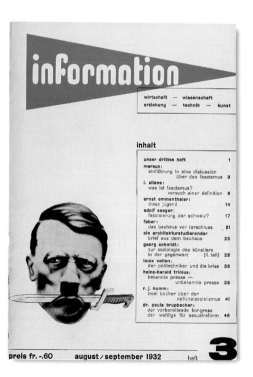

BLOK
CZASOPISMO AWANGARDY artystycznej

CENA 3 Złp.

№ **3—4**

Warszawa, czerwiec 1924 r. — Redakcja i Administracja: ulica Wspólna № 20, m. 39.

REDAKCJA: Henryk Stażewski, Teresa Żarnowerówna, Mieczysław Szczuka, Edmund Miller.

Nous prions nos amis de nous envoyer des clichés, photographies, dessins et articles en les adressant: Varsovie — Pologne, ul. Wspólna 20 m. 39.

Unsere Freunde werden gebeten uns Clichés Photographien, Zeichnungen und Artikel schicken zu wollen. Adresse: Warschau — Polen, ul. Wspólna 20, m. 39.

Nous ouvrous une enquête concernant l'éducation artistique.

Wir eröffnen eine Enquete betreffs Künstlererziehung.

HP I CZŁOWIEK PRZY MASZYNIE 10000 HP = 800000 LUDZI BEZMASZYNOWYCH

„RONALDSHAY" STATEK-DRAGA Z WYSTAWY IMPERJUM BRYTYJSKIEGO 1924 r.

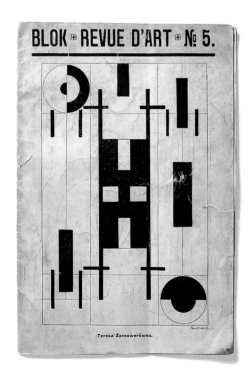

BLOK ✶ REVUE D'ART ✶ № 5.

Teresa Żarnowerówna.

KURJER BLOKU
BLOK
Spezielle Informationsnummer
REVUE INTERNATIONALE D'AVANGARDE

Varsovie-Pologne Wspólna 20.

B

№ 6—7 ——

WYSTAWA MIĘDZYNARODOWA ARCHITEKTURY NOWOCZESNEJ w WARSZAWIE w Tow. Zachęty Sztuk Pięknych

OD 27.II DO 25.III

BLOK 11
Revue internationale d'avant-garde
Varsovie-Pologne, Wspólna 20 m. 39

Redaction: T. Żarnower & M. Szczuka
Editeur Szczęsny, Rutkowski

1 marzec 1926   rok III

Udział biorą:
Belgja
Czechosłowacja
Francja
Holandja
Niemcy
Rosja
Polska

Cena 5 zł.

simultaneity of events and combined pictorial elements – through what he described as an 'intangible lyrical quality'. His most powerful work combined type and image (and the colour red) into a poem by Anatol Stern entitled 'Europa', which became a paradigm of Polish avant-garde design.

The New Typography signalled vanguard activity and this was true of the covers of *Praesens*, a magazine of art, architecture and social concerns that followed *Blok*'s demise in 1927 and was edited in Warsaw by Szymon Syrkus (1893–1964), A Pronaszko (1888–1961) and Henryk Stażewski (1894–1988). Stażewski's dissonant typography on the covers – which were usually more adventurous than the interior format – was consistent with other modern journals yet often revealed the influence of Dada. This organ of a group of Polish architects and designers, also known as Praesens, followed the Soviet avant-garde model, such as the reductive covers of *CA*, and promoted Constructivism.

All the European 'isms' conformed to some common tenets but followed their own paths. *Zenit* (*Revue International pour l'Art Nouveau*), published from 1921 to 1926 (43 numbers) and edited by Ljubomir Micić (1896–1966) in Zagreb and Belgrade, conformed to the machine-age ideologies of the day. It published free verse ('words in space') that was the equivalent to Futurist experiments and was replete with manifestos and proclamations calling for a modern spirit. *Zenit* was designed by Micić in a variety of formats, influenced initially by Expressionism and later by Constructivism. It was also printed on variegated paper stocks. The works reproduced in its pages were indeed the linchpins of modernism, and included work by artists such as Vladimir Mayakovsky, Vladimir Tatlin, George Grosz and Theo van Doesburg. The names of other frequent contributors are also familiar: FT Marinetti, Michel Seuphor and Herwarth Walden. And, once again, the peripatetic El Lissitzky rears his head as guest editor (with Ilya Ehrenburg) of the 1922 'Russian issue', which introduces Constructivism and Bolshevism to the editorial mix.

But this was not a copy-cat movement. The term 'Zenitism' is original, representing a quasi-mystical synthesis of Futurism and Expressionism that evolved into even more radical modernism. Zenitism had a virulent militant side, and promoted a new era of Balkan culture – or, in the words of Micić, the 'Balkanization of Europe'. Micić used modernism to bolster his own nationalist, post-war agenda. 'Zenitism acknowledged indigenous roots, which, it believed, could introduce fresh blood and awaken healthy, young, original and forceful tissue in a fatigued and war-exhausted European civilization,' says historian Irina Subotić.[3] The new art and design was a tool in this rehabilitation. Zenitism was linked to the modernist/progressive artistic affinities within Yugoslavia – the

Opposite, clockwise from top: **Blok**, no.3–4, 1924, cover designer unknown; no.11, March 1926, cover design by Wladyslaw Strzeminski; no.6–7, 1925, cover design by Henryk Stażewski; no.5, 1924, cover design by Teresa Zarnowerówna. *Blok*, the Polish avant-garde review, was edited and designed by Mieczyslaw Szczuka. The covers were a confluence of various progressive tendencies; no.11 reflects Constructivist sensibilities, while no.6–7 reveals a hint of Dada. The cover of no.3–4 was produced to look more like a conventional newspaper yet it was printed in an unconventional horizontal format.

Above: **Praesens**, no.2, 1930. The cover of *Praesens*, which was edited by Szymon Syrkus, A Pronaszko and Henryk Stażewski, rejected the pictorial in favour of typographic imagery. The type serves as both information and abstract composition which was common in avant-garde design at the time.

Zenit group's first congress was held in Belgrade at the International Exposition in 1924 – and served as an outlet for Micić's anti-European, pro-Serbian nationalism. Micić's world-view was often at odds with many within the pan-European avant-garde, to the point that *Zenit*'s manifestos were not only condemned by Yugoslav officials for blaspheming against the king and government, but also by previously supportive fellow-travellers. Micić had to endure harsh criticism and the confiscation of *Zenit* until, in its fifth year, official banning forced the periodical to close for ever.

Despite *Zenit*'s inauspicious demise, Constructivism continued to flourish within the Slovenian avant-garde, which promoted itself in the periodical *Tank*. This was edited and designed by Avgust Cernigoj (1898–1985), who, along with Ferdo Delak (1905–68) was a key Slovenian progressive. Like Zenitism, the Slovenian movement sought to uproot the traditions that dominated culture and, in consequence, faced strict government censorship. *Tank* provided the arts – painting, music, literature and graphic design – with a forum for their respective ideas and, therefore, published manifestos that assailed convention. Ostensibly modelled on *Zenit*, *Tank* was published in a smaller format with less visual razzmatazz, but Cernigoj's typography and collage was rooted in Constructivist tenets, including horizontal and vertical composition of type and image. Variations in the scale and organization of type further added to the

dynamism of some of *Tank*'s pages. The cover of the first issue was consistent with this principle; that of the second was less dynamic in its overall appearance, but its receding logo was a unique design conceit. Large exclamation points and question marks were employed as editorial commentaries on the texts within, forcing the reader to navigate in unusual ways. Breaking up words in sentences and paragraphs was used to express movement and sound, or to simulate the workings of mechanical objects.

Tank's international troupe of contributors included Herwarth Walden, Tristan Tzara and Kurt Schwitters, along with some former members of the Zenit group. But only two issues were actually published (the oddly numbered 1^1/$_2$ and 1^1/$_2$–3); a third issue was produced but banned before coming off the printing press. Eventually, some of the leading contributors to *Zenit* and *Tank* joined the ranks of the post-war Communist regime.

Hungary was perhaps a little more hospitable to an avant-garde. In 1909 a group of radical artists known as Keresok (The Seekers, aka The Eight), followed in the footsteps of the post-Impressionist masters and embraced Cubism and other French developments. Although vital inside Hungary, this group was unable to find a place within the international community and, in consequence, gave way to a more internationalist, revolutionary manifestation called The Activist Group. This band of radicals aggressively

Below left and centre: **Zenit**, covers of no.25, February 1925, by Mihailo S Petrov; no.41, May 1926, by Dimitri Moor. The organ of the Zenit Movement and brainchild of Ljubomir Micić, who also edited and designed the magazine, *Zenit* was designed in different sizes and shapes with continually changing logos and typographic schemes. The logo was set here in both Roman and Cyrillic letters.

Below right: **Tank**, cover of no.1^1/$_2$ – 3, 1927. Avgust Cernigoj edited and designed two issues of *Tank*. For no.1^1/$_2$–3 a simple typeset logo was repeated along the contour of the right-angle triangle that carves the image space in half.

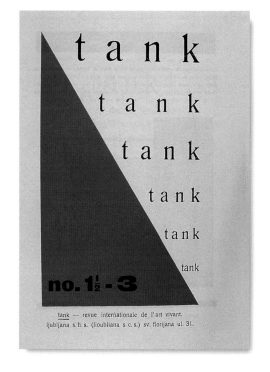

publicized its aesthetic and political goals through journals that were edited and designed by the writer and artist Lajos Kassák (1887–1967). *A Tett* (Deed) and *MA* (Today) promulgated German Expressionism, Italian Futurism and the various arts of central and eastern Europe. Unlike the Futurists, Kassák's editorials were avowedly anti-war. *A Tett*, the Budapest-based political/sociological, literature and art fortnightly, founded by Kassák in 1915, was the more incendiary and so shorter-lived, although less graphically progressive, of the two publications. A few issues had been confiscated prior to September 1916 when it was banned, charged with 'insulting the nation' owing to its anti-war stance.

Two months later, the first number of *MA* appeared featuring an article by Kassák titled 'The Poster and the New Painting', which clearly established The Activist Group's interrelationship with the plastic arts. *MA*, which was published in Budapest from 1916 to 1919 and then in Vienna from 1920 to 1926, was the organ for the activist movement of the same name. *MA* had briefly embraced the ideas of Dadaism, then shifted emphasis to Suprematism and Constructivism and eventually adopted De Stijl as part of its overall theoretical and aesthetic approach.

Kassák directed the magazine and the movement with the heartfelt belief that political and artistic revolutions were united, and that Constructivism was the most

revolutionary manifestation of the new social commitment. The magazine (and ancillary posters and books) clearly reflected this world-view by virtue of graphics and typography that conformed to the rational modern aesthetic. Along with Kassák, László Moholy-Nagy (before moving on to the Bauhaus) played an active role in Budapest and Vienna in producing and propagating radical new art in *MA* and other publications. In 1922 the two colleagues published *Buch neuer Künstler* (Book of New Artists), designed with an emblematic Constructivist cover that echoed the *MA* layout. It was proposed as a yearly almanac of contemporary attempts to link art to the modern industrial world but did not continue beyond the first issue.

By 1926 the modern avant-garde had passed its high-water mark. The new art and design born of rebellion and forged from crisis had become institutionalized in schools like the Bauhaus. Since *MA* was published in Vienna, not Budapest, at this time, Kassák had lost touch with his Hungarian supporters and the intensity of experimentation had dwindled. *MA* had run its course and Kassák returned to Budapest where he published other avant-garde arts magazines. His Constructivist journal *Dokumentum* (1926 to 1927) was established to rival another distinct avant-garde journal, *Uj Föld* (New Earth), co-edited and designed by the painter and graphic designer Sándor Bortnyik (1893–1976). Although at philosophical odds on the leftist

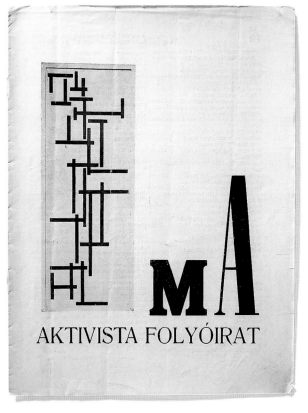

spectrum, both publications furthered the principles of the New Typography. However, neither could weather the increasingly right-wing political storms of the time and both ceased in 1927 owing to financial problems exacerbated by harassment from the authorities.

Radical modernism was more stable in Czechoslovakia, where an impressive number of avant-garde periodicals held sway over a wide swath of cultural activity. Among the most notable was *Red: Mésićnik pro Moderní Kulturu* (A Monthly for Modern Culture), edited in Prague by Vitezslav Nezval and the architect, graphic designer, photographer, poet and typographer, Karel Teige (1900–51). The latter was a member of Devetstil, the Czech section of the International Union of Artists of the Revolutionary Avant-garde which, akin to the other radical 'isms' and 'stils' of the Twenties, promoted artistic, architectural and typographical practice within a socialist environment. Of all the artist/editors working in Europe, Teige was more totally in sync with the holistic view of art – yet it is surprising that until recently he was less well known than the ubiquitous modern luminaries. He was a disciple rather than an originator and was deeply influenced by both Russian Constructivism and Dutch De Stijl. Yet he also applied a wide range of methodologies, from Dada to the New Typography, in diverse media that ranged from books to magazines, including the periodical *Devetstil*. He was a vocal editor of journals on Czech and international culture and wrote provocative essays and manifestos on the theory and criticism of art and architecture. His most important publication, *Red*, was issued between 1927 and 1931 and exposed Czech readers to foreign ideas by including analyses of all the major cultural movements. Teige's issues devoted to such modernist themes as 'Photo, Film, Typo', 'The Russian Revolution' and 'The Bauhaus' influenced Devetstil and other groups.

Red's strongest visual attribute – its cover – adhered to a strict format with certain variations. Each cover had a colour band under the masthead, which changed colour with every issue, along with the stencil-type logo and large issue number. The rest of the image area under the logo conformed to the contents of the magazine, alternately featuring a photo, collage or headline text. Teige applied similar principles, though even more rigidly in terms of type, colour and white space, to the design for the avant-garde architectural journal *Stavba* (Architecture), which was published between 1922 and 1935. Here he was the editorial director and under his tutelage international architects, including Le Corbusier, Neutra, Van Doesburg, Gropius and Oud, were introduced to Czech culture. Teige was indefatigable in his mission to edit and design with ideological exactitude, as was the case with his intimate

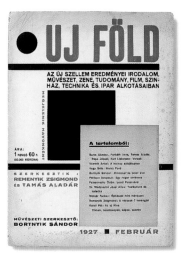
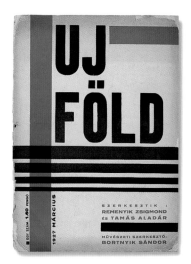

Above, clockwise from top left: **Dokumentum**, covers both 1927, with designs by László Moholy-Nagy. **Uj Föld**, covers of vol.1 no.2, March 1927; vol.1 no.1, February 1927, both designed by Sándor Bortnyik.

Hungary was fertile ground for the avant-garde and *Dokumentum*, designed and edited by Lajos Kassák and *Uj Föld*, designed by Sándor Bortnyik and edited by Bortnyik and Remenyik Zsigmond, used the bold geometric themes current at the time.

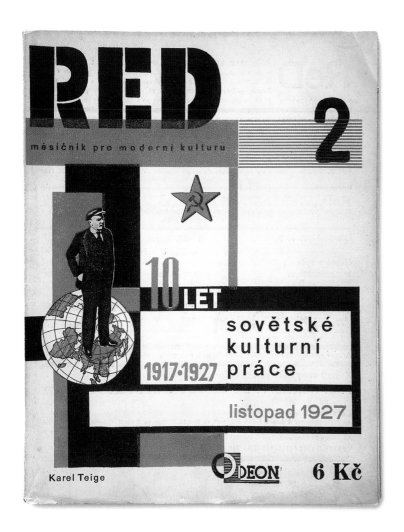

RED 2

měsíčník pro moderní kulturu

10 LET

sovětské
kulturní
práce

1917·1927

listopad 1927

Karel Teige

ODEON 6 Kč

RED 4

měsíčník pro moderní kulturu

spolupracovníci:
collaborateurs:
mitarbeiter:

Hans Arp, J. Babel,
Willi Baumeister, Konstantin Biebl, Pierre
Albert Birot, C. Brancussi, Le Corbusier &
Pierre Jeanneret, Max
Ernst, J. Fučík, L. Feininger, J. Honzl, Paul
Klee, Lautréamont, E.
Linhart, Jacques Lipchitz, El. Lissickij,
Jiří Mařánek, Pierre
Minet, Moholy-Nagy, Murayama, F. Picabia, E.
Piscator, V. J. Průša,
Man Ray, Z. Rossmann,
J. Seifert, Ives Tanguy, V. Tatlin, L. Theremin, Tristan Tzara,
B. Václavek, J. Voskovec, F. C. Weiskopf

leden 1928

Jacques Lipchitz

ODEON 6 Kč

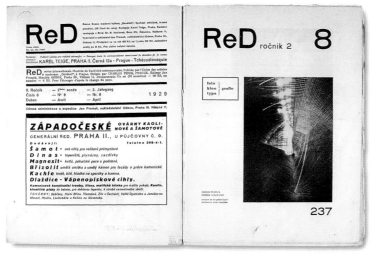

ReD

ReD ročník 2 8

foto
kino grafie
typo

237

Above, clockwise from top left: **Red**, vol.3 no.2, November 1927, cover design by Karel Teige; vol.4 no.4, January 1928, cover design by Jacques Lipchitz; vol.4 no.8, 1929, inside spread design by Karel Teige. Teige designed the Czech periodical *Red* and edited it with Vitezslav Nezval. It was a review of the Czech avant-garde art movement, Devetstil, whose format remained constant throughout its duration. The stencil type of the logo complemented the constructed rules and bars that defined the avant-garde graphic style.

involvement in yet another journal devoted to modernism, *MSA: Mezinárodní Soudobá Architektura* (International Contemporary Architecture) that ran from 1929 to 1930.

Teige's graphic design was not as pristine or as economical as that of a fellow Czech designer Ladislav Sutnar (1897–1976) who also designed books, posters, children's toys, exhibitions, household utensils and, most notably, book jackets for the publishing house DP (Druzstevní Prace – Cooperative Works). With his periodical design, Sutnar outdid the Bauhaus in creating standardized formats. *O Bydlení* (About Living), an avant-garde interior design magazine co-edited by Sutnar and published in 1932 by Svaz Ceskoslovenského Díla (The Union of Czechoslovak Industries), continued where *Stavba* left off in proposing contemporary approaches to the design of interior environments. Sutnar's covers were progressive, contemporary and timeless even by today's standards. The magazine's logo was a simple lower-case sans-serif typeface that was positioned wherever it was convenient on the image area. Photographs of furniture were silhouetted and placed strategically at angles against coloured backgrounds or otherwise empty fields to heighten the drama of ordinary pictures. The typographic format was economical to a fault, allowing the schematic illustrations and photographs to be the focus.

Sutnar redoubled his progressive methods for the magazine *Zijeme: Obrázkový Magazin Dnešní Doby* (For Life: An Illustrated Magazine of Modern Times), one of the most popular monthly Czech magazines of the Thirties. For each issue he created a photomontage that suggested, rather than literally illustrated, themes relating to modern life. While these covers formally refer to earlier covers by Rodchenko for *Novyi Lef* and other journals, Sutnar's signature typofoto compositions are distinctively his own. As with *O Bydlení*, photographs are tightly cropped or silhouetted, allowing for exaggerations in scale that inject a sense of dimensionality on to the flat plane. In fact, these covers are more akin to book jackets or posters than to conventional magazine covers. While *Zijeme* was not an alternative avant-garde periodical, it offered its readers the most progressive view of contemporary applied arts.

Romania was another thriving source for avant-garde periodicals on Constructivism. *Contimporanul*, the most influential, was published in Bucharest from 1924 to 1929 with former Dadaist Marcel Janco (1895–1984) as its artistic director. It contained works of progressive art from eastern and western Europe and the contributors included Tristan Tzara, Lajos Kassák and other leaders of the modern movement. Janco showed an obvious bias for modernist and abstract tendencies through the art and poetry that he selected, and his covers attempt to bridge the divide between Dada and Constructivist sensibilities. Janco contributed to another Constructivist review, *Punct*, directed by Scarlat Callimachi (1884–1944) with painters Victor Brauner (1903–66), Stephan Roll and Ilarie Voronca as editors, and published in Bucharest from 1924 to 1925. Its contributing editors included Romanian artists as well as the international cabal of Schwitters, Van Doesburg and Philippe Soupault, as well as the Yugoslav Micić.

Punct was characterized by the abstract linoleum cuts of Janco and Brauner that were an amalgam of Constructivist and Dada styles. Janco further developed a formal alphabet for the magazine and Brauner freely experimented with graphic ideas, leading to his eventual fascination with Surrealism. In 1924 Brauner also co-edited a single issue of a fledgeling periodical *75HP* where he pioneered a technique called 'pictopoetry' (consistent with other word-image modern art forms), which involved using words and word fragments in paintings. The words were chosen for their visual and organic properties, giving them equal emphasis to the more abstract shapes and designs.

The revolutionary fervour of Constructivism in Romania was as high-pitched as it was in Russia and the periodical *Integral* was a leading proselytizer. Owing to the inhospitable authorities, it began in Bucharest in 1925 and soon moved to Paris where it ceased publication in 1928. In the meantime,

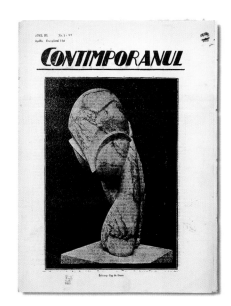

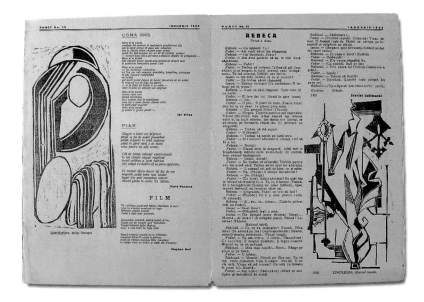

Opposite top, from left: **Stavba**, cover of vol.2 no.2, 1923. **O Bydlení**, cover of 1932 issue. *Opposite bottom, from left*: **Zijeme**, covers of vol.1 no.2, May 1931; vol.1 no.3, June 1931; vol.1 no.4–5, July–August 1931.

Karel Teige, who also edited the magazine, designed *Stavba* no.2 in an economical, rationalist manner with symbols of architecture as the only illustrative element. Ladislav Sutnar, who designed these covers of *O Bydlení* and *Zijeme*, refined the modernist visual language with systematic formats and rational layouts. *O Bydlení* was edited by

Karel Herain, Sutnar and Ladislav Žák. *Zijeme* was published by Druzstevní Prace.

Above, clockwise from top left: **Contimporanul**, vol.3 no.1, 1927, cover art by Constantin Brancusi; **Punct**, no.10, 1925, cover by Victor Brauner and inside spread.

Contimporanul's artistic director was Marcel Janco and the editor was Scarlat Callimachi. It went through various design incarnations, from a traditional newspaper to a modern typographic look. *Punct*, another Romanian avant-garde periodical, was designed by Victor Brauner who also co-edited it with Callimachi.

the magazine provided an outlet for international artists as diverse as Picasso and Fortunato Depero, and movements including Cubism and Dada. As a successor to *Punct*, it surveyed a broad range of formal phenomena, especially typography and film. Its editorial stance was in opposition to Surrealism which was beginning to take hold in Romania during the late Twenties. *Integral*'s editors included Max Herman Maxy, Ilarie Voronca, I Calugaru and F Brunea, each of whom were influenced by Constructivism. Their covers were quintessential Constructivist designs, dominated by a logo built from type-case materials evoking a Futuristic aura. The colour palette was limited to black, red and sometimes blue, and the typographic forms were restricted to circles, squares and rectangles.

Not all modern reviews were rooted in Constructivist visual idioms. *L'Esprit Nouveau*, France's most renowned and historically influential magazine of architecture, art and literature from 1920 to 1925, was hospitable to every manifestation of modernism and its design was contemporary but not in step with any of the dominant movements. Published under the direction of Paul Dermée, it drew on the inspirational guidance of Amédée Ozenfant (1886–1966) and Le Corbusier (1887–1965), who coined the term Esprit Nouveau and co-founded the magazine as a reaction against the conservative Ecole des Beaux Arts. Their ideas developed into an aesthetic philosophy called Purism that evolved as a response to both the artistic and the political conditions in post-World War I Paris. It was manifest almost exclusively in painting and architecture, though typography was under its sway, and championed a traditional classicism with a formal focus on clean geometries. It also embraced new materials and the machine aesthetic. *L'Esprit Nouveau* ardently emphasized the need for a new architecture in tune with the developments of the machine age.

This same machine age hit American shores in the early Thirties like a tidal wave and was the impetus for an industrial design revolution aimed at reinvigorating the stagnant economy. But modernism was not the same radical avant-garde experiment in the US as it was in Europe. Of course, painters and poets pushed the vocabulary of art, but in the realm of graphics, advertising and industrial design, modernism was a tool of business utilized by progressive designers in the service of corporate capitalism. The periodicals that promoted modernist graphic design in the US helped tame the renegade elements to make them compatible with a broad culture that was content with its status quo.

America's own form of modernism became known as Streamline and was built on speed as the end product of twentieth-century technology. This resulted in increased aerodynamics in new products that sometimes heightened performance (as in cars and aeroplanes) and sometimes

Right: **75HP**, no.1, 1924, cover with art by Victor Brauner and inside spreads. *75HP* was edited by Victor Brauner, F Brunea, Mihail Cosma, Miguel Donville and Stephan Roll, and designed by Victor Brauner. Issue no.1 combined abstraction and Constructivism into a unique form of visual poetry (or 'pictopoezie').

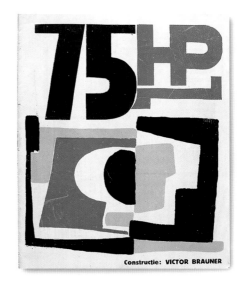

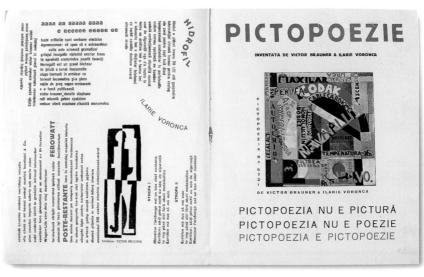

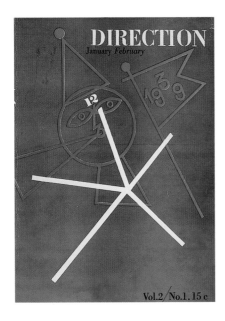

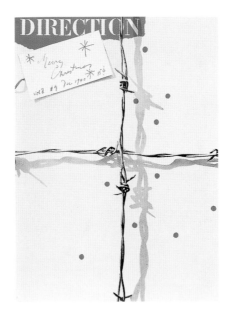

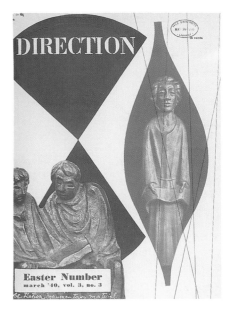

did not (as in pencil sharpeners and toasters). In terms of graphic design, Streamline was ersatz modernism, which meant that modernistic veneers were applied to type and layout through the application of asymmetric composition and airbrush rendering. In the US, it was contemporary trade magazines (see Chapter 6) rather than zealous avant-garde periodicals that advanced the New Typography and the exponents thereof.

Few of the American periodicals exhibited progressive design attributes that were similar to those of the European periodicals discussed earlier in this chapter. In fact, only one, *Direction*, followed the traditions of the Bauhaus and expanded upon its visual language. This was evident on some of its covers, especially those designed by Paul Rand (1914–96), who embraced the concept of modern art and transformed it into a personal method that defined progressive design in America. *Direction*, founded by Marguerite Tjader Harris in 1938, was a left-leaning political and cultural journal with an anti-Fascist bias. Rand's covers complemented rather than mimicked the editorial content, providing an additional level of expression. About these covers, Rand said, 'I was working in the spirit of Van Doesburg, Léger and Picasso. It was not old-fashioned. To be old-fashioned is, in a way, a sin.'[4]

Each cover of *Direction* illustrated a particular theme. The first, and Rand's most politically astute, showed a map of Czechoslovakia torn in half, representing the nation's evisceration by the Nazis. The 1940 'Merry Christmas' cover was a visual pun that substituted barbed wire for gift-wrap ribbon. Messages had to be conveyed quickly and efficiently. Since there was no budget for materials, Rand used handwriting instead of type for many of the covers and he also pieced together the stencilled masthead from examples in type catalogues. His images were often assembled from a variety of elements. 'Collages don't imitate reality,' Rand stated. 'The machine aesthetic dictated that you don't do things by hand any more.'[6] The *Direction* covers did not slavishly conform to all modern principles, however, and drawings by hand were used on occasion. None the less, *Direction* was the end product of two decades of modern, rational graphic design experimentation, significant for the synthesis of modern attributes – collage, montage, geometric abstraction and economical typography – that later had an impact on the post-World War II generation of mass-market magazine design.

The legacy of the rational modernists was two-fold. On the one hand, their methods evolved during the Fifties into a universal (or international) corporate design style that embodied the ethics of multinational industry. On the other, it became a touchstone which later avant-garde magazines either rebelled against or parodied.

Opposite, top row from left: **Direction**, covers of vol.2 no.1, January–February 1939; vol.2 no.9, December 1940; vol.3 no.3, March 1940; *centre row*: vol.3 no.4, April 1940; vol.3 no.6, Summer 1940; vol.3, no.7, October 1940; *bottom row*: vol.4 no.1, January 1941; vol.5 no.3, 1942; vol.6 no.4, Christmas 1943, all designed by Paul Rand. *Below*: vol.1 no.9, December 1938, cover design by Paul Rand. American modernist Paul Rand used *Direction* magazine covers as a laboratory, those shown here represent among others, Christmas after the outbreak of war, the Nazi occupation of Czechoslovakia, hunger at Christmas time, and the axis of Fascist evil. Each uses photomontage and metaphoric symbolism to express clear polemical and political messages. *Direction* was edited by Marguerite Tjader Harris as a progressive arts and culture journal with an anti-Fascist editorial policy.

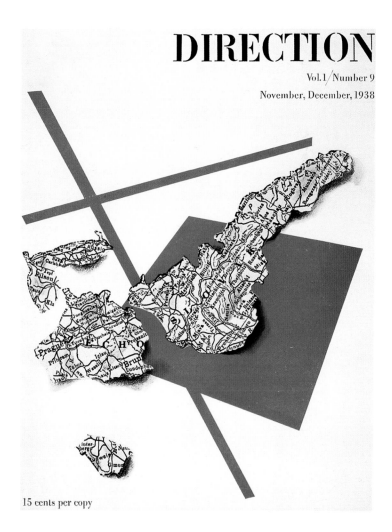

DIRECTION

Vol.1/Number 9

November, December, 1938

15 cents per copy

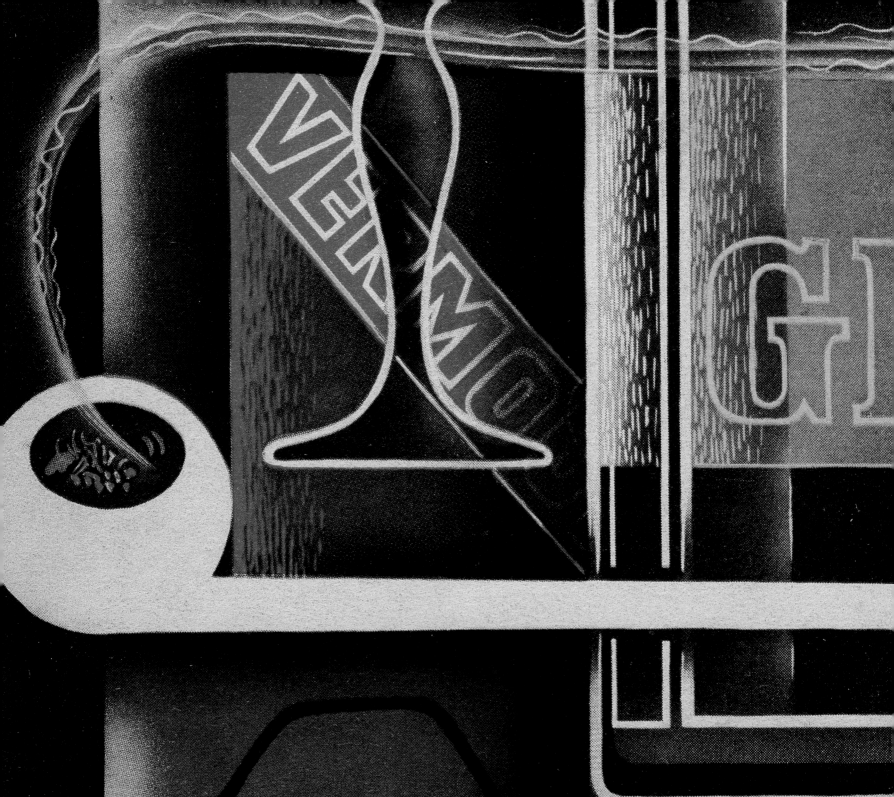

ALLEINVERTRETER
VON NORD-AMER
SERVICE COMPAN
SOLE REPRESENTATIVE FOR THE UNITED STA

N

HERAUSGEBER · PROF. H. K. FRENZEL · EIDTOR

PHÖNIX ILLUSTRATIONSDRUCK U. VERLAG GMBH

BERLIN SW 61, BELLE-ALLIANCE-PLATZ 7-8

6

R DIE VEREINIGTEN STA

A UND KANADA: THE B PO

15 EAST 40TH STREET,

S OF AMERICA AND CANADA

Guerrillas of Commerce:
The Journals of Radical Design

The purpose of a trade magazine is to disseminate accepted professional standards. It serves rather than leads. Yet, while serving, graphic design trade magazines often pump new ideas and novel methods into the professional mainstream. During the late nineteenth century, professional periodicals that were targeted at printers represented organizations devoted to the crafts of printing, type manufacture and book production. The actual design process was secondary to the latest hardware and technologies but, all the same, the business dictated that printers provided layout and design services to their customers. Graphic design or commercial art quickly evolved out of this secondary service into an independent profession and gave impetus to editors of magazines aimed at the printing trade to analyse layout and typography in different media and commercial circumstances.

Many periodicals became ersatz specimen books that showed *au courant* styles and encouraged printers and designers to follow specific templates that they set forth. And rather than being objective observers of the current design scene, these journals were exemplars of unconventional design. Today these publications provide historical evidence of how particular styles developed during the nascent period of graphic design.

The graphic styles of any given era – especially during the late nineteenth and early twentieth centuries – share the same traits in part because trade magazines held a tight grip on professional activity. The styles they proffered made it easy for the printer/designer to satisfy the needs of clients who did not want their printed matter to be perplexingly quirky – although, in retrospect, the Victorian and Art Nouveau styles were indeed quirky. In context, however, the widespread conformity of such eccentric styles as Victorian decorated fat typefaces and bifurcated Tuscan types, among other characteristics, was not avant-garde but rather a common vernacular rooted in a need to capture the viewer's eye. At the time, graphic design was not perceived or practised as an art *per se*, and typography was the common language of communications and the stylistic lure for guiding an audience towards a message. Anything that distracted or confused this audience was unacceptable.

Trade periodicals cautiously tampered with the status quo. Formats were neutral but every so often, within an otherwise staid framework, editors published articles, illustrations and even facsimiles that were radical in design terms. Sometimes these illustrations accompanied bitter, reactionary critiques of new phenomena, but at other times editors took a vicarious pleasure in exhibiting convention-busting creations even while refusing to practise such methods themselves. The editors and designers who sidestepped change in their personal practices could not

Previous page:
Gebrauchsgraphik, detail of vol.8 no.11, November 1931, cover artist unknown.

Clockwise from top left:
Das Plakat, covers of vol.7 no.1, January 1916, by Lucian Bernhard; vol.8 no.1, January 1917, by Mihaly Biro; vol.12 no.2, September 1921, artist unknown; vol.12 no.6, June 1921, by Walter Kampmann; vol.11 no.7, July 1920, by Karl Michel. *Das Plakat*, which was edited by Hans Josef Sachs, introduced on its covers scores of commercial artists – some progressive – from Germany and throughout Europe. They worked in diverse styles from decorative to expressionist, and from representational to abstract.

entirely ignore the intriguing new developments occurring in *fin de siècle* European modern art that had both a rejuvenating effect and a definitive influence on aspects of commercial art. Impressionism, Expressionism and later Cubism were leaving their respective marks on the design and use of type and image in many media, from publications to packages. Gradually, commercial artists who were practising in the highly visible domain of the advertising poster assimilated new ideas concerning spatial composition, perspective, colour and even abstraction.

This was profoundly felt in France during the late nineteenth century and early twentieth centuries where progressive advertising approaches, notably in the form of posters, were challenging stolid academic art conventions. In France during the 1890s, advertising art represented the Fauves and Impressionists created by the likes of posterists Jules Chéret (1836–1932) and Henri de Toulouse-Lautrec (1864–1901). The French poster brought avant-garde art to the people: the Parisian streets were plastered with colourful advertisements displaying sensual images and bold typography. And in *Maîtres de l'Affiche* (1895–1900), the leading journal for late-nineteenth-century French poster artists and enthusiasts, popular new poster art was reproduced as pristine miniature prints (today they are almost as valuable as the original posters). While this magazine did not alter the status quo of publication design, it provided a beautifully printed record of the latest work and was a source from which other designers the world over could draw inspiration.

Other journals of the advertising trade that published throughout Europe and in the United States after the turn of the century were not as meticulous about the quality of their reproductions yet none the less promoted the most current and popular work. But one magazine set itself apart from this group of quotidian periodicals and became an influential outlet for both acceptable and risk-taking work. The Berlin-based *Das Plakat* (The Poster) did not pretend to be avant-garde yet it freely published provocative and unconventional covers by renowned *and* unknown artists, and its coverage ranged from representational to abstract design. It subverted commonplace expectations, broadened the horizons of the profession and was both the clarion call for German poster invention and the gospel of contemporary graphic design between 1910 and 1921.

Das Plakat was founded in 1910 as the official journal of the Verein der Plakat Freunde (Society for Friends of the Poster), which was established in 1905, with cells throughout Germany, to champion the collecting of art posters and increase scholarship among amateurs and professionals. During its comparatively short lifespan, *Das Plakat* covered the whole poster scene and raised aesthetic,

cultural and legal issues about the art of publicity. In addition to surveying the most significant German (and ultimately international) work, the magazine addressed plagiarism and originality, art in the service of commerce, and the art of politics and propaganda. Over the years, its influence on the practice of design grew, as did its circulation from an initial print-run of a mere 200 copies to over 10,000 at its peak.

Das Plakat was the creation of Hans Josef Sachs (1881–c.1960), a chemist by training and a dentist by profession, who collected French posters and became the leading private collector in Germany with his thousands of acquisitions. At the age of twenty-four, he co-founded the Verein der Plakat Freunde with Hannes Meyer and built it into a formidable self-supporting organization. In 1909 he proposed to his board of directors the idea of publishing a journal that would represent the organization yet, under his auspices, become an expanded chronicle of poster art.

Sachs was inspired by the German advertising artists known as the Berliner Plakat, which enlivened the city's grand boulevards with posters that transformed the dominant commercial graphic style from painterly and decorative to graphic and conceptually witty. In the early 1900s, a Berlin printing firm and advertising agency, Hollerbaum & Schmidt, introduced a new style of poster, Sachplakat (object poster), that welded the fluidity of French Art Nouveau and the bold linearity of German Jugenstil into a form that was comparatively economical and stark. In 1906 a novice graphic artist named Lucian Bernhard (1883–1972) became the style's founder when he won a competition that further changed the nature of poster design. Bernhard designed an unprecedented, reductive composition that became the hallmark of Sachplakat, which was characterized by the rejection of ornamental excess in favour of an unambiguous image of the product – the only text being the brand name in block letters. The Sachplakat monumentalized the ordinary – be it a typewriter, shoes or a light bulb. Compared to the more ornate posters on the Berlin hoardings, Bernhard's poster for Priester matches showed only two red-and-yellow tipped wooden matches but was a real eye-stopper. It also confirmed its creator as Berlin's foremost poster-maker. Sachs immediately invited Bernhard to design the Society's logo and stationery – and to become one of its board members. That Das Plakat favoured the Sachplakat sensibilities was no accident: Bernhard had strong ties with Hollerbaum & Schmidt and they, in turn, took many advertising pages in the magazine.

Sachs had little interest in the actual business of advertising. As a connoisseur rather than a professional, he had the freedom to study the poster more for its formal attributes than for its functional requirements. Yet he was

not a dilettante, nor was Das Plakat an arcane journal laden with academic art-historical jargon. Given the stiff conventions of German writing and typography at the time, the magazine's text was accessible and informative. From the visual standpoint, generous use of expensive colour plates and tip-in facsimiles made Das Plakat the most ambitious magazine published at that time – and not only among art and design periodicals.

In the tradition of German (and European) art/culture magazines that preceded it, the cover and masthead of each issue of the bi-monthly Das Plakat was different. The covers were designed as mini-posters with the emphasis on a central, often abstract image. Most covers were printed on a heavy, uncoated cover paper, which allowed for concentrated colour saturation, and occasionally a special paper or ink was used for tactile effect. The interior layout was consistent – mostly a Black Letter type (Antiqua designed by Bernhard) set in justified columns. The illustrations were frequently mortised out of the columns and framed inside black borders. The magazine's format preceded the era of white space and cinematic pacing of images that became so common in magazines during the Fifties.

The popularity of the poster, and other forms of Gebrauchsgraphik (advertising art), during the 1910s was similar to the boom in television use in the Fifties. More than a mere sales tool, the poster was street art that addressed the public in both utilitarian and aesthetic ways. This fascination with the object accounted for the increase in membership of the Society for Friends of the Poster and the concomitant rise in Das Plakat's readership. In 1914 Sachs was drafted into the army and his editorial duties were assumed by Hannes Meyer and another director, Rudi Bleistein, but in 1915 Sachs's collaborators were also drafted and he was released from army service to assume sole editorship and authorship (using different pen names).

Without Sachs's passion, the magazine would have succumbed to wartime privations, but he maintained his operation by attending to the propaganda needs of the imperial German government. Articles in Das Plakat reported on war bond design and it reproduced posters of both allied and belligerent nations. After the War, Sachs published a supplement exclusively devoted to political posters in an attempt to summarize the paper war that had challenged so many artists and advertising creators. Moreover, Das Plakat turned its attention to media other than posters, including articles on trademarks and typefaces.

Das Plakat is a document of the early period of European commercialization and industrialization, as seen through the lens of graphic art and design. It was also rooted in a pre-modern aesthetic, adhering to a format that was soon labelled as antiquated – characterized by Black Letter type and central-axis typography. The magazine acknowledged the modern avant-garde in a few issues but never embraced it wholeheartedly. Nor was it given the opportunity to do so. *Das Plakat* continued to publish until 1921, when internal disagreements among the Society's members and its board of directors negatively affected operating decisions. Embittered, Sachs closed the magazine.

By the time of *Das Plakat*'s demise, even mass periodical design was coming under the spell of modernism – Futurism, De Stijl, Constructivism – at least through the introduction of sans-serif typefaces and asymmetrical page compositions. These new ideas were cautiously and incrementally adopted as the keepers of tradition ventured into realms and methods that had previously been anathema. Revolution in politics, culture and technology was unseating the accepted world-view, and design certainly echoed changes that were manifest in radical art movements that sought to influence public perception through a new mass art.

Jan Tschichold (discussed in Chapter 5) codified the daring leaps in graphics from the old to new. When members of the German Printers' Association based in Leipzig received the October 1925 edition of their monthly journal, *Typographische Mitteilungen*, they were shocked by the contents. Founded in 1903, the magazine showcased

conventional German typography and used an array of spiky Black Letter typefaces common to German publication design at the time. Occasionally, examples of Art Moderne typefaces and logotypes were reproduced. However, the October issue, guest-edited by Tschichold, who in 1928 authored the seminal design handbook, *Die Neue Typographie*, was not only a departure from the norm – it was a revolution in form that integrated graphic methods developed for avant-garde art into commercial graphic design. Nevertheless, at the time it was published, this issue of *Typographische Mitteilungen* was an aberration.

Tschichold, a typographic prodigy, admired the experimental typography produced by avant-gardes in Russia, Holland, Czechoslovakia, Poland and Germany (Chapters 4 and 5) and had amassed an impressive specimen collection which, in 1925, the magazine's otherwise conservative editorial board invited him to show in a special issue entitled 'Elementare Typographie'. To the consternation of the editors, its signature Black Letter was removed (except in the paid advertisements) and the publication's interior format was entirely redesigned using sans-serif, lower-case grotesques of varying weights to frame a sampling of the most ascetic 'modern' compositions.

This was the first time that the German printing establishment had a full dose of the type and layout

produced by aesthetic radicals. In fact, this issue of *Typographische Mitteilungen* was not only an aesthetic deviation – it ignited political debate. The advent of the Weimar Republic gave rise to major polarities on the political spectrum among right, centrist and left-wing parties, all vying for governmental dominance and popular support. It is clear from the political broadsheets and posters issued during the Weimar period of 1919–33 that German political parties allowed ideology to influence design and sans-serif typefaces had a symbolic, indeed Communist/Socialist, connotation.

Since the magazine was not just distributed to members of the Printers' Association, which was apolitical in nature, but to printing and design professionals throughout Germany, Austria and Switzerland, the ideological issues of the New Typography caused some alarm. Throughout the Twenties, Austrian and Swiss designers eschewed asymmetry as aesthetically unacceptable. Only intense lobbying within the profession forced a sea change in design attitudes. Although *Typographische Mitteilungen* never intended to radicalize the design industries, the political implications of the New Typography did affect literary organizations that supported book design, such as the Social Democratic-leaning Büchergilde Gutenberg, which encouraged the use of sans-serif and other novel typography in contemporary

books. Aligning themselves along political lines, German publishers directed their in-house design departments to work either in the modern or traditional manners.

Typographische Mitteilungen was usually moderate about experimental typography, without showing a preference for any particular style or movement. Its responsibility was to report, not criticize. The editors accepted Tschichold's authority in this area and in showcasing the so-called form-givers, El Lissitzky, Kurt Schwitters, Theo van Doesburg, Karel Teige and others, they felt justified in devoting an entire issue to the subject. Other trade magazines of the period, including *Gebrauchsgraphik* (the leading advertising arts magazine to follow *Das Plakat*), *Reklame* and *Archiv*, featured their share of avant-garde-inspired approaches too.

By the late Twenties, the concepts that Tschichold had codified were being mainstreamed in various ways into mass commercial art and touted by commercial arts clubs and magazines as 'dynamic' and 'streamlined', or, to paraphrase László Moholy-Nagy, a mechanical art for a mechanical age.

Various professional periodicals followed the trends closely and celebrated the exponents as much, if not more, than the proponents. A list of such magazines is not necessary here, but there were a few progressive

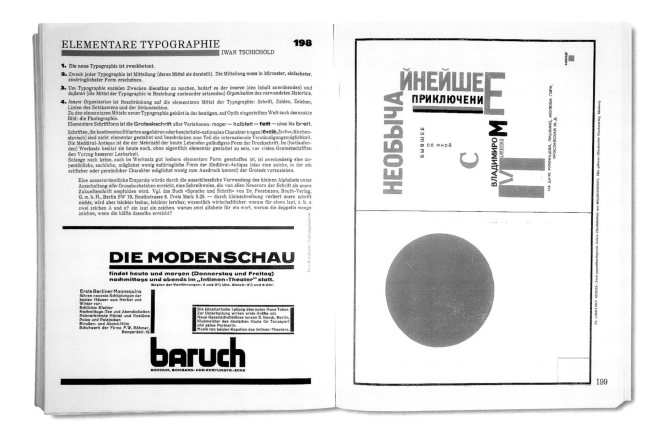

publications which, like *Das Plakat*, trod the fine line
between reporting and trend-setting. The periodicals
discussed in the rest of this chapter defined themselves by
linking their respective editorial policies to the Zeitgeist.

The premier German advertising arts magazine,
Gebrauchsgraphik, edited by Dr H K Frenzel (1882–1937) and
founded in Berlin in 1923 just as the devastating period of
post-war economic inflation came to a close, was the direct
heir of *Das Plakat* as the chronicle of 'new' international
graphic arts. Published in two languages (German and
English), it promoted advertising art as a force for good in
the world. Borrowing the ideas of Futurism, De Stijl and
Constructivism, Frenzel believed that utilitarian art
educated the public because, in fact, it was the public's
art. 'He saw advertising as the great mediator between
peoples, the facilitator of world understanding, and through
that understanding, world peace,'¹ wrote the historian
Virginia Smith.

Gebrauchsgraphik was a professional, not an avant-
garde, journal. It had no ties to any ideological or philosophical
groups. Nevertheless, owing to its independence the
magazine encouraged acceptance of unprecedented work.
Frenzel sought to navigate through traditional and progressive
design with the goal of investing the latter's attributes into
German industrial arts. He understood the psychology of
the public mind and knew that its stimulation must be
achieved through novel visual approaches. And yet his
favourite *Gebrauchsgraphikers* were designers who exhibited
considerably more than style: they had to have vision. So
he used the Bauhaus as a model for how to integrate graphic
and other design disciplines into a single practice, and
supported those artists who adhered to such tenets through
the magazine, books and other means. A few Bauhaus
masters, notably Herbert Bayer, were featured in portfolios
and on *Gebrauchsgraphik*'s prestigious monthly covers.

When compared to Jan Tschichold's issue of
Typographische Mitteilungen, Frenzel's magazine was
a more neutral showcase for all manner of contemporary
work. Its layout was clean, simple, unadorned, and did
not obstruct the diverse work that it featured with over-
designed pages. He used classic typefaces, framed pages
with generous white space, and routinely followed the same
grid in every issue. Moreover, Frenzel's advocacy for the new
stopped short of creating avant-garde design himself. While
catholic in his appreciation of avant-gardisms, he did not
support illegibility. Nothing promoted through his magazine
could be mistaken as art for the sake of art – or design for
the sake of design. Sadly, *Gebrauchsgraphik* survived, as
did various other trade magazines, into the Third Reich.
Although on the surface Frenzel's vision remained intact
during these difficult years, the fact that Nazi principles

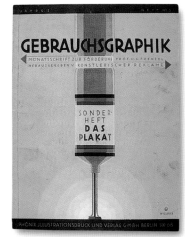

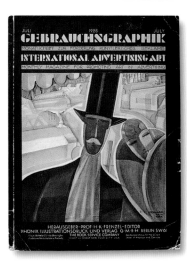

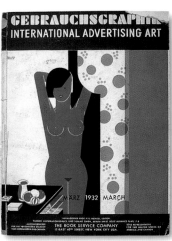

gradually took hold is evidenced by the elimination of features about unsanctioned design. After Frenzel's death in 1937 in an automobile accident (purportedly suicide), *Gebrauchsgraphik* cautioned *Gebrauchsgraphikers* to avoid Impressionism, Expressionism, Cubism and Futurism, and thus officially ended the period of German avant-gardism.

Meanwhile, in the United States progressive design was promoted only after the dust had settled in Europe. During the Twenties and Thirties, the American advertising industry was cautious about changing its conventional methods of selling products because words (or slogans), not images, had historically been the most effective means of addressing the public. There were few advocates of advertising or commercial art as a utopian force rather than as a tool of capitalism, as there were in Europe. However, within the advertising and design industries two magazines were often compared to *Gebrauchsgraphik*. Neither was avant-garde in the strict sense but, like Frenzel's periodical, *Advertising Arts* and *PM/AD* advanced progressive notions of design developed by émigré European designers.

The first issue of *Advertising Arts* on 8 January 1930 marked a new way of addressing graphic and advertising art. This trade magazine integrated modern art into the stodgy mainstream commercial culture. While other American trade journals promoted the status quo,

Advertising Arts, a perfect-bound monthly supplement of the weekly trade magazine *Advertising and Selling*, proposed ways to integrate new design fashions and progressive ideas 'adopted by radicals' into conventional practice. Although it could only report on, rather than actually originate, these developments, the magazine advocated them with such fervency that it became the centre of progressive American graphic and industrial design of the era.

Yet *Advertising Arts* is not to be confused with the radical European design manifestos that introduced the New Typography and changed visual practice and perception. In Europe, quotidian 'publicity' was more image-oriented and modern avant-garde design was an alternative to antiquated aesthetics born of bourgeois culture and politics. In the United States of the Twenties, which did not have a design or advertising avant-garde, modernistic design was a product of the commercial concept known as 'style obsolescence', devised by advertising supremo Earnest Elmo Calkins (1868–1964) as an acceptable way of encouraging consumers to 'move the goods' despite the ravages of a worldwide economic downturn.

When *Advertising Arts* made its debut during the Great Depression, the economy was at its nadir and desperation was at its zenith. Unless advertising and public-relations experts like Calkins could help resuscitate the economy, the nation would plummet further into the abyss – and with it the

Below: **Gebrauchsgraphik,** cover and inside spread from vol.7 no.8, September 1930. This cover illustrating hot metal type composition reveals how difficult it was to prepare even the most traditional layouts – such as the letter heads on the spread – and suggests why outlandish experimental approaches were so hard to achieve.

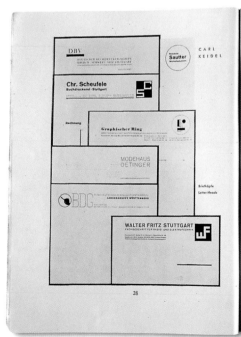

advertising industry. *Advertising Arts*, edited by Frederick C Kendall and Ruth Fleischer, was developed as a vehicle to encourage innovative work and celebrate the determination of advertising designers to manipulate popular perception using pseudo-science. It was a magazine with a mission. So, rather than publish the usual diet of gossip, trade talk and technical notices, Kendall and Fleischer tapped the movers and shakers of what was then called 'art for industry' to flag the new progressivism. Touting their own achievements as 'artists' and imbuing art with commercial value was a massive public-relations effort that required the most articulate practitioners. Granted, the readers of *Advertising Arts* were primarily other advertising artists and designers, but nevertheless the magazine gained authority within the offices and boardrooms of industry.

The magazine was a blueprint for how to market modernity as both an ethos and a style – in print, in packaging and as industrial wares. For their part, the writers, who included influential graphic and industrial artists such as Lucian Bernhard, René Clark, Clarence P Hornung, Paul Hollister, Norman Bel Geddes and Rockwell Kent, passionately advocated the new. In an article entitled 'Modern Layouts Must Sell Rather than Startle', design pundit Frank H Young wrote: 'Daring originality in the use of new forms, new patterns, new methods of organization and bizarre color effects is the keynote of modern layout and is achieving the startling results we see today.' At the same time, *Advertising Arts* cautioned against excess: 'In some instances enthusiasm for modernism has overshadowed good judgment and the all-import selling message is completely destroyed,'[2] continued Young. The design of the magazine itself lived up to these words. Each issue had a striking cover by a contemporary commercial artist, but the interior typography was always neutral. Printing, paper and embossing samples were frequently inserted to give the periodical more visual excitement.

Advertising Arts promulgated a progressive design approach (and style) unique to the United States during the early Thirties, called Streamline. Unlike the elegant austerity of the Bauhaus, where economy and simplicity was paramount, Streamline was a uniquely American futuristic mannerism based on sleek aerodynamic design born of science and technology. Planes, trains and cars were given the swooped-back appearance that both symbolized and physically accelerated speed. Consequently, type and image were designed to echo that sensibility, the result being that the airbrush became the medium of choice and all futuristic traits, be they practical or symbolic, were encouraged. The clarion call was to 'Make it Modern' – and 'it' was anything that could be designed.

Below from left: **Advertising Arts**, covers of January 1930, by Gustav Jensen; January 1932, by Anton Bruehl; May 1933, by Warren Chappel. *Advertising Arts*, edited by Frederick C Kendall and Ruth Fleischer, adhered to the motto 'Most Advanced Yet Acceptable' in terms of what it chose to publish. Each cover, designed by a progressive artist, exemplified the diversity of modernism.

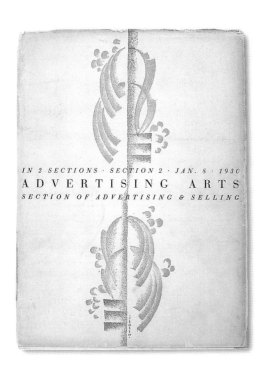

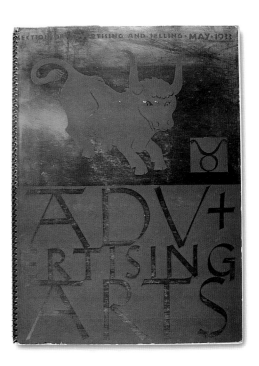

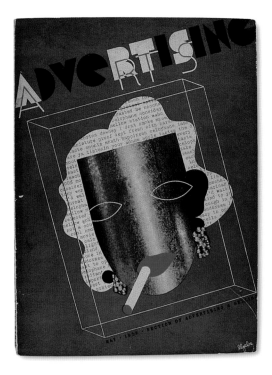

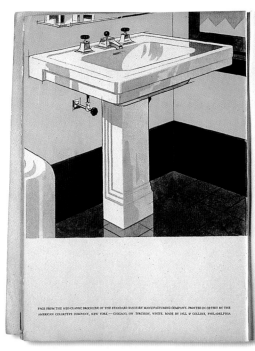

HOT and COLD

By GEORGE SAKIER

Neo-Classic fittings designed for the Standard Sanitary Manufacturing Company by George Sakier

For some mysterious reason the bathroom is one of today's better topics of conversation. At dinner, when my partner feels it about time to ask what I do, I generally, albeit I have more romantic wares to offer, answer that I design bathtubs. The response is electric, earnest and most gratifying. I am now sure of her complete attention for at least three courses. My hostess beams and forgives me for not playing bridge. I become a social asset.

There may be one or two people who have not written a play, but there is probably no one who has not a dream bathroom. There is no one who has not some unfulfilled bathroom desire . . . artistically . . . or mechanically. It may be for crystal tubs and porphyry floors, for the voluptuous luxury of super-sybaritic comforts; mayhap to satisfy that long-lost memory of marble halls . . . "when I was King in Babylon and you were a Christian slave" . . . and vice-versa. Or it may be, nation of small boys that we are, the irresistible hankering for some Joe Cook contraption to reduce effort to its irreducible minimum . . . no matter how much work it requires. In the complete privacy of our bathroom we can indulge freely in the flights of fancy which we lack the courage to gratify in less private places.

Therefore I was surprised to find, in an otherwise shrewd and seasoned article in Creative Arts the following footnote: ". . . Our own manufacturers of tubs and washstands have so debased their product with a romantic flub-dub, their rendering of what they conceive to be Superior Culture, to wit, "art moderne" from Paris, that the American bathroom threatens to become idiotic."

More in levity than in seriousness (for Mr. Haskell's attitude is refreshing, considering the flock of parlor engineers who are frothing at the mouth in print for a "pure industrial art") I take up his own bludgeon to gently reproach him for running down "romantic flub-dub" so puritanically and homelessly . . . for calling our endearing frailties—flub-dub!

Mr. Haskell complains of functional beauty destroyed by our romanticizing Europe, and yet, is shrewd enough to admit that "functionalism" is Europe's romanticizing America's hard boiled engineering technique. And now our young aesthetes are importing "functionalism" . . . romanticizing Europe's romanticizing America. If that isn't super-romantic flub-dub—Pardon Me! It's very like the chap who goes to the trouble to buy imported Virginia cigarettes. But I myself occasionally smoke an English cigarette, and though it is made from an American-grown tobacco, somehow its English package seems to make it taste delightfully "different."

Anyway if Louis Quatorze is flub-dub, so is Functionalism, or any of the four "modern" styles. And, whatever you call it, we like it. And we hope it sells our wares. A skilful designer should know when, where and how to apply it.

To do this with scientific method, as far as such intangible elements can be so treated, we have, in the Bureau of Design Development of the American-Radiator and Standard Sanitary Corporation constructed a number of bathrooms in a variety of current styles. Together they are a synthesis of the types of bathrooms the Great American Public feels it wants.

We have built these rooms that we might study the

PAGE FROM THE NEO-CLASSIC BROCHURE OF THE STANDARD SANITARY MANUFACTURING COMPANY. PRINTED IN OFFSET BY THE AMERICAN COLORTYPE COMPANY, NEW YORK—CHICAGO, ON TORCHON, WHITE, MADE BY HILL & COLLINS, PHILADELPHIA.

11

TRADEMARKING GOVERNMENT ACTIVITIES

● When the government adopted its now famous Blue Eagle a little over a year ago, the administration took one of the most progressive steps ever made in this country in the direction of successful trademarking. It seemed at the time of its adoption that this emblem might be the beginning of the earmarking of other governmental activities. We had every reason to believe that the National Recovery Administration had set a high standard and a precedent that other agencies would follow. Since March 4, new departments have sprung up in great numbers in Washington, and at the present writing we find twenty-eight important governmental activities designated by initials, such as AAA, CAB, ICC, etc. NRA stands alone with its consumer appeal as symbolized by the Blue Eagle.

Many of these other governmental activities could be successfully dramatized and popularized through a series of intelligently designed devices. On this and the opposite page, we show five marks created by Clarence Hornung, New York designer, to show what can be done in this direction.

18

Federal Coordinator of Transportation

Reconstruction Finance Corporation

Grain Futures Administration

Eastern Zone Army Air Corps Mail Operations

19

Lucian Bernhard (1883–1972), the German poster artist who designed some of the era's most emblematic typefaces (including Bernhard Gothic) after emigrating to the United States, suggested in an *Advertising Arts* article that the modernistic designer must be responsible for recasting American products. *Advertising Arts* viewed modernization as the panacea for the world's ills (and, if Calkins was to be believed, it was the cure for all the economic woes of the United States). It is therefore curious that in the first issue of *Advertising Arts* the editors featured 'The Bolshevik Billboard' as a possible direction that should be taken by capitalist advertising agencies. Given its progressive stand, circulation was never as high as other mainstream American trade journals. *Advertising Arts* ceased publishing when the weekly magazine *Advertising and Selling* folded, prior to the *New York World's Fair: The World of Tomorrow* of 1939, where so many of the modern graphic, packaging and industrial design concepts championed by the magazine were put into practise.

By then *Advertising Arts* also had a viable competitor entitled *PM* (Production Manager), later called *AD* (Art Director), launched by a leading New York type business, Composing Room Inc., and published bi-monthly between 1934 and 1942. Founded by Dr Robert Lincoln (Doc) Leslie (1885–1987), *PM: An Intimate Journal for Production Managers, Art Directors and Their Associates*, was initially the Composing Room's house organ. With its co-editor Percy Seitlin, a former newspaperman, this 15.25 x 20.25 cm (6 x 8 in.) 'journal' developed into the leading outlet for traditional and progressive work. It explored a variety of print media, covered industry news, and developed a strong prejudice in favour of asymmetric typography and design. It was also one of the first journals to showcase recently arrived European émigrés such as Bayer, Will Burtin, Gustav Jensen, Joseph Binder, M F Agha, as well as native-grown moderns Lester Beall, Joseph Sinel and Paul Rand. While covering the commercial scene, its editors delved deeper into the Bauhaus and the New Typography because the Composing Room of New York was no mere type shop. It was the principle centre of progressive design activity from the late Thirties until the late Sixties. No other typographic business promoted itself more aggressively, or so fervently advanced the art and craft of type design. What began as a campaign to attract typesetting business from New York's advertising agencies and book and magazine publishers evolved into one of the most ambitious educational programmes that the field had known. It initiated type clinics, lecture series, exhibitions, catalogues and its influential graphic arts periodical.

The programme, conceived and sustained for almost forty years by the Composing Room's co-founder, Leslie,

was rooted in graphic arts traditions yet was motivated by his personal willingness to identify and promote significant new approaches even if they rejected tradition. What made the Composing Room so profoundly influential, in addition to being a recognized leader in quality metal type and eventually photo-typesetting, was a commitment to explore design approaches while turning a blind eye towards style or ideology. Despite his own preference for classical practice, Leslie gave young progressive designers a platform on which to exhibit their wares.

Leslie believed that a well-informed professional would be a more discerning customer and so, in a corner of his shop, he created a graphic arts salon. Regularly frequented by Ladislav Sutnar and Herbert Bayer, this put his shop at the centre of what would now be called a 'design discourse' but was then practical design talk. The Composing Room's unparalleled efforts to elevate the level of graphic arts and typography may have been driven by commercial priorities but none the less it formed a solid foundation for the celebration and documentation of graphic design.

In 1939 the name *PM* was changed to *AD*, which, coincidentally, reflected a creative shift within the profession from production managers to art directors – marking a gradual transition from craft to art. Each cover of *PM* and *AD* featured an original image with a redesigned logo. E McKnight Kauffer's was characteristically Cubistic; Paul Rand's was playfully modern; Lucian Bernhard's was suitably gothic; and Matthew Leibowitz's prefigured the New Wave in its Dada-inspired juxtaposition of discordant decorative old wood-types.

Three years after starting *PM* Leslie took over a small office in the Composing Room which, with the addition of a display case and bright lights, was transformed into the PM Gallery, the first exhibition space in New York dedicated to graphic design and its affinities. The magazine and gallery were symbiotic. Often, a feature in one would lead to an exhibition in the other or vice versa. Leslie believed that there was an enthusiastic audience for a showcase featuring the work of artists in industry; and, furthermore, that the audience was larger than anyone had ever imagined.

In April–May 1942 the editors, Leslie and Seitlin, published this note: '*AD* is such a small segment of this wartime world that it is almost with embarrassment, and certainly with humility, that we announce the suspension of its publication ... for the duration ... The reasons are easy to understand: shortage of men and materials, shrinkage of the advertising business whose professional workers *AD* has served, and all-out digging in for Victory ...'[3] The magazine, which did not resume publishing after the War, left a documentary record of a period when American and European designers began to forge an international design language in the service of business. World War II had killed the idealistic stage of avant-garde design and dispersed its proponents. *PM* and *AD* helped to launch its commercial stage.

Graphic design was covered in professional magazines but, with the exception of small articles in general design or consumer journals, it rarely featured as an integral art form. After all, graphic design is a service to commerce and politics but not an end in itself – or a message of its own – as the European avant-gardes believed. So, all the magazines surveyed in this chapter must be seen as insular, addressing an audience of professionals rather than a larger public. Indeed, there has been only one magazine during the twentieth century to attempt to break out of the trade ghetto and that was the American *Portfolio*. In its day it was avant-garde on two counts: it was ahead of the curve in terms of design and content and it accepted no advertising. Even *Graphis*, the upmarket, Swiss-based, multilingual, international design magazine founded in 1946, took advertising aimed at its decidedly professional audience. Conversely, *Portfolio*, founded in 1949, charted new territory all the way from its editorial content to its format design.

Although only three issues of *Portfolio* were published between 1949 and 1951, it was such an exquisite integration of content and design that even today it offers a standard against which all design magazines must ultimately be judged. Modelled on *Minotaure* – the lavish, Surrealist art magazine (see Chapter 7) – this was not a typical printing or advertising trade journal. The editor, Frank Zachary (b.1914), explained that the physical size itself was meant to be 'a graphic experience'.[4] Indeed, the 22.75 x 30.5 cm (9 x 12 in.) publication, designed and art-directed by Alexey Brodovitch (1898–1971), the art director of *Harper's Bazaar*, was a virtual museum between covers, incorporating all kinds of tactile inserts, including wrapping and wallpaper samples, printing specimens and 3D glasses with which to view a special section on stereoscopy. Articles on the relationship of letter forms to abstract painting, Alexander Calder's sculpture, and Jackson Pollock's action painting (with photographs by Hans Namuth) were seamlessly interwoven with essays on commercial culture, vintage advertising from 1900, Paul Rand's trademarks, and western cattle brands. Zachary and his partner, publisher George Rosenthal, Jr., a photographer and disciple of Moholy-Nagy, left no stone unturned, followed any leads, and spared no expense in expanding the parochial definition of graphic design from service to art.

The reason for founding the magazine, however, was rather pedestrian. 'I was out of work and I had to think up something to make some money,' explained Zachary. 'I also

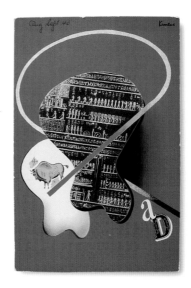

had a long-standing idea of doing an American *Graphis,* but done in such a way that the magazine itself would be a model of design, and at the same time communicate the contents in a very original, innovative and inspirational manner.'[5] In 1948 Zachary wrote a letter outlining his idea for *Portfolio* to George Rosenthal, Sr., the scion of a large Cincinnati publishing family that published *Writers' Digest* and *MiniCam* magazines. The partners received $25,000 out of which a direct mail campaign was launched, with a four-page prospectus designed by Paul Rand that outlined a prospective table of contents. The goal was to attract 20,000 subscribers once the magazine got rolling. They succeeded in attracting 12,000.

For the job of art director, Zachary fixed his sights on Alexey Brodovitch. 'I approached him cold; told him what I wanted to do, and he decided to do it'[6] for a design fee of $3,000 per issue. So, with the finest magazine designer in America in place, Zachary's job was to build a premier issue from the most desirable material in the proposed table of contents. The first issue contained photographs by leading American photographers, Richard Avedon and Irving Penn and articles on Giambattista Bodoni, early xerography, trademarks by Paul Rand, Giantism (grand monuments

of popular culture), design from the field of mathematics, good-looking package design from major department stores, a profile of E McKnight Kauffer, and a portfolio of Saul Steinberg's cartoons. It was an eclectic though complementary mix that spoke of the essence of visual culture and the role of design in that culture. Zachary wrote many of the articles himself, but in later issues spread a wider net for journalists and essayists who avoided the clichés of trade reportage.

Brodovitch's design process fascinated Zachary. The latter delivered the material for the respective issues to the art director's apartment and then waited for layouts. Brodovitch's usual technique was to reproduce the material in photostat form in an infinite variety of sizes. 'Actually, the damn stat bill was the biggest single burden we had to bear,' recalled Zachary. He would come back the next day, when he described Brodovitch as 'running around picking stats up here and there; and out of this morass of stats, he would assemble a 6- or 8-page layout. It was absolutely beautiful to watch!'[7] Layouts were shown to Zachary and Rosenthal on big white sheets of paper. Once they had assembled what they thought was the final content, the three of them would edit out and reposition the various

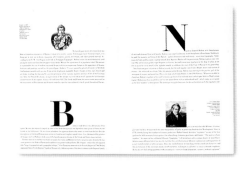

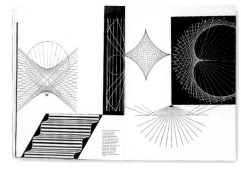

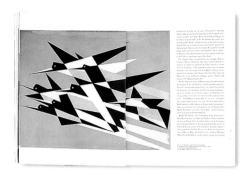

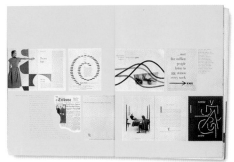

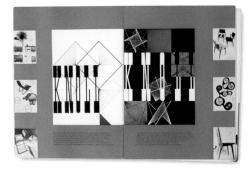

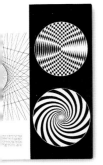

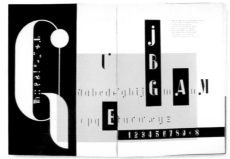
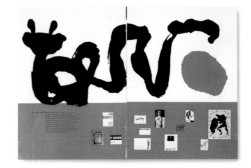

spreads. There were so many pages that Zachary rented a room at New York's Gotham Hotel where Brodovitch laid them out in the hallway after eleven o'clock at night.

Brodovitch's first cover was a type-only composition that was unique for both professional *and* consumer magazines. He selected a stencilled typeface for the first issue's name-plate that was dropped out in white against black, and overlaid it with transparent primary-colour rectangles. The word *Portfolio* ran vertically down the centre of the cover without any headlines promoting the contents, either on the front or the back (which simply repeated the transparent colour rectangles). It was artful though tame, especially for an art director known for his photographic *tours de force*.

Portfolio was intended to be a quarterly, but the high production costs reduced the frequency. To support *Portfolio*, Zachary and Rosenthal decided to accept limited advertising, and Rosenthal Sr. sold six pages of ads to the Radio Corporation of America and other prestigious advertisers. When the two editors saw the low quality of their ads they decided not to run any advertising at all. 'We hated the ads we got,' insists Zachary. 'So we said, "Hell, we're not going to mar our beautiful magazine with crummy ads."'[8] Rosenthal Sr. thought it was an unorthodox idea, but humoured the young partners because he respected the achievement of the magazine.

Portfolio was a hybrid – part book and part magazine. Issue no.3 even had a 'french fold' jacket wrapped over the flimsy cover boards. Inside was elegant, functional, yet always had (even by today's standards) surprising pace. Without ads to interrupt the flow, Brodovitch kinetically paced the layouts so that they were modulated for highs, mediums and lows. Few magazine designers truly understand notions of balance and scale in the same way – or are able to move the reader's eye (and mind) along from story to story with such ease.

Brodovitch designed *Portfolio* with a symphonic breadth. Each issue opened with a quiet prologue. Whereas, today, tables of contents are sprinkled with pictorial teasers and word bites, Brodovitch's were subdued – indeed delicately minimal. The first feature began with a full-page image complemented by an elegant headline with body-text blocks framed by generous white space. Indeed, white space was a transparent but major instrument in his symphony. Images would be selected for their compositional and informational weight, but positioned on the page both according to how well they told the visual story and how well they complemented or contrasted with each other. Brodovitch's mastery was in keeping a long story moving without any redundancy, and presenting a short story as visually powerful but without being overly jarring. Text

Right from top: **Portfolio**, covers of no.2, 1950, art by Charles Eames; no.3, 1951, film stills by Herbert Matter. The covers for *Portfolio* nos. 2 and 3 were designed to address uncommon aspects of everyday design. Kites are beautiful and graphic, and the multiple frames from Herbert Matter's film *Constellations* are dramatic when used as a tableau.

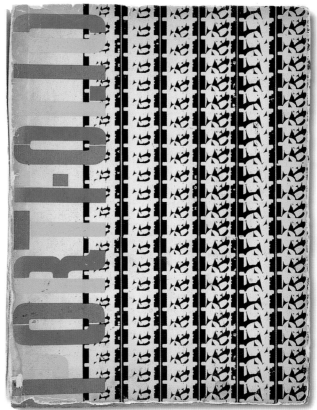

spreads sandwiched purely visual essays, but never in a predictable way. The reader could never anticipate what the next page would bring. Surprise was everything. While each of the three issues has its own defining moments, in totality they are linked by a prevailing aesthetic point of view.

There was some irony (and risk) in publishing an advertisement-free magazine that celebrated the high end of commercial culture. And Zachary and Rosenthal were constantly trying to raise additional funds in order to produce the magazine to the highest standards. But the increasing lag between issues did not bode well. Zachary was resolved to continue publishing, and even while issue no.3 was on the press, he began working on issue no.4 (the cover was to be done by Fernand Léger). But with no funds remaining in the coffers, he had little option but to try to sell the magazine intact. He unsuccessfully approached Henry Luce, publisher of *Time* and *Life*, as a possible buyer. Unfortunately, late in 1951 Zachary was laid low with appendicitis, during which time George Rosenthal, Sr. decided to kill *Portfolio* rather than incur further losses.

Although a handful of significant design and typography magazines that emphasized art and commerce were published in the late Forties and early Fifties – including *Alphabet and Image* in England, *Graphis* in Switzerland and *Print* in the United States – *Portfolio* was the only one to truly celebrate the interdisciplinary nature of graphic design. It therefore helped to define a decidedly American late modernist sensibility. *Portfolio* levelled the playing field between what critics call high and low art by finding the common denominator. Since its demise, other magazines have published: *Novum Gebrauchsgraphik*, *Print* and *Communication Arts* are among the oldest, continuous trade magazines, while *Neue Grafik*, *Typographica* and *U&lc* have long passed from view. Some of these (such as *Eye* and *Baseline*) have made an impact but few have truly bridged the gap between the professional and cultural journal in the manner of *Portfolio*.

Below from left: **Alphabet and Image**, cover of no.5, 1947. **Graphis**, vol.4 no.23, 1948, cover design by Joseph Binder. **Print**, vol.7 no.3, June 1953, cover design and art directed by George A Shealy.

Edited by Robert Harling, *Alphabet and Image* combined ornate Victorian letters with modern notions of scale and economy. The contrast of the boisterous A and I against empty space contributes to the dynamism of the cover. Binder's thrust to the heavens for the cover of Swiss design magazine *Graphis*, edited by Walter Herdeg, suggests an Italian Futurist influence, while this 1953 *Print* cover resembles a Dada composition. *Print* was published by William Edwin Rudge and edited by Lawrence A Audrain.

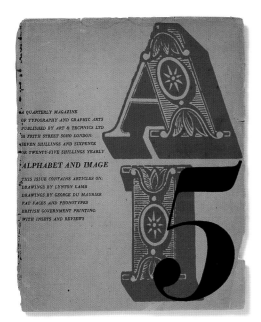

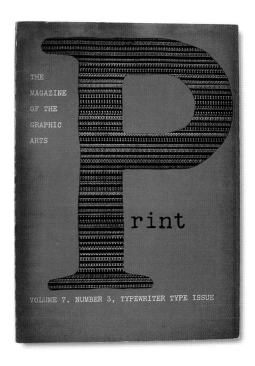

THE MODERN MAGAZINE

50c

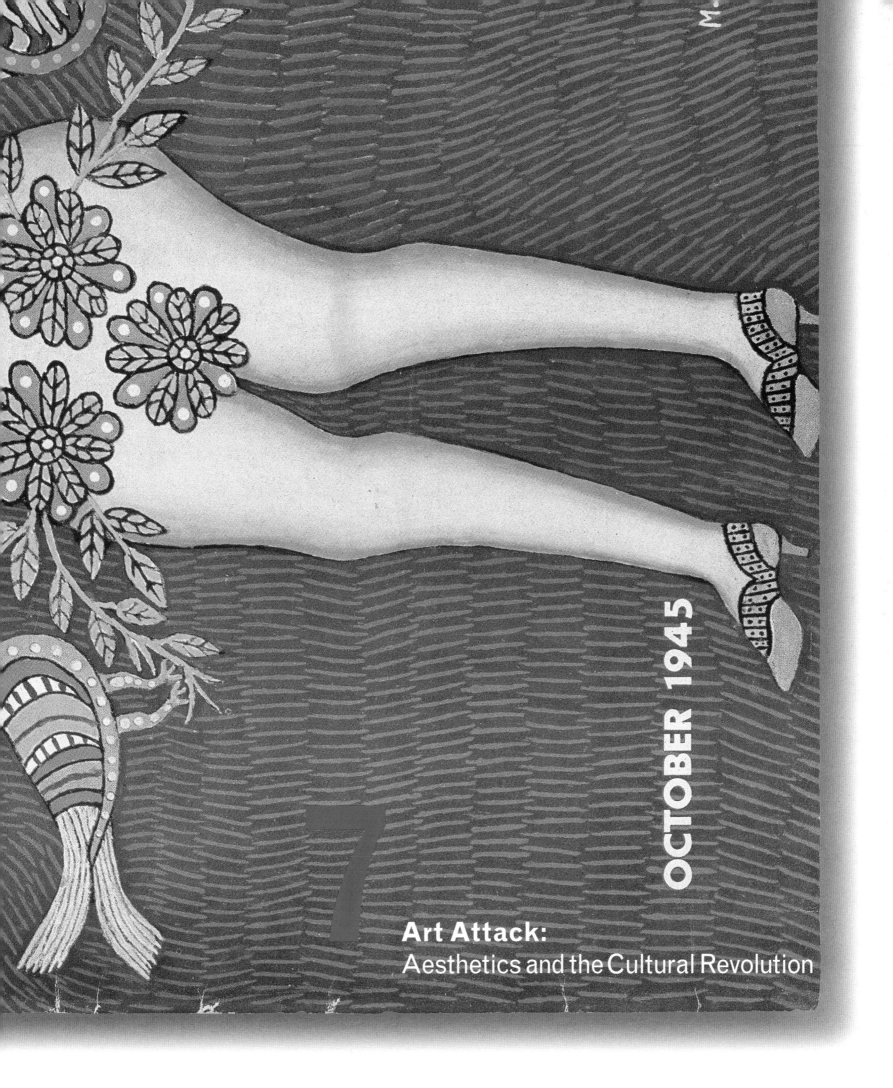

OCTOBER 1945

7

Art Attack:
Aesthetics and the Cultural Revolution

aux camara des cubistes .

LE CUBISME EST PEINTURE BOCHE
Voilà l'injure où descendent ses adversaires.
TELUM IMBELLE

En rétablissant construction & infusant synthèse, le Cubisme ouvrait chantier de sensibilité. Car il n'est de sensibilité que RATIONNELLE, rien ne pouvant se greffer à l'inconsistance.
Et c'est par la sensibilité rationnelle que se caractérisent à la fois le Cubisme & le « *CLAIR GÉNIE DE NOTRE RACE* ».
A moins que n'apparaisse mieux imprégnée de ce génie la phrase suivante :
« Hier encore le Cubisme, végétation monstrueuse, décorait dignement la boutonnière de nos snobs. La rose malodorante était toute l'originalité dont nous nous piquions. »
(ÉMILE BAYARD.)

LE CUBISME SERAIT BOCHE
Simple question :
— « Lui connaîtriez-vous un précurseur allemand ? »
— Non, _____MAIS
DÈS qu'apparut le Cubisme les Allemands se mirent

à l'imiter » (CAMILLE MAUCLAIR)
? ? ?

?

Ajoutons, à titre surérogatoire, que l'Allemagne ne fournit pas plus d'imitateurs que de précurseurs :
« Berlin méprisait les Welches tombés dans l'aberration cubiste. »
(CAMILLE MAUCLAIR.)

Et de proclamer — cela va de soi — la fin du Cubisme avec menace aux essais de résurrection qu'APRÈS LA GUERRE il voudrait tenter.

après la guerre ?

Souffrez que nous devancions l'appel.

C'est au cours de la guerre, pendant les loisirs de la tranchée, que

BRAQUE, DERAIN, de LA FRESNAYE, LÉGER, L.-A. MOREAU,

A.-D. de SEGONZAC

ALLARD, APOLLINAIRE & tant d'autres

s'obstinent — ô paradoxe! — à
perpétrer ou prôner . . .
LA PEINTURE BOCHE

Appréciable réplique aux annonces de décès, si tant est que la vie se prouve par le mouvement.

J. GRANIÉ

Although Dada and Surrealism were closely linked through shared members and political affinities, they were aesthetically and philosophically opposed. Unlike the brutish reality on which Dada (especially German Dada) was based, Surrealism ventured into the subconscious. Surrealism projected the inner demons onto the outer world. Dada and Surrealist periodicals propagated these distinct points of view in many ways, including typography and design. Dada (see Chapters 3 and 4) was more raucous than Surrealism, which was curiously refined. Dada publishing clearly influenced design approaches in Sixties Underground and Seventies Punk but Surrealist publications had more resonance, with eclectic art movements (tied to Surrealism itself) that spanned the post-World War II period well into the Seventies and Eighties. This chapter surveys the most important Surrealist journals and some of the many offshoots that arguably grew from a seminal tree, André Breton's (1896–1966) proto-Surrealist periodical *Littérature.*

In 1922, two years before Breton officially launched the revolutionary artistic movement with his first 'Manifesto of Surrealism', he defined Surrealism in *Littérature* by referring to it as pure psychic automation intended to express, either verbally or in any other way, the true functioning of thought. This was a kind of thought, he noted, that was dictated in the absence of any control exerted by reason and outside any aesthetic or moral preoccupation. Artists had, of course, probed subliminal realms centuries before the advent of Surrealism. But as the new movement was making its way down the birth canal the despair caused by a lengthy, horrifyingly bloody world war in the first decades of the twentieth century had wreaked havoc on the psyches of artists and writers.

At this time, as a medical student and member of the French Army medical corps, Breton saw the carnage first-hand. Surrealism was his tool to cope with, and describe, such repugnance. What began as a literary movement during Dada's heyday eventually overtook Dada, on the grounds that the latter had failed because it was nihilistic and lacked the belief system held by Surrealism. Breton, who was proprietor of the burgeoning movement along with Philippe Soupault (1897–1990), Louis Aragon (1897–1982) and Paul Eluard (1895–1952), searched for a new spirituality born of the past but dedicated to the future.

Even before *Littérature* began, a wartime periodical called *L'Elan*, founded in 1915 and edited by Amédée Ozenfant (1886–1966), published arts and letters about the war by allied soldier-artists who had been interested in Cubism. Many of *L'Elan*'s contributors would ultimately influence, or participate in, what became Breton's *Littérature* circle. Surrealism needed time to gestate and much of this evolutionary period was documented in Breton's interim

Previous page: **View**, detail of vol.5 no.3, October 1945, cover by Morris Hirshfield.

Opposite, clockwise from top left: **L'Elan**, covers of no.1, 15 April 1915; no.3, 15 May 1915; inside spread from no.1, 15 April 1915.

Right from top: **Les Chroniques du Jour**, vol.7 no.3, 15 May 1926, cover art by Amedeo Modigliani; cover of vol.10 no.5, March 1930.

As the cover art shows, *L'Elan*, published and edited by Amédée Ozenfant, presented anti-German satire with an avant-garde accent. Gualtieri di San Lazzaro's *Les Chroniques du Jour*, however, was concerned with the post-war French avant-garde.

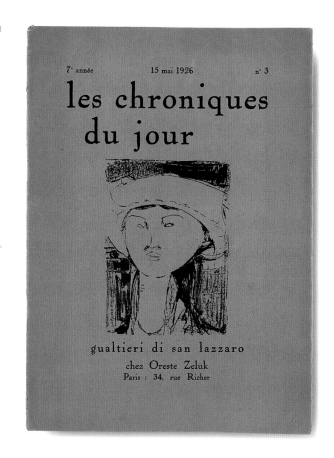

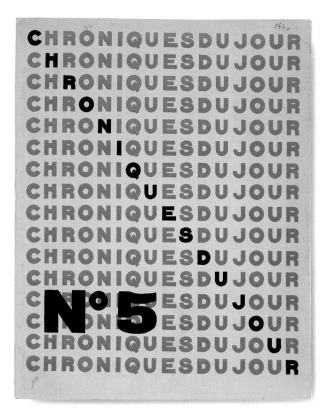

review which began in 1919 and lasted until 1924 (the name *Littérature* was suggested by the poet Paul Valéry). In 1920 *Les Chroniques du Jour*, edited by Gualtieri di San Lazzaro in Paris until 1930, also addressed avant-garde concerns but without the same resonance on vanguard thinking.

In the beginning, *Littérature* was eclectic. However, it adamantly refused to be considered simply an heir of earlier Parisian avant-gardes. Breton was initially unmoved by both Dada (the movement) and *Dada* the review (particularly the first two issues), but he was taken with *Dada* no.3, in which Tristan Tzara published his first Dada manifesto and radically altered its persona (see Chapter 3) into a fount of graphic experimentation. Hence Breton invited Tzara, after his arrival in Paris from Zurich in 1920, to take a role in *Littérature*, which by then showcased a pot-pourri of Dada and Surrealist poems and texts as well as announcements of Dada art exhibitions. Nevertheless, Breton maintained a certain wary ambivalence towards many Dada activities, with the noticeable exception of his high praise in *Littérature* for an exhibition of Max Ernst's collages.

Despite its flirtation with Dada, *Littérature* was not influenced by what Breton referred to as *Dada*'s typographical 'tricks'. Neither typographic invention nor novelty was pursued for its own sake. *Littérature* maintained a rather conservative format (like the first two issues of *Dada*): a yellow cover with a simple masthead set in an elongated, Ultra-Bodoni (fat- and thin-stemmed) typeface. Rejecting the boisterous post-war typographic styles, *Littérature* did not veer far from its original literary format. However, subtle rule-breaking variations were employed when needed, such as alternately setting poems in italic and roman characters. Different type families were also permissible if the content could benefit from it. But other demonstrative graphic approaches were frowned upon and even illustration was eschewed for most of the issues.

Experiments with dream analysis and automatic writing between 1922 and 1924 marked Breton's attack on past artistic verities. He further instituted a new look for *Littérature*: a larger-sized, revised cover format, and a variable hand-scrawled masthead for each number. Abstruse cover illustrations were introduced: two covers had line drawings of a top hat, two depicted sacred hearts, and issue nos. 4 to 12 featured drawings by Francis Picabia (1879–1953) who had become a contributor to *Littérature* at the time that Tzara moved to Paris. Although the magazine concentrated on prose and poetry, Breton retained a passionate interest in painting, and wrote frequently on the visual arts. So art gradually appeared on full pages in *Littérature*, including work by key influences on Surrealism: Marcel Duchamp (1887–1968), Pablo Picasso (1881–1973), Giorgio de Chirico (1888–1978) and Max Ernst (1891–1976).

Below: **Littérature**, advertisement for *Littérature*, 23 January 1920. *Opposite, from left*: covers of vol.2 no.1, 1 March 1922, and vol.2 no.5, 1 October 1922.

Littérature, which was edited by André Breton, was the mouthpiece for the proto-Surrealists. The calligraphic logo emerging from the nineteenth-century top hat reveals the avant-garde's ironic use of nineteenth-century graphic forms. Francis Picabia's satiric cover drawing for issue no.5 is indicative of the periodical's embrace of twentieth-century sexual taboos.

PREMIER VENDREDI

DE LITTÉRATURE

Le 23 janvier 1920, à 16 h. 30
AU PALAIS DES FÊTES 199, rue Saint-Martin

M. André Salmon parlera
DE LA CRISE DU CHANGE

Poèmes de
MM. Max Jacob, André Salmon, Pierre Reverdy, Blaise Cendrars, Maurice Raynal, Francis Picabia, Louis Aragon, Tristan Tzara, André Breton, Jean Cocteau, Georges Ribemont-Dessaignes, Philippe Soupault, Pierre Drieu la Rochelle, Paul Eluard, Raymond Radiguet.

lus par
Mademoiselle Valentine Tessier; MM. Herrand, Bertin et Fraenkel; MM. Louis Aragon, André Breton, Jean Cocteau, Pierre Drieu la Rochelle, Raymond Radiguet.

On présentera des toiles de
MM. Juan Gris, Georges Ribemont-Dessaignes, Georges de Chirico, Fernand Léger, Francis Picabia.
et des sculptures de
M. Jacques Lipchitz.

On interprétera la musique de
MM. Georges Auric, Darius Milhaud, Francis Poulenc, Henri Cliquet.
Au piano Madame Marcelle Meyer.

ENTRÉE : 2 FRANCS

Breton further published an important essay in *Littérature* on Duchamp's 'ready-mades'. Yet by 1924, the year Breton issued his first 'Manifesto of Surrealism', *Littérature*, which was ostensibly apolitical, had outlived its usefulness. The publication ceased because all involved agreed that a new, totally dedicated journal was necessary to establish a viable place for Surrealism in culture.

Littérature was succeeded by Breton's new review, *La Révolution Surréaliste*. As the title suggests, Breton propelled Surrealism towards cultural *and* political revolution. 'The activity of interpreting the world must continue to be linked with the activity of a changing world,' he wrote in his book *Manifestos of Surrealism*. 'We maintain that it is the poet's, the artist's role to study the human problem in depth in all its forms, that it is precisely the unlimited advance of his mind in this direction that has a potential value for changing the world.' He professed that his revolution was rooted in the social and economic aims of Marxism proffered by the French Communist Party (PCF), but for Breton this was something of a critical paradox since the Party kept its followers under a single ideological banner. Refusing to allow himself or Surrealism to be a slave to political expediency, Breton claimed independence of the PCF and incessantly argued with its leaders over cultural matters. He flirted with party policies that promoted proletarian realism, but used surreality as a weapon in the revolution against French culture and materialism. He demanded that his group should change the world by addressing art as an encompassing endeavour and fought to keep the avant-garde from being viewed with suspicion by Party leaders. Breton did his utmost to maintain a balance between art and ideology, and in 1941, with Diego Rivera (1886–1957),

he wrote a 'Manifesto for a Revolutionary Independent', published in the *Partisan Review*.

La Révolution Surréaliste was the nexus of Surrealist art and politics. The magazine first appeared in 1924, after a few smaller yet unsuccessful attempts at publishing Surrealist reviews, and ceased in 1929. Issue nos.1 and 2 were edited by Pierre Naville (1906–94) and Benjamin Péret (1899–1959), issue no.3 by Antonin Artaud (1896–1948), and issue nos.4 to 12 by Breton himself. Although Breton's followers had outlets in other art publications, they preferred one that was dedicated to their needs, unfettered by outside editorial constraints. Also, Breton felt that it was not advantageous to undermine the critical mass of Surrealist thought by dribbling away its members' contributions in diverse periodicals, as was done among the Dadaists (see Chapter 3).

Originally, *La Révolution Surréaliste* was to be produced in an eccentric manner with raggedly-cut papers, unpredictable inserts and typographic disruptions. But Pierre Naville suggested a more ironic, conservative look based on the austere format of *La Nature*, a popular mainstream *revue des sciences*. *La Révolution Surréaliste* adopted a staid typographic approach that was purposely scientific-looking to suggest that Surrealism was not stylistic but phenomenological.

La Révolution Surréaliste was not meant to be a *beaux arts* review. The cover included a conventionally fixed masthead sitting over a small black-and-white photograph above a table of contents that announced the regular sections: *Textes surréalistes*, *Poèmes*, *Rêves* and *Chroniques*. The interior typography was equally restrained: two justified columns per page with small, tasteful headlines. Poems were in italic, save for the occasional Dada-styled typographic composition. Despite the academic air, the startling illustrations – line drawings, sketches and paintings – that appeared throughout, by Picasso, Ernst, Yves Tanguy (1900–55), André Masson (1896–1987), Joan Miró (1893–1983), Man Ray (1890–1976) and Paul Klee (1879–1940), were somewhat shocking in this context. Cover images, however, were alternately conventional portraits, ironic reportage or flamboyantly surreal imagery. In issue no.11, the article 'Le Cinquantenaire de L'Hystérie' includes an animated series of photographs of a young woman in the throes of hysteria. Other articles in *La Révolution Surréaliste* ran the gamut of Surrealist interest, from psychoanalysis to death. The final issue, no.12, includes the scenario of the 1928 Surrealist film *Un Chien Andalou*, directed by Luis Buñuel and Salvador Dalí, as well as Breton's lengthy 'Second Manifesto of Surrealism', its opening page illustrated with lipstick imprints.

The first two issues, edited by Naville and Péret, presented a view of Surrealism in its pure, or as Breton called it, 'naïve state'. Dream power was stressed as a means of reclaiming a personal inner depth. Yet despair (*désespéré*

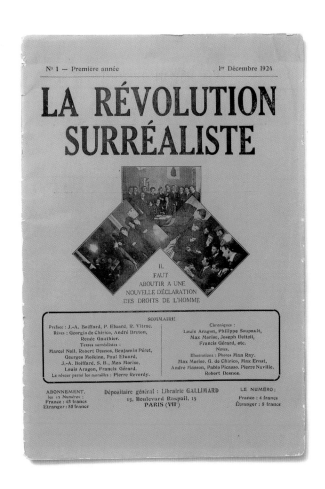

Nº 5 — Première année   15 Octobre 1925

LA RÉVOLUTION SURRÉALISTE

LE PASSÉ

SOMMAIRE

Une lettre : E. Gengenbach.

TEXTES SURRÉALISTES :
Pierre Brasseur, Raymond Queneau, Paul Éluard, Dédé Sunbeam, Monny de Boully.

POÈMES :
Giorgio de Chirico, Michel Leiris, Paul Éluard, Robert Desnos, Marco Ristitch, Pierre Brasseur.

RÊVES :
Michel Leiris, Max Morise.
Décadence de la Vie : Jacques Baron.
Le Vampire : F. N.
Lettre aux voyantes : André Breton.

Nouvelle lettre sur moi-même : Antonin Artaud.
Ces animaux de la famille : Benjamin Péret.

CHRONIQUES :
Au bout du quai les arts décoratifs :
Louis Aragon.
Le Paradis perdu : Robert Desnos.
Léon Trotsky : Lénine : André Breton.
Pierre de Massot : Saint-Just : Paul Éluard.
Revue de la Presse : P. Éluard et B. Péret.
Correspondance, etc.

ILLUSTRATIONS :
Giorgio de Chirico, Max Ernst, André Masson, Joan Miró, Picasso, etc.

ADMINISTRATION : *42, Rue Fontaine,* PARIS (IXe)

ABONNEMENT.
les 12 Numéros :
France : 45 francs
Étranger : 55 francs

Dépositaire général : Librairie GALLIMARD
15, Boulevard Raspail, 15
PARIS (VIIe)

LE NUMÉRO :
France : 4 francs
Étranger : 5 francs

SECOND MANIFESTE DU SURRÉALISME

En dépit des démarches particulières à chacun de ceux qui s'en sont réclamés ou s'en réclament, on finira bien par accorder que le surréalisme ne tendit à rien tant qu'à provoquer, au point de vue intellectuel et moral, une *crise de conscience* de l'espèce la plus générale et la plus grave et que l'obtention ou la non-obtention de ce résultat peut seule décider de sa réussite ou de son échec historique.

Au point de vue intellectuel il s'agissait, il s'agit encore d'éprouver par tous les moyens et de faire reconnaître à tout prix le caractère factice des vieilles antinomies destinées hypocritement à prévenir toute agitation insolite de la part de l'homme, ne serait-ce qu'en lui donnant une idée indigente de ses moyens, qu'en le défiant d'échapper dans une mesure valable à la contrainte universelle. L'épouvantail de la mort, les cafés-chantants de l'au-delà, le naufrage de la plus belle raison dans le sommeil, l'écrasant rideau de l'avenir, les tours de Babel, les miroirs d'inconsistance, l'infranchissable mur d'argent éclaboussé de cervelle, ces images trop saisissantes de la catastrophe humaine ne sont peut-être que des images. Tout porte à croire qu'il existe un certain point de l'esprit d'où la vie et la mort, le réel et l'imaginaire, le passé et le futur, le communicable et l'incommunicable, le haut et le bas cessent d'être perçus contradictoirement. Or, c'est en vain qu'on chercherait à l'activité surréaliste un autre mobile que l'espoir de détermination de ce point. On voit assez par là combien il serait absurde de lui prêter un sens uniquement destructeur, ou constructeur : le point dont il est question est *a fortiori* celui où la construction et la destruction cessent de pouvoir être brandies l'une contre l'autre. Il est clair, aussi, que le surréalisme n'est pas intéressé à tenir grand compte de ce qui se produit à côté de lui sous prétexte d'art, voire d'anti-art, de philosophie ou d'anti-philosophie, en un mot de tout ce qui n'a pas pour fin l'anéantissement de l'être en un brillant, intérieur et aveugle, qui ne soit pas plus l'âme de la glace que celle du feu. Que pourraient bien attendre de l'expérience surréaliste ceux qui gardent quelque souci de la place qu'ils occuperont *dans le monde?* En ce lieu mental d'où l'on ne peut plus entreprendre que pour soi-même une périlleuse mais, pensons-nous, une suprême reconnaissance, il ne saurait être question non plus d'attacher la moindre importance aux pas de ceux qui arrivent ou aux pas de ceux qui sortent, ces pas se produisant dans

---

LA RÉVOLUTION SURRÉALISTE

Directeur :
André BRETON
42, Rue Fontaine, PARIS (IXe)   Tél. Trudaine 38-18

ÉDITIONS SURRÉALISTES

COLLECTION DE BOULES DE NEIGE

Nº 1

HOMMAGE A PICASSO
Vient de paraître

Il a été tiré de cette boule 100 exemplaires numérotés de 1 à 100
L'exemplaire, 60 fr.
Le moule a été détruit après le tirage.

Prochainement :

Boules par : Man Ray, Tanguy, Malkine, Picasso, Arp, etc (d'après des maquettes originales).

MAN RAY

REVOLVING DOORS
1 volume avec 10 reproductions en couleurs d'après les aquarelles originales de Man Ray.

En Octobre

Anthologie de la Poésie moderne

10 disques phonographiques.
Lectures par : Louis Aragon, Antonin Artaud, André Breton, Robert Desnos, Paul Éluard, Max Morise, Benjamin Péret, Philippe Soupault.

Ma**S**son
Tang**U**y
Chi**R**ico
Man **R**ay
Rrose S**É**lavy
Pic**A**bia
Ma**L**kine
M**I**ro
Pica**S**so
Erns**T**

GALERIE   Objets Sauvages

Paris (VIe)

16, Rue Jacques-Callot

Man Ray

L'ENCLUME DES FORCES

Ce fleuve, cette nausée, ces lanières, c'est dans *ceci* que commence le Feu. Le feu de langues. Le feu tissé en torsades de langues dans le miroitement de la terre qui s'ouvre comme un ventre en gésine, aux entrailles de miel et de sucre. De toute sa blessure obscène ce bâille ce ventre mou, mais le feu bâille par-dessus en langues tordues et ardentes qui portent à leur pointe des soupiraux comme de la soif. Ce feu tordu comme des nuages dans l'eau limpide, avec à côté la lumière qui trace une règle et des cils.

Et la terre de toutes parts entr'ouverte et montrant d'arides secrets. Des secrets comme des surfaces. La terre et ses nerfs, et ses préhistoriques solitudes, la terre aux géologies primitives où se découvrent des pans du monde dans une ombre noire comme le charbon. La terre est mère sous la glace du feu. Voyez le feu dans les trois rayons, avec le couronnement de sa crinière où grouillent des yeux. Myriades de myriapodes d'yeux. Le centre ardent et convulsé de ce feu est comme la pointe écartelée du tonnerre à la cime du firmament. Un absolu d'éclat de la force. La pointe épouvantable de la force qui se brise dans un tintamarre tout bleu.

Les trois rayons font un éventail dont les branches tombent à pic et convergent vers le même centre. Mais ce centre est un disque laiteux recouvert d'une spirale d'éclipses.

was the movement's mantra) was the underlying tone of these issues, evidenced by frequent inquiries into suicide (a recurring theme), although without seeming to obliterate the Surrealist's curious ode to life. The first issue was hyperbolically poetical; the next mounted a more polemical attack on the propriety of bourgeois society with a call to open the prisons and disband the army. Then, under Antonin Artaud's editorship, the third issue turned its attention to the ironic aspects of Surrealism. Artaud took command of the so-called Bureau of Surrealist Research, which he asserted was established to ironically rupture and disqualify logic and to support the spontaneous reclassification of things following an order which is deeper and subtler, and impossible to elucidate using the means of ordinary reason. Artaud wrapped himself in irony to mask an irrepressible rage that found expression through a curious confluence of mysticism and revolution. Breton, however, believed this was both contrived and counter-productive and so assumed the editorship of the journal with the fourth issue as a means to inject Surrealism into the current socio-political debate.

The cover of issue no.5, Breton's second as editor, is revealing in this regard. A photograph showing a pile of contemporary avant-garde magazines, including *Littérature*, *Dada 3*, *Mouvement Dada* and, ironically, this very number of *La Révolution Surréaliste*, appears above the words 'Le Passé'. From this issue forward, Breton led the movement through the labyrinth of *realpolitik* wed to Surrealism. He asserted that a political goal of the movement was to help transfer the dominance of power from the bourgeoisie to the proletariat, yet he maintained that this would not be accomplished at the expense of personal expression. Of course, here is where the immovable forces of party politics and the philosophical movement collided. Although Breton eventually joined the Communist Party, the alliance was fraught with disparities that could never be resolved. And in the 'Second Manifesto of Surrealism' he addresses his inability to embrace an ideology that insisted he forsake Surrealism. Yet, although he referred to the Party ideologues as 'narrow revolutionaries', he continued to support revolutionary action, as he defined it. The 'Second Manifesto', as published in 1929 in *La Révolution Surréaliste*, was the capstone of the first stage of Surrealism, which introduced a more politically entrenched and contentious movement. Yet it was as much for political as for aesthetic reasons that *La Révolution Surréaliste* ended its run later in the year because it was unable to forge the two halves into a viable whole. The contradictions that were inherent in art and politics were reasons for founding other journals.

The journal *Bifur*, eight issues of which were published in Paris between 1929 and 1931 was directed by Georges Ribemont-Dessaignes (1884–1974) and edited by Pierre G

Lévy. It was a transitory review intended to bridge Surrealism and other avant-gardes, but from the look of it *Bifur* did not challenge any tenets of graphic style. Instead it published illustrations by a few Surrealists, including De Chirico, Man Ray, Ernst and Arp, and the work of writers as diverse as Langston Hughes and James Joyce. In addition, film stills were commonly reproduced from movies by such Russian progressives as Sergei Eisenstein and Vsevold Meyerhold, as well as by the American comedian Buster Keaton. But the energy needed to make this a vital long-term review simply never materialized. Anticipating a vacuum, Breton founded *Le Surréalisme au Service de la Révolution*, published intermittently between 1930 and 1933. According to Breton, it was 'by far the richest [of all the Surrealist journals] in the sense that mattered to us: the most balanced, the best put together, as well as the most fully alive (with a thrilling and dangerous life). It was in this magazine that Surrealism burned with the most intense flame. For a time, we all saw nothing but this flame, and were not afraid to be consumed by it'.[1] However, it earned the least circulation of his magazines to date, an average of 350 compared to *La Révolution Surréaliste*'s 1,000.

Le Surréalisme au Service de la Révolution was physically smaller and typographically more austere than *La Révolution Surréaliste*. The first cover had a masthead with the words 'Le Surréalisme' set large across the top and 'au Service de la Révolution' set smaller underneath. The sole cover image, sitting on an empty field save for the numeral one, was a heraldic shield impressed with the astrological signs belonging to Aragon, Breton and Eluard. The title was something of a concession to the French Communist Party and the Moscow-based International Bureau of Revolutionary Literature, the Communist organ that regulated art in the service of the Party. The earlier title, *La Révolution Surréaliste*, was suspect because it implied an insular revolution that suggested the potential rejection of Party agendas. The newer title, which was coined by Aragon, indicated the anti-individualist creed integral to the Communist Party. *Le Surréalisme au Service de la Révolution* lived up to Party requirements not in a design sense, but insofar as it included Communist tracts from various groups in Europe, South America and Japan. In the first issue, Breton made it quite clear that he was committed to fight for the Communist cause and vowed to engage in pure Surrealist activity. Yet there are significant policy shifts in *Le Surréalisme au Service de la Révolution*: automatic writing and dream analysis were more or less eliminated as superfluous to Party concerns. Poetry still received considerable space, but more political and theoretical texts were included. The pantheon of Surrealism's heroes was also reassessed and Sigmund Freud (1856–1939), whose influence had been pervasive, was critiqued for not providing a concrete enough philosophical foundation for the political demands of the movement. Conversely, the Marquis de Sade rose to the level of hero as revolutionary, atheist and sexual fantasist – perverse sexuality was always a leitmotif of Surrealist art and literature.

The visuals in *Le Surréalisme au Service de la Révolution* are more fantastical in certain ways than in previous Surrealist journals. Romantic dream- and fantasy-based imagery by the newcomer René Magritte (1898–1967), as well as by Giorgio de Chirico, Salvador Dalí (1904–89), Man Ray, Hans Arp and Alberto Giacometti (1901–66) graced the pages – yet these surrealisms seriously challenged the Party's concept of revolutionary art. The schism between devout Surrealists and unyielding Party members played itself out through the pages of *Le Surréalisme au Service de la Révolution.* Dalí, for example, was attacked by a PCF 'control commission' for a text he had written deemed anti-revolutionary and pornographic. Dalí put forth the notion that paranoiac thought could produce imagery and objects that addressed the fragile constructs of perception, and his thesis that an individual could perceive two truths (or illusions) at one time went counter to the Party's anti-individualist dogma. The Party was vociferous in its condemnation but Breton argued, even though he was never totally comfortable with Dalí, that his expressive liberty was endemic to revolutionary literature and art.

The contradictions in *Le Surréalisme au Service de la Révolution* underscored the incompatability of social revolution and individual behaviour. Despite Breton's commitment to ideological politics, he was an artist first and an ideologue second. Breton allowed *Le Surréalisme au Service de la Révolution* to cease its run because it could no longer support itself after the simultaneous publication of the fifth and sixth numbers in May 1933. The double issue was packed with evidence of the controversy that had split the Surrealist factions, notably arguments between Breton and Aragon. But, more to the point, the journal had a negligible income due to its small circulation. In fact, the only advertisement (presumably paid) in the final issue was for another Surrealist art magazine, which had launched a few months earlier and was destined to become the vessel of Surrealism for the next six years.

Minotaure was its name, and it was the most visually evocative and professionally produced alternative review of its day. Breton commented years later, in an interview with André Parinaud, that it had taken a while for an autonomous Surrealist magazine to emerge after the fall of *Le Surréalisme au Service de la Révolution*. 'The movement was reduced to splitting its activity into two parts,' he said, 'one expressed in tracts ... the other seeking the widest possible development in the sumptuously produced magazine *Minotaure*.' At first the magazine was eclectic, embracing a wide range of modern and ancient art, but as Breton noted in the interview, 'Surrealism gained territory with every issue, until finally it took over completely. From this viewpoint, and because of its external splendour, it gave Surrealism a dimension that we hadn't had before this.'[2]

Below left: **Bifur**, cover of no.5, September 1930. *Bifur*'s cover design was less than neutral so as not to show preference for any one avant-garde movement or style. The magazine was directed by Georges Ribemont-Dessaignes and edited by Pierre G Lévy.

Below, centre and right: **Le Surréalisme au Service de la Révolution**, no.1, July 1930, cover and detail of inside page with artwork by Salvador Dalí. The editor, André Breton, downplayed the graphic look of the cover of *Le Surréalisme au Service de la Révolution*, which was in sharp contrast to its incendiary contents, as a concession to the French Communist Party which rejected artistic ostentation. This picture by Dalí, however, did not follow this ideological mandate.

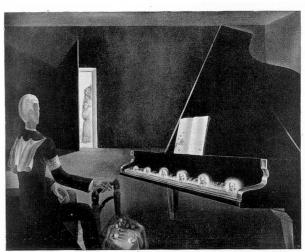

Minotaure premiered in Paris in 1933 as an artistic and literary review with Albert Skira (1904–73) as the administrative director and E Tériade as artistic director. Its professed aim was to integrate many of the contemporary arts and artists under one banner. Originally Picasso suggested calling it *Feather Duster*, as in a 'clean sweep of the art world', but then, as Skira noted, the playwright, Roger Vitrac (1899–1952), came up with *Minotaure*. 'We all agreed that it sounded more inspired,' he said. 'Picasso sparked to it right away, and created a whole series of drawings based on the legendary beast, which have since become very famous.'[3]

Minotaure was not just a review of information, announced its editors, and indeed it published a large number of literary texts, together with histories of objects, religions, mythologies and psychoanalysis. Though dutifully eclectic, this lavish magazine – the first so-called avant-garde magazine to employ full-colour printing and fine typography – served as a record of Surrealism and its affinities. *Minotaure* was resolutely apolitical, and unlike the ad hoc appearance of the more politically dogmatic periodicals that had preceded it, its graphic look was consistent with conventions established for other rotogravure picture magazines. It afforded generous space to spreads of contemporary and documentary art. The noteworthy picture essays included Paul Eluard's personal collection of turn-of-the-century comic and fantasy postcards – naïve Surrealism – that showed erotically contorted women in farcical poses; Man Ray's feature of curious pin-ups by the French photojournalist and portraitist Nadar (1820–1910) and Bill Brandt's (1904–83) photographs of antique ships' figureheads. Other curiosities were published along with contemporary paintings, drawings and sculptures by Masson, Arp and Giacometti.

Minotaure gave artists the opportunity to explore new dimensions of art on an ambitious scale. With the earlier magazines images were reduced to dark, colourless blotches, but in this publication they were lavishly displayed. Dalí played with found objects in collage, and one of his most kinetic two-dimensional works was a montage of closely cropped heads of different scales and sizes, a cinematic panoply of expressions, used to illustrate an essay, 'The Phenomenon of Ecstasy'. The magazine's covers were its most visually exciting feature: with each issue a different artist, including Picasso, Dalí, Duchamp, Henri Matisse, Joan Miró, Ernst and André Derain, created an original concept on the theme of the title – the bull-man living alone in a labyrinth, seeking love and truth. Each interpretation was different from the next, and even the masthead was routinely hand-lettered as a principal component of the original artwork.

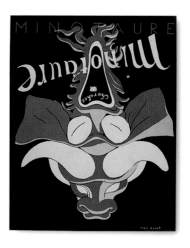

Clockwise from left:
Minotaure, covers of vol.1 no.2, 1933, by Gaston-Louis Roux; vol.1 no.3–4, 1933, by Man Ray; vol.3, no.11, 1938 by Max Ernst; vol.3 no.12–13, 1939, by Diego Rivera; vol.3 no.8, 1936, by Salvador Dalí. *Opposite*: cover of vol.1 no.1, June 1933, by Pablo Picasso. Edited by Albert Skira and E Tériade, *Minotaure: Revue Artistique Littéraire*, was a platform for leading Surrealist artists, and was the most elegant and graphically provocative of all the Surrealist reviews. These covers all displayed surreal interpretations of the theme of the mythical man/beast.

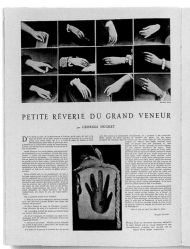

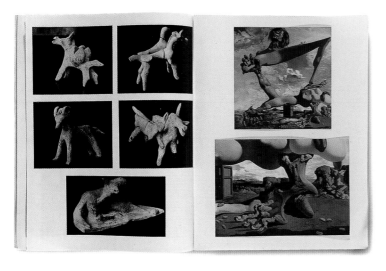

The ever-present Breton used *Minotaure* as an outlet for ideas about spirituality and psychology, as well as automatism. In the sixth issue Breton published his essay 'Bride stripped bare by her bachelors even', which brilliantly explained the mysteries of Duchamp's seminal Surrealistic erotic work. Breton also explored new ways of making art, which had been one of Surrealism's most significant missions since the mid-Twenties. One such process was decalcomania, which involved covering a sheet of white glazed paper with black gouache and then pressing another sheet of paper on top and peeling it off to reveal ad hoc designs and topologies. By the ninth issue of *Minotaure*, Breton took an even more active editorial role and became a member of the editorial committee comprised entirely of Surrealists. By issue no.12, Breton and his cronies were injecting politics into the editorial mix and railing against encroaching nationalism and the rise of Fascism throughout Europe.

Paradoxically, once the clouds of war darkened, and the PCF was in the throes of its concerted battle against the right, the Communists became less critical of governmental policies. And, always at odds with prevailing views, the Bretonian Surrealists severed from Communism over this issue.

In 1937 a group of heretical Surrealists (as in anti-Breton), led by the writer Georges Bataille (1897–1962), joined forces in Paris to found *Acéphale*, which lasted four numbers. The magazine was set up to analyse religion, sociology and philosophy through a militant Surrealist perspective, since its initiators had maintained their ties with the Communists. Articles included critical examinations of Nietzsche and the Fascists and, on a more ethereal plane, Dionysus, god of wine and ecstasy. The images used on its covers and within the magazine, including drawings by Masson, were more spiritual than confrontational but, as the world was on its trajectory towards cataclysm, the reality of politics could not be avoided.

Surrealism's survival as a revolutionary movement was threatened by the rise of the Right during the late Thirties and *Minotaure* provided a wall behind which the artists could take refuge if they desired. It was also a fortress for Breton. He saw that the Left, threatened by the coming new order, imposed intractable requirements for art. Breton wanted to remain perpetually outside the establishment of arts and letters and Communism had initially promised an absolute and continuous revolution. Yet, as the Soviet system became more entrenched, Breton and Surrealism became estranged from it. It was the inevitability of world war that forced a shift in Surrealism and the closure of *Minotaure* in 1939 with its final number, 12–13.

Attempts were made to continue the political debate through a few short-lived periodicals. The French newspaper *Clé (Bulletin Mensuel de la Fédération Internationale de*

Opposite, clockwise from top left: **Minotaure**, spreads from no.3–4, 1933, two spreads with artwork by Salvador Dalí; no.6, 1935, artwork by Hans Bellmer; no.12–13, 1939 photography by Alvarez Bravo; no.9, 1936, artwork by Salvador Dalí; no.5, 1934, artwork by Giorgio de Chirico. Some interior pages of *Minotaure* were quite spare, others were cinematic displays of artistic obsession, such the essay on Hans Bellmer's erotic dolls. *Minotaure* was designed using traditionally elegant printing types, composed in a fairly neutral manner to frame its radical photography, paintings and drawings.

Below: **Acéphale**, no.1–2, 21 January 1937, cover art by André Masson. *Acéphale* was published in Paris and edited by George Ambrosino, Georges Bataille and Pierre Klossowski. The cover suggests the religiously mystical symbology practiced throughout Surrealism.

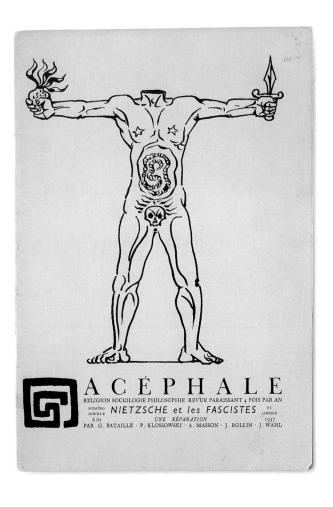

l'Art Révolutionnaire Indépendant) was founded in 1939
by Maurice Nadeau and C C P Acker as an organ of
independent and Surrealist artists to resist the rise of
Fascism and totalitarianism. Despite the best efforts of
the editorial committee, of which Breton was one, the
publication was unable to prevent the rise of the French
Right and closed after just two issues. Once the Germans
occupied Paris in 1940, the centre of Surrealism, and
modern art, moved to New York.

Art in the service of left-wing politics had been
practised in New York since the end of World War I.
From 1919 until 1924, Egmont Arens (1877–1966) published
Playboy, an arts magazine that ran to nine numbers
and which, through literature and poetry, tangentially
addressed leftist political concerns. Among his visual
contributors were Stuart Davis (1894–1964; the former
art editor of the more overt socialist organ, *The Masses*),
William Gropper (1897–1977) and Henry Glintenkamp
(1887–1946), who produced cartoons and vignettes that
worked on both aesthetic and polemical levels. The covers
were often woodcuts or coloured line drawings, and while
the interior design was not as radical as Futurist or Dada
periodicals of a similar period and earlier, neither was
it as conventional as some other literary journals. *New
Masses*, which began in 1926, devoted considerable space

Right: **Clé**, cover of no.1,
1 January 1939. A wide
range of metaphoric
and allegoric Surrealist
drawings, addressing
issues of mortality and
immortality, such as the
one shown here, were
common as cover art for
the majority of Surrealism's
later journals. *Clé* was
edited by Maurice Nadeau
and C C P Acker.

Below from left: **Playboy**,
vol.2 no.1, 1923, cover
art by Hugo Gellert, and
inside spread with artwork
by William Gropper and
unknown artist. *Playboy*
covers were different for
each issue. The interior,
printed on heavy paper
stock, employed generous
empty margin space
allowing the type to
breathe. The magazine was
edited by Egmont Arens.

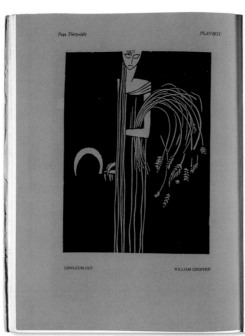

to promoting art as a propaganda tool. And in 1934 *Art Front*, subtitled 'We Have Just Begun to Fight', the organ of the Artists' Union, included Aragon, Ernst and Paul Klee, as well as American artists, as contributors in the war against capitalist-inspired, traditional American art. It was not a Surrealist magazine and had no intention of becoming one; indeed, the first attempt at Surrealism in an American periodical would be quite different in form and content.

New York's first Surrealist journal, *View: Through the Eyes of Poets*, appeared in September 1940 as a six-page tabloid edited by the poet Charles Henri Ford (1908–2002), the former American editor of the *London Bulletin*, the British Surrealist review published by the London Gallery between 1938 and 1940. *View*'s mission for its seven-year duration (36 numbers in 32 issues) was to fill the void that existed due to the closure of numerous European avant-garde periodicals because of the war. It was avant-garde, Surrealist and not ideologically Communist. In fact, Ford positioned his publication between the 'little magazine' *Transition* – the vanguard journal edited in Paris by Eugene Jolas (1894–1945) and Elliot Paul (1891–1958) between 1927 and 1938 – and *Minotaure.* After *View*'s special 'Surrealist issue' of 1941, edited by Nicolas Calas (b.1907), it became the most important American Surrealist publication,

featuring text and visual contributions from the principal members of the circle.

By 1943 *View* shifted from a tabloid to a more standard magazine format printed on slick paper with full-colour covers and the occasional gatefold. This increased the financial burden of production far beyond what could be borne by a maximum paid circulation of 3,000. Ford accepted relatively expensive advertisements for fashions and perfumes, among those he already included for books, periodicals and cultural events, in order to maintain a regular quarterly publishing schedule. Associate editor Parker Tyler (1904–74) was in charge of *View*'s typography and graphic design and produced a highly sophisticated graphic persona on a par with *Minotaure* and yet unique to *View*. The covers created by Surrealist standard-bearers André Masson, Man Ray, Kurt Seligmann (1900–62) and Marcel Duchamp, as well as by other modern artists, including Alexander Calder (1898–1976), Fernand Léger (1881–1955) and Georgia O'Keeffe (1887–1986), were the most adventurous of any American magazine. Moreover, these were not paintings arbitrarily placed on the covers but images designed especially for this context. Occasionally, the *View* masthead (set in a Bodoni typeface) was designed by the cover artist: Isamu Noguchi's (1904–88) cover of 1946 is a superb example of this transformation. Here the letters

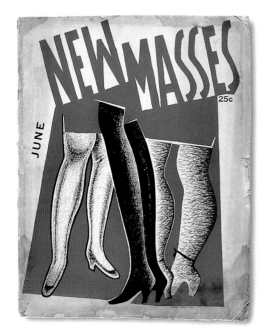

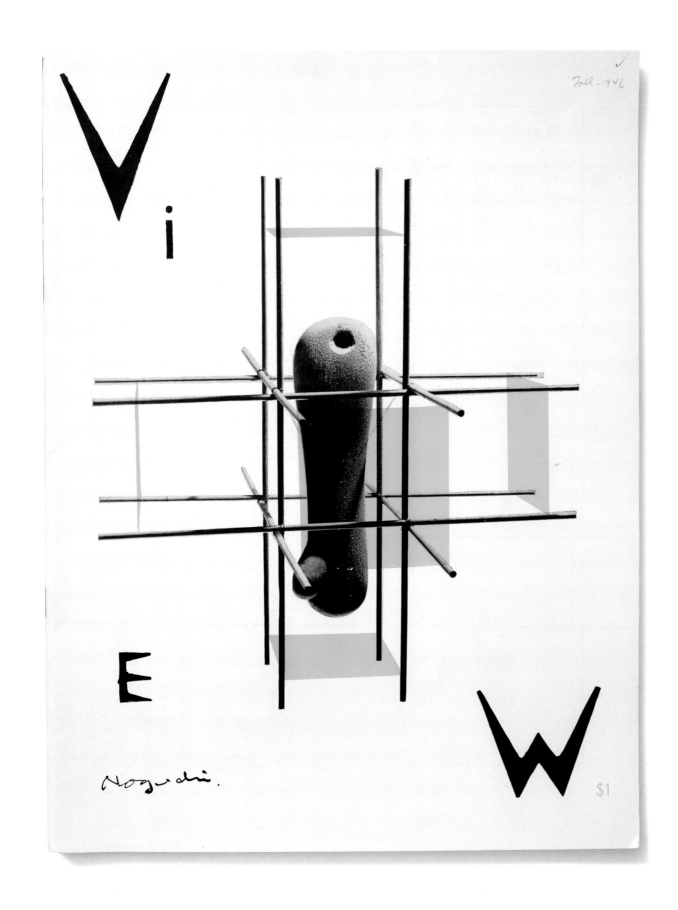

of *View* are graphic approximations of sculptural elements that read diagonally down and mingle with the actual piece of sculpture in the centre of the page.

View not only covered the Surrealism experience but also served to introduce the key Surrealists to New York. André Breton's first American interview was published here in issue no.7–8, October–November 1941. An entire issue (no.1, April 1942) was devoted to Max Ernst, with an article on him by Breton, and a spectacular issue (no.1, March 1945) featured Duchamp, complete with layouts designed by the artist – this being the first monograph ever published of his work. An essay by Peter Lindamood described the technical machinations involved in the creation of Duchamp's *View* cover, a montage of a smoking wine bottle. He explained how this master of 'art-plumbing expediency' rigged up a smoke pipe under the bottle and then manipulated the various half-tone layers to achieve the desired effect. In this and other articles, *View* gave Surrealist art a human context, a rationale based on the passions and fixations of its artists, that was absent in the hyper-analysis of the pseudo-scientific writing found in the European journals.

Coverage of the European vanguard was only part of the editorial menu. Ford felt a duty to bridge the transatlantic gap by bringing Americans into the Surrealist fold and, in 1943, *View* was the first magazine to publish Joseph Cornell's (1903–72) earliest 'found art' compositions (*The Crystal Cage: Portrait of Berenice*). It provided an outlet for the emerging American vanguard writers and artist-writers, including Henry Miller, Marianne Moore, William Carlos Williams and Alexander Calder, and for some of the naïve and self-taught Surrealists, notably the African-American artist Paul Childs (dates unknown). Morris Hirshfield (1872–1946), whose beguilingly detailed folk paintings were discovered by Sidney Janis in the Thirties, was also part of the *View* community. Hirshfield's intricately rendered cover of a cleverly veiled nude, of 1945, was Surrealism at its most slyly innocent.

View celebrated the artist as visionary and Surrealism as a fount of artistic eccentricity. In its role as avant-garde seer, the magazine often overstepped the bounds of propriety and, in 1944, was banned by the US postal service, presumably for publishing nudes by Picasso and Michelangelo. However, despite its confrontational stance and the debates about Marxism, Communism and Trotskyism that were carried on in European Surrealist circles, *View* did not advocate ideological political activity, but rather supported the right of individual artistic freedom – and eclecticism. '*View*'s editors thought it delusional to believe that art could ever serve any cause other than its own,'[4] wrote historian Catrina Neiman, who further noted

Opposite: **View**, vol.7 no.1, October 1946, cover artwork by Isamu Noguchi. *Below from left to right*: covers of vol.4 no.3, October 1944, by Fernand Léger; vol.5 no.1, March 1945, by Marcel Duchamp; vol.5 no.3, October 1945, by Morris Hirshfield. Following the lead of *Minotaure*, *View* covers became showcases for experimental art that pushed the boundaries of both aesthetics and content.

that while certain poets of the day urged opposition to the inevitable world war, *View* printed no editorials denouncing it, even though the magazine maintained a pacifist stance that supported conscientious objection.

View invariably came in for its share of acrimony among the skirmishing groups who sought dominance for their respective art forms. Surrealism was not universally admired and the *Partisan Review*, a left-leaning intellectual journal established in 1934, declared that it was both decadent and dead, endorsing abstract art as the new avant-garde art. This was no mere preferential disagreement but a contest for what genre and which artists would dominate the museums, galleries and private collections. *View* tried to preserve the importance of Surrealism and so ignored the backbiting, yet this was not so much due to militancy over an ideological cause as a campaign for the hegemony of style.

View was not only a significant outlet for Surrealism; it also became an instrument for popularizing the avant-garde. Surrealism as a style was, no pun intended, ready-made as an advertising trope. 'Ford did not disdain commercial avenues of support,' states Catrina Neiman, '... on the contrary, he knew not only how to navigate capitalism but how to appreciate (appropriate) its imagery, namely through the lens of camp, a "view" that converged with Surrealism then and with Pop Art twenty years later.'[5] Despite the paid advertisements, *View* ceased publication in 1949.

Breton was so enraged by the appropriation of Surrealism in commercial advertisements that he excommunicated Dalí from the movement because he felt he had turned the Surrealist style into a commodity. For similar reasons he maintained a tenuous relationship with *View* and in 1942 helped found a rival New York-based periodical and Surrealist mouthpiece, *VVV* or *Triple V*, not dissimilar from *Minotaure*, which represented his purist notions of Surrealism through poetry, art, anthropology, sociology and psychology. It lasted only two years because Breton neither accepted advertising nor franchised the Surrealist identity to the highest bidder, but during its short run *VVV* exerted an impact on the practice of art in America. Breton used the magazine as a means to integrate exiled Surrealists and American artists. His hand-picked editor, the photographer and sculptor David Hare (1917–91), was certainly sympathetic to Breton's beliefs. He was also young enough (twenty-five years old) to be in awe of Surrealism's father, which meant that Breton's editorial will prevailed.

Breton explained the meaning of the three V's of the title (inspired by the Allies' sign for Victory) in an interview with André Parinaud: 'Victory over the forces of regression and death ... and that double Victory, again over all that is opposed to the emancipation of the spirit ... or again, the View around us, the eye turned towards the external world

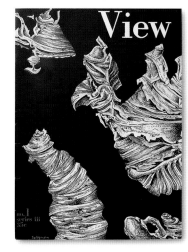
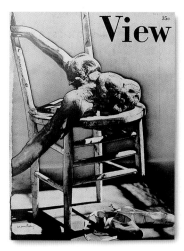
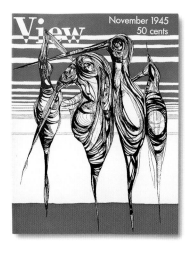

Clockwise from top left: **View**, covers of vol.2 no.3, October 1942, artwork by Hanani Miller; vol.3 no.1, April 1943, by Kurt Seligmann; vol.5 no.4, November 1945, by Leon Kelly; vol.6 no.4, May 1946, by Jean Hélion; vol.3 no.3, June 1943, by Man Ray. Edited by Charles Henri Ford, *View* was a veritable beauty pageant of avant-garde art. Its covers showed work by a range of international Surrealists – both primitive and self-conscious.

Opposite: **View**, two spreads from vol.5 no.1, March 1945, designed by Parker Tyler with artwork by Marcel Duchamp. *View*'s 'Duchamp Issue' was filled with the artist's autobiographical collages including the 'Duchamp Triptych' that contains views of his New York studio and a timeline of his life.

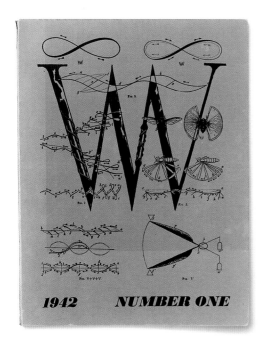

1942   **NUMBER ONE**

Five Prizes

Number 2-3

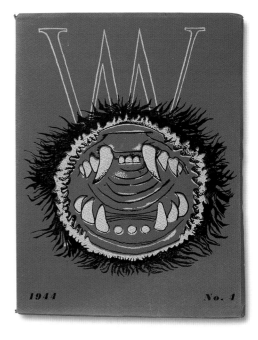

1944   *No. 4*

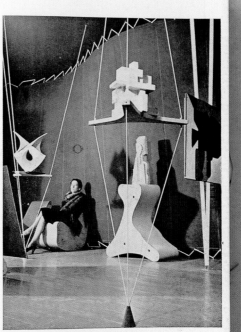

Photo: Pix   *Frederick J. Kiesler*

DETAIL OF GALLERY FOR ABSTRACT ART "ART OF THIS CENTURY"

... towards a total view, VVV, which translates all the reactions of the eternal upon the actual.'[6] The intent of the publication, which included an editorial board comprised of Duchamp and Ernst, was to propagate the Surrealist faith, but as Breton also noted in the interview, liberation from the Nazi yoke took precedence over everything else.

Roberto Matta (b.1911) illustrated Breton's 'Prologomena to a Third Manifesto of Surrealism or Else'. This *VVV* tract cited the need for integrity within the movement and attacked, among other heretics, the artist 'Avida Dollars', the anagram for Salvador Dalí, who became, in Breton's eyes, an opportunist after moving to America. Breton further declared that it was necessary to keep the nonconformist spirit of Surrealism alive and to create a new myth while in temporary exile.

VVV gathered a 'Who's Who' of cross-cultural artists and writers (most of whom already published in *View*), including William Carlos Williams, Benjamin Péret, Pavel Tchelitchew (1898–1957), André Masson and the emerging painter Robert Motherwell (1915–91). It also continued the now common practice of inviting artists to create its covers; Ernst designed the first. The magazine published numerous colour reproductions of new works, often on fine paper stock. The inconsistency of type styles, variations in paper colour and the use of contemporary drawings and old engravings heightened *VVV*'s visual appeal. Duchamp contributed an image that looked like a blood-soaked American flag bandage to the 1944 issue, no.4, but it never ran; it had been commissioned for a *Vogue* cover but rejected because it was too lugubrious.

Breton, who never really learned English, used *VVV* as a means to disseminate his ideas and capture the minds of American youth. He extolled Surrealism's legacy from World War I to World War II, and condemned the 'impatient gravediggers' who were writing about Surrealism's demise in other journals. He claimed that Surrealism was the only defence against the rationalism and 'good sense' of adult generations that had twice brought catastrophe upon humanity within the space of just twenty years. But the editorial thrust of *VVV* was not pacifist like that of *View*. Instead, *VVV* integrated occult science, indigenous art by indigenous peoples and a fascination with science fiction (i.e., H P Lovecraft and pulp fiction) with the existing European Surrealist liturgy. *VVV* was intellectually vital in breaking conventions, yet it was also mired in its own editorial egalitarianism, wherein every contributor had a percentage of space allotted regardless of quality. An even more fatal problem was the extravagant manner in which the magazine was produced; this quickly took its toll, causing its demise in 1944, just two years after it had begun, and leaving the new artistic centre-stage clear, in

Opposite, clockwise from top left: **VVV**, no.1, June 1942, cover by Max Ernst; no.2–3, March 1943, back cover by Max Ernst; no.4, February 1944, cover by Roberto Matta; no.2–3, March 1943, inside spread with artwork by Max Ernst. *VVV*, edited by David Hare with André Breton and Max Ernst, was a striking magazine produced on limited funds. Issue nos. 1 and 4 were resolutely Surreal. On the covers *VVV* made do with only two colours. The interior pages shown here included die-cuts and other special effects that enhanced the graphic illusions. The back cover for issue no.2–3 was a die-cut of a human torso which was covered with a piece of chicken-wire fencing, thereby revealing the last inside page.

Below: **La Séance Continué**, cover of no.1, 1941. Edited by 'Art and Liberty', *La Séance Continué* was published in Cairo with texts in French. The cover symbolized 'art and liberty', the theme on which the magazine was based.

the United States at any rate, for *View* to continue without a rival until 1947.

The United States was not the only wartime haven for Surrealism or the cultural avant-garde. *La Séance Continué*, which began in 1941, was edited by the group 'Art and Liberty' in Cairo and represented Egyptian Surrealism. South and Central America also had vital pockets of activity. None was more respected than the magazine, *Dyn*, founded in Mexico in 1942 by Wolfgang Paalen (1907–59) as an alternative to – in fact, a slap in the face of – Breton's socio-idealistic brand of Surrealism. Paalen had been a member in good standing of Breton's group and on very cordial terms with him since moving to Mexico in 1939. And yet, underneath, he was growing disillusioned with Breton's concessions to politics. In the first issue of his own magazine he penned an editorial announcing 'the death of Surrealism', and that his own group would go 'beyond Surrealism'. None the less, Paalen and his contributing artists kept faith with the Surrealist aesthetic. Although published in Mexico, *Dyn*'s articles were in English and French, not Spanish, and were targeted at a New York audience of exiles and natives. In this way, Paalen hoped to influence his readership to see him as the centre of a new artistic manifestation. But despite his rift with orthodox Surrealism, Paalen's interest in

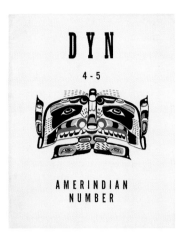

Above from left: **Dyn**, cover of no.1, April–May 1942; no.4–5, December 1943, cover typography by Diaz de León. *Right:* no.2, July–August 1942, inside spread with artwork by Wolfgang Paalen. *Dyn* announced 'the death of Surrealism', yet what the journal really espoused was a new form of abstract Surrealism, as typified on the cover of no.1. The cover of issue no.4–5, the 'Amerinidan number' illustrates the Surrealist connection to native American art. *Dyn* was edited and designed by Wolfgang Paalen.

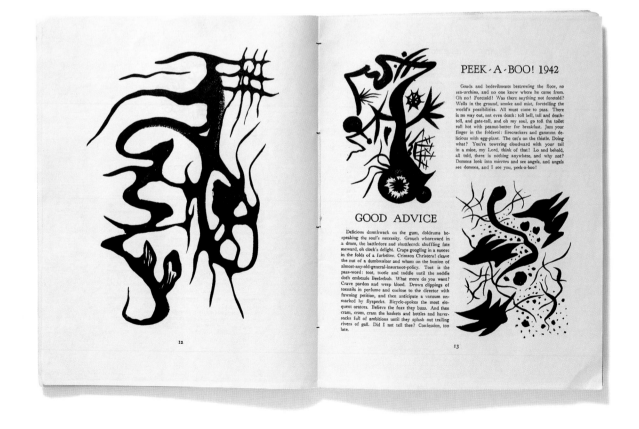

indigenous peoples and art was consistent with the Surrealist respect for native origins. *Dyn* contained articles devoted to North and West Coast Indian art, with an article by the famous caricaturist Miguel Covarrubias (1904–57), who became one of the world's leading experts on pre-Columbian art.

Dyn was elegantly subdued. Its covers were sparsely illustrated and the ethereally hand-drawn, abstract, calligraphic masthead of the first issue indicated that the magazine was not composed by a printer but rather designed by an artist. The interior layouts were functional, without the flamboyance or flourish of *View*, typographically conservative but with a generous number of documentary illustrations. The last issue of *Dyn* appeared in 1944, shortly after the demise of *VVV*, after just six numbers. Paalen had established a rather prophetic view of the future of what he called 'Abstract Surrealism' that may have influenced the Abstract Expressionists of the Fifties.

In 1948 André Breton returned to Paris and gathered together a corps of younger Surrealists to launch the newspaper *Néon* (*N'être rien Etre tout Ouvrir l'être*) as an outlet for the continuation of orthodox Surrealist dominance in post-war French culture. It was printed on poor-quality paper and its expressive, sculptural typography, called 'typoplastique', bore a curious resemblance to the earlier

Stieglitz journal, *291*. The second number of *Néon*, designed by Frederick Kiesler (1890–1965), ran a graphic black serpent running through all four of its pages. Yet even with its expansive format and dynamic page design the publication lasted only five numbers, for just over a year, before it ran out of steam in March 1949. In the same year that *Néon* was launched, a semi-Surrealist, rather conservative-looking journal, *K: Revue de la Poésie*, edited by Alain Gheerbrant and Henri Parisot (1889–1945), was founded in Paris. Its first issue was dedicated to Antonin Artaud but *K* did not remain as devoted to Surrealism once shifts in other art forms made their impact on culture. It continued to publish intermittently until some time after 1970.

Despite the efforts of its more ideological leaders, Surrealism had been adopted as a commercial style. The vocabulary of disparate, dream-like forms proved irresistible for advertising in both post-war Europe and in the United States. The leading advertising firms used the progressive conceits of modern art as a code for 'new and improved' products, a veneer that imbued commodities with a stylish contemporaneity. Dalí was among the most notorious style-mongers but he was not unique among artists who applied their Surrealist affinities to advertising, editorial layout and package design.

Below from left: **Néon**, cover of no.2, February 1948. The designer, Frederick Kiesler, developed a constructive typographic art form called 'typoplastique' for *Néon*. The magazine was edited by Sarane Alexandrian, Jindrich Heisler, Ver Herold, Stanislas Rodanski and Claude Tarnaud.

K: Revue de la Poésie, cover of no.3, May 1949. This cover was devoted to the concept of terror-humour and was dedicated to its mentor Kurt Schwitters. The magazine was edited by Alain Gheerbrant and Henri Parisot.

Labyrinthe, vol.1 no.8, 15 May 1945, cover with photography by Brassaï. *Labyrinthe*, which was edited by Albert Skira, had a newspaper format and covered the European avant-garde.

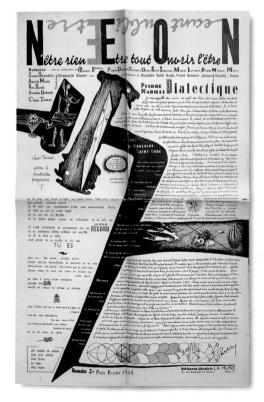

The failure of Surrealism to perpetuate its revolution through the post-war era prompted a spate of avant-garde journals promoting a broader realm of artistic sensibilities. Among these was the monthly newspaper *Labyrinthe*, published in Geneva from 1944 until 1946 by Albert Skira, formerly the editorial director of *Minotaure* and a leading art publisher in his own right. Skira used a newspaper format because it was 'more direct and spontaneous', inexpensive, and could reach a broad public. 'I wished to open a door to many writers and artists who had been unable to express themselves during long years of suffering and oppression,'[7] he wrote. The layouts, Skira noted, were calculated to be dynamic and refined at the same time, creating a feeling of luxury in a modest frame. The newspaper covered the rebuilding of the European avant-garde and included contributions by, and articles on, Matisse, Giacometti, Eluard, Maillol, Braque and Chagall that collectively helped the European art community to regroup and re-establish its sense of centrality.

A year after the war ended, in 1946, *Intermède* was published in Paris for two numbers, edited by Eric de Grolier, with the aim of covering French film, theatre and dance. Although its design was enticing in a late modern style, this was not enough to sustain a solid following. It was also difficult to physically produce an avant-garde magazine owing to the scarcity of materials – ink and paper – and distribution networks were uncertain. In 1948 an existentialist writer, Lionel Abel (1911–2001), published six issues of *Instead*, a review that promoted art and literature in the aftermath of World War II and included the work of a range of artists and writers involved with the Surrealists and other groups. Among the notable contributors were Parker Tyler, Jacques Prévert, Max Ernst and Matta, who designed at least one of its covers. A long, narrow, vertical format gave *Instead* an ad hoc aesthetic that set it apart from the rest of the 'little magazines' at the time.

By 1949 Paris was once again a publishing centre for the avant-garde, and during the next decade it saw the rise (and fall) of various non-Surrealist periodicals that covered art in a more catholic manner. *Art d'Aujourd'Hui: Revue d'Art Contemporain*, edited by André Bloc from 1949 to 1954, was the first of the new Paris-based general art publications with avant-garde affinities. It attempted to contextualize Expressionism, Cubism, Fauvism, Futurism, etc. and to give these genres post-war relevance. It was also the most ambitious in terms of design. Various artists contributed covers to the magazine, each of which was a demonstrative poster that elegantly married Constructivist and Abstract approaches, setting the stage for the adoption of these striking design forms by the popular media.

The following year saw the first issue of *Cahiers du Collège de 'Pataphysique*, which continued intermittently

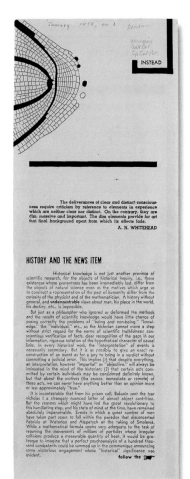

Opposite, clockwise from top left: **Intermède**, covers of no.1, 1946; no.2, 1947. **Instead**, no.3, March 1948; no.1, January 1948, both covers illustrated by Roberto Matta.

The two covers of *Intermède*, edited by Eric de Grolier, were devoted to French theatre and dance, and were illustrated in a representational and romantic manner. In contrast, New York-based *Instead*, edited by Lionel Abel, was concerned with the philosophy of art, and was designed without any superfluities.

Right: **Art d'Aujourd 'Hui**, vol.4 no.2, March 1953, cover artwork by M Bidoilleau. *Art d'Aujourd 'Hui*, which was edited by André Bloc, had covers that changed with each number. While on occasion representational art would appear, Constructivist-inspired geometric abstraction was more common and gave the magazine its distinction.

ART D'AUJOURD'HUI

REVUE D'ART CONTEMPORAIN ● SÉRIE 4 ● N° 2 ● MARS 1953 ● 300 FRS

until 1982. It was founded to propagate the ideas of Alfred Jarry (1873–1907), the author and illustrator of the fantastic *Ubu Roi*. This surprisingly sedate-looking journal (considering the radical nature of Jarry's hand drawings and lettering) was the source for the followers of 'Pataphysics, Jarry's pseudo-scientific art, who included Boris Vian (1920–59), Eugene Ionesco (1912–94), Jacques Prévert (1900–77), Jean Dubuffet (1901–85) and other writers and artists engrossed in the farcical and the fanciful. In addition to its journal, the Collège de 'Pataphysique produced scores of pamphlets, catalogues and tracts.

In 1954 Surrealism reared its head once again. René Magritte published the first of his own quirky journals from Brussels, *La Carte D'Après Nature*, a typographically simple publication that addressed the poetic sensibility endemic to Surrealist painting. Then there was Jean-Jacques Pauvert's *Bizarre: Revue Periodique Nouvelle Series*, edited by Pauvert and M Laclos, an irregular quarterly from 1953 to 1966 which was an absurdist journal based upon the eccentricities of Surrealism. The quarto-sized magazine had covers by leading artists, including Dubuffet and Ernst, and introduced a new breed of eastern European Surrealists who had emigrated to Paris from elsewhere in once-occupied Europe. One was Roland Topor (1938–97), whose satiric line and political/erotic imagery became a mainstay

of European cartoon art during the next decade. *Bizarre* was indeed bizarre, if not in form (it was a standard quarto) then in content: in keeping with Surrealist tradition, it published eerie sexual imagery which had an incredible influence on the manner in which illustration and design was practised in Sixties France.

In 1956 Pauvert launched André Breton's next Surrealist journal, *Le Surréalisme, Même*, which during its six numbers (lasting until 1959) projected a distinctly modernist aura with its minimalist one-colour covers, square format, colour reproductions and variegated interior typography. While Breton had been a contributor to *Bizarre* and other post-war Surrealist reviews, *Le Surréalisme, Même* was stamped with his unmistakable personality and further continued the tradition of *View* and *VVV* by concentrating on specific themes and individuals. Breton now made a point of introducing to the Surrealist orbit new blood, such as Adolf Wölffli, a Swiss schizophrenic who, when not engulfed in a catatonic state, produced remarkable fantasy paintings on wood.

Shortly before *Le Surréalisme, Même* published its final number, in 1959, Gérard Legrand (b.1927), a younger member of the Surrealist conclave, founded *Bief: Jonction Surréaliste* in Paris. Its masthead was typeset in a late-nineteenth-century, slab-serif decorative typeface that prefigured by

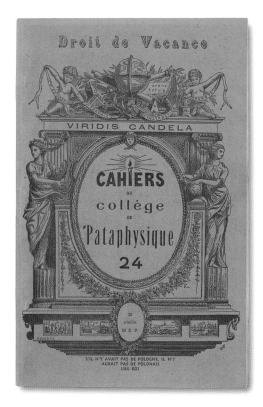

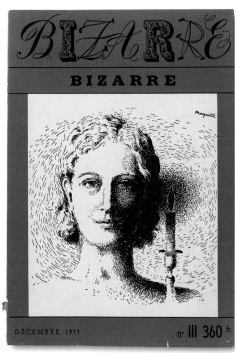

almost a decade the appropriation of the same kinds of fonts by psychedelic poster designers in the US. The covers were designed on a strict modern grid with the masthead always positioned in the upper left corner and a black-and-white photograph (of a diverse subject) placed squarely into the modernist grid. Each issue number was prominent in the lower left. The contributors to *Bief* included the old guard and new waves of Surrealism, André Breton among them. Editorially, it attempted to extend their legacy while addressing newer metaphysical themes. By this time politics had been superseded by the aesthetic and spiritual aspects of the movement. But Breton was still politically active, and while happy to see a renewal of interest among a younger generation, he was a watchdog when it came to maintaining Surrealism's outsider status.

Surrealism none the less continued to express itself through a variety of means. In 1958 *L'Arc: Revue Trimestrielle* was published in Aix-en-Provence and initially concerned itself with the pioneers of Surrealism, featuring work by Breton, Magritte and Dalí. The magazine continued through the Sixties, although not entirely focusing on Surrealist themes. *La Brèche: Action Surréaliste*, founded in 1961, again by Breton in Paris, continued to conscript the younger generation for one further ideological hurrah. Like *Bief*, the magazine had a fairly rigid format, though it is by no means

Right: **Bief**, cover, of no.1, 15 November 1958. Edited by Gérard Legrand, the faux modernism of *Bief* is reflected in its anachronistic Victorian logotype.

Below from left: **La Brèche**, cover of no.6, June 1964. *La Brèche*, edited by André Breton, was a conventional art review.

Cahiers Dada Surréalisme, no.3, 1968, cover artwork by Raoul Hausmann. **The Dreamer**, no.12, March 1971, cover artwork by Brian Mills.

With the demise of Surrealism the avant-garde splintered into various groups, each represented by a periodical designed to reflect their idiosyncrasies. *The Dreamer*, edited and designed by Brian Mills, was absurdist, and *Cahiers Dada Surréalism*, edited by Dominique Baudouin, incorporates the original Hausmann design for *Club Dada* on its own cover.

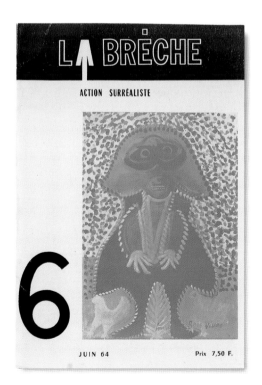

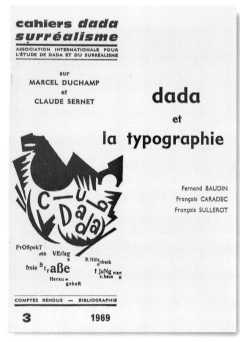

unappealing to the eye. A fixed masthead above an area that frames rectangular images in an empty field evokes modernity and eccentricity. *La Brèche* folded in 1965 after eight numbers, and Breton died the following year.

Breton had held Surrealism together by the sheer strength of his will and ego. After his death the movement, which had already long ago splintered and fragmented, lost much of its relevancy except for a few latter-day Surrealist revivals, one in the form of *Cahiers Dada Surréalisme*, edited by Dominique Baudouin, a typographically quiet scholarly journal devoted to the study of these forms. Another eccentrically designed publication, *The Dreamer* from Derby in England, mixed hand-drawn and mechanically typeset type with comic-style images. The magazine was inspired by Max Ernst and lasted for twelve issues, from 1970 to 1971 – one of a number of short-lived acolyte periodicals that reprised Surrealism.

In the early Fifties, members of the avant-garde who had been dispersed to escape the war were beginning to regroup as an international network. Founded in 1955 in Paris, *Phases: Cahiers Internationaux des Recherches Littéraires et Plastiques*, edited by Edouard Jaguer, attempted to cover the contemporary scene with contributions from countries as diverse as Denmark and Haiti, and wherever else the seeds of the vanguard had been planted. Likewise, *Edda: Cahier International de Documentation sur la Poésie et la Avant-garde*, published from 1959 to 1964 in Brussels, addressed younger adherents of the amorphous avant-garde. *KWY: Revue Trimestrielle d'Art Actuel* began in the late Fifties under the direction of Portuguese editors living in Paris who were part of the KWY group of painters and printmakers. The magazine, which published for twelve numbers until 1963, included original, numbered serigraphs (silkscreens) that were heavily layered abstract combinations of lettering and image. The ad hoc nature of its design prefigures similar methods of the Underground press of the Sixties.

Not every post-war periodical was, however, published in France, Belgium or the United States, nor were they all influenced by Surrealism or Breton. Despite the failure of Futurism and its regrettable tie to Fascism, Italy was still trying to regain its status as a wellspring of modern art. One periodical that reflected this aim was *Documenti D'Arte D'Oggi*, the organ of a Milanese artists' group. Although published in New York through George Wittenborn Inc., a well-respected publisher and bookstore devoted to publishing documents of modern art, its contributors, including Enrico Baj (b.1924), were all Italian. Another, *Documento-Sud*, a handsome journal representing the Naples avant-garde, was founded in 1959 and lasted for one year (six numbers) under the editorship of Luca Luigi

Castellano, and in the Futurist tradition it published manifestos extolling art as a cultural saviour. The design was minimal with covers that combined modernism with eclecticism – the logo, made from a late-nineteenth-century ornamental typeface, sat above a stark field of colour with a simple image in the centre of the page.

Throughout the late Fifties the cultural avant-garde hobbled along without a central driving force to give it focus. Nor did it have a fixed location, although Paris and New York continued to draw the lion's share of attention. Pop Art was beginning to supersede Abstract Expressionism in museums and galleries, but the confluence of diverse aesthetic and cultural influences in the art world had diluted its progressivism. With the Sixties, however, there was something of a renaissance and a reawakening of art as a social weapon, yet only a few periodicals expressed this activist sensibility.

In 1957 the most invasive new avant-garde movement, the Situationist International, was founded by Guy Debord (1932–94) and Raoul Vaneigem (b. *c.*1937) at a conference that was set up in Italy to politically meld activist writers and artists from several European vanguards. According to David Crowley in *Eye* magazine, the group took aim at 'the reign of the technocrats, "invisible" experts who shape the modern world by dint of their claims on science, alienation,

Right from top: **Documento-Sud**, covers of no.4, 1959 and no.5, 1960. *Documento-Sud* was edited and designed by Luca Luigi Castellano. The design combines a nineteenth-century novelty typeface with twentieth-century minimalist layout.

Below from left: **The Situationist Times**, cover of no.6, May 1967, and inside pages with artwork by Roland Topor and Antonio Saura. *The Situationist Times* was edited by Constance De Jong and published in Paris, Holland, London and Copenhagen. The covers of each issue were designed in a similar fashion, while inside were portfolios of variegated drawings and prints by key collaborators, among them Pierre Alechinsky, Asger Jorn and Max Bucaille.

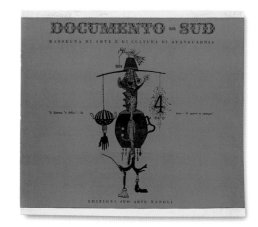

the numbing sense of being detached from society, from the environment and even from one's self; as well as the empty cravings of consumerism.'[8] Debord's *bête noire* was what he called 'The Spectacle' – the capitalist trinity of advertisements, public relations and brands that made people into passive sheep in the dynamics of consumer culture – as explained in his book, *The Society of Spectacle* (1968). Debord believed that the confluence of Western capitalist strategies – the propagation of illusions of desire used to capture the hearts, minds and wallets of its citizenry – could only be defeated through counter-spectacles. In the Sixties, Debord's writings ignited an anti-consumerist ethic and launched the practice of design co-option (now called culture jamming) that subversively, through irony, pirated mainstream advertising techniques to undermine the dominant culture. He called this hijacking of conventional economic and social principles 'Détournement'.

The Situationist Times was launched in 1962 and continued until 1967. Edited by Constance De Jong (and, on occasion, by Vaneigem), different 'international' numbers originated in Hengelo (Holland), Copenhagen, London and Paris. Texts were published in French, German and English, according to the origins and preferences of contributors. The covers were designed in an ad hoc fashion with scrawled graphics and distressed lettering for the masthead,

with the word 'Times' lettered in the *New York Times* Old English type style. Each number had different contents: issue no.6, for example, was the most lavish and included thirty-three original full-page lithographs by, among others, Pierre Alechinsky, Asger Jorn, Wifredo Lam, Lea Lublin, Matta, Christina Martinez, Hannes Postma, Antonio Saura and Roland Topor. The movement challenged the function of capitalist society and the periodical was but one tool working towards this aim. In fact, the publication was a much less effective confrontational weapon than the demonstrations and events through which the movement's adherents derided the power structure. Nevertheless, *The Situationist Times* was a prototype for the eventual rise of Sixties Underground and a number of alternative cultural/political newspapers.

During the Sixties, a spate of newer art journals that either revived the past or charted new territory began publishing throughout Europe. Among the retro periodicals, *Ex*, edited by poets Emilio Villa, Mario Diacono and Gianni Debernardi in Rome in 1963, attempted a return to Dadaesque concrete poetry but, with the exception of the style of typefaces employed, did not significantly advance its aims. *Metro*, published in Milan for seventeen numbers from 1960 to 1970, went further in presenting a new face of contemporary art. Edited by Bruno Alfieri,

*Below from left: **Ex**, cover of no.2, 1963. **Metro**, cover of no.3, 1961; no.12, March 1967 cover artwork by Leo Lionni.*

By the Sixties and Seventies avant-garde art periodicals started to exhibit certain 'professional' design traits. Edited by Emilio Villa, Mario Diacono and Gianni Debernardi, *Ex* was inspired by Dada typography, but *Metro*, edited by Bruno Alfieri, with its Helvetica type, followed a late modernist style.

Metro lent abstract painting the same weight as Surrealism, and focused attention equally on Ben Shahn (1898–1969), Jasper Johns (b.1930) and the former *Fortune* magazine art director Leo Lionni (1910–2000) who was also painting in a symbolic manner. *Metro*'s design changed radically from issue to issue and symbolized the new inclusiveness of the avant-garde. Yet another Italian periodical, *Bit: Arte Oggi in Italia*, published in Milan and edited by Daniela Palazzoli during 1967–8, was perhaps the most sophisticated of the new generation of art magazines. With texts in Italian and English, it covered art from Rome, Milan and Turin. What set it apart from other art reviews was its contemporary graphic design, which was influenced by advertising layout with its emphasis on close-cropped, staged photography and conceptual illustration. The lower case 'b.t', set in a variation of Classic Bodoni (with a period stuck between the letters to represent the 'i'), was constant but not fixed in one location on the cover. Unlike most others, this avant-garde magazine exhibited a distinctly professional design hand.

In contrast to the internationalism of many avant-garde publications, *Location*, published in New York from 1963, edited by art critics Thomas B Hess (1920–78) and Harold Rosenberg (1906–78) and author Donald Barthelme (1931–89), was devoted to exploring the new art and

Right: **Location**, cover of vol.1 no.1, spring 1963. Larry River's cover for *Location*, which was edited by Thomas B Hess, Harold Rosenberg and Donald Barthelme, was at the cutting-edge of contemporary, post-abstract Expressionism.

Below from left: **Bit**, cover and inside spread from vol.2 no.1, April 1968. *Opposite:* cover of vol.2 no.3, June 1968. *Bit*, edited by Daniela Palazzoli, had a very sophisticated design format that was consistent with the modernist sensibility in Italy at that time.

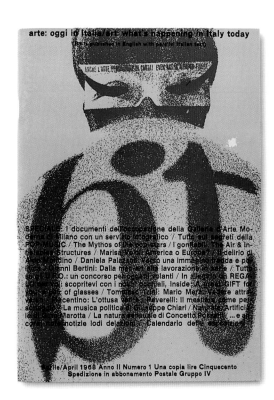

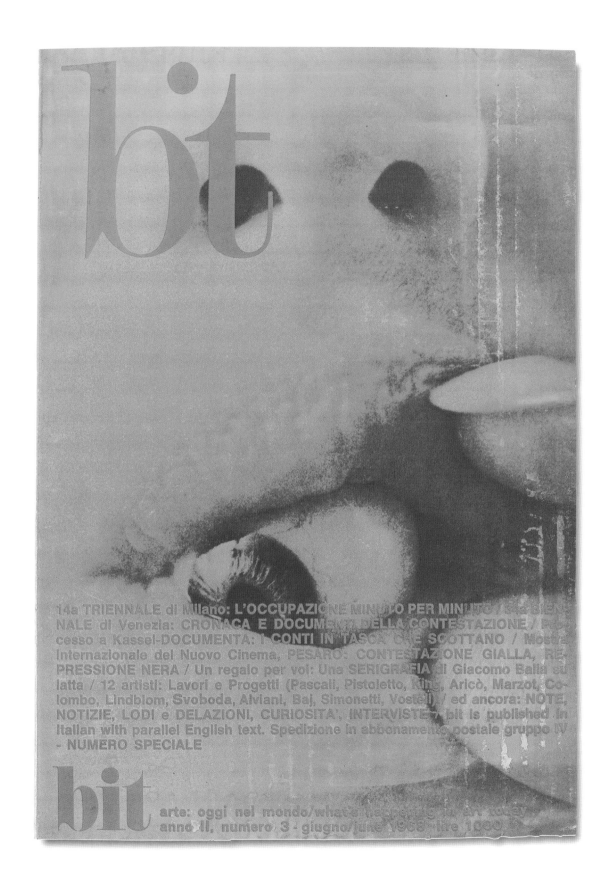

bit

14a TRIENNALE di Milano: L'OCCUPAZIONE MINUTO PER MINUTO / 34 BIEN-
NALE di Venezia: CRONACA E DOCUMENTI DELLA CONTESTAZIONE / Pro-
cesso a Kassel-DOCUMENTA: I CONTI IN TASCA CHE SCOTTANO / Mostra
Internazionale del Nuovo Cinema, PESARO: CONTESTAZIONE GIALLA, RE-
PRESSIONE NERA / Un regalo per voi: Una SERIGRAFIA di Giacomo Balla su
latta / 12 artisti: Lavori e Progetti (Pascali, Pistoletto, King, Aricò, Marzot, Co-
lombo, Lindblom, Svoboda, Alviani, Baj, Simonetti, Vostell) / ed ancora: NOTE,
NOTIZIE, LODI e DELAZIONI, CURIOSITA', INTERVISTE / bit is published in
Italian with parallel English text. Spedizione in abbonamento postale gruppo IV
- NUMERO SPECIALE

bit

arte: oggi nel mondo/what's happening in art today
anno II, numero 3 - giugno/june 1968 - lire 1000

literature and its social ramifications in America. Reading like a catalogue of veteran and contemporary members of the avant-garde, its first issue included an early appearance by Marshall McLuhan, soon to be the philosopher of late-twentieth-century mass communication. *Location*'s square format, alterable masthead and conceptually illustrated covers emphasized its progressive air.

The sheer number of periodicals rose sharply as setting type and printing with offset lithography became increasingly inexpensive. Some new publications were produced by small arts groups, others covered a broader range of contemporary activity. Many during the mid- to late Sixties were dedicated to the growing art of concrete poetry and the novel typographic manifestations endemic to this visual form of literature. Among the notable journals, *Spur* was published in Munich from 1960 to 1961 and covered the machinations of the group of that name. *Futura*, launched in Stuttgart in 1965, with a cover designed in the iconic Futura typeface, was a folded sheet that opened into a poster; it published the concrete poetry of French, German, British and American artists. In 1964 *Die Schastrommel*, from Cologne, was the organ for the German Action Group of Performance Artists and published reports of its activities. *L'Art Brut*, published in Paris from 1964 to 1967 and edited by Jean Dubuffet, focused on the unschooled and often psychotic art that became known as the L'Art Brut genre – and later, style. *Geiger*, published in Turin from 1967 to 1970, introduced various concrete poets and their visual approaches to the Italian art world. *Agentzia* was produced in Paris in 1968 and was also devoted to concrete poetry and Pop Art; while *Archigram* was published from London in 1967 with an emphasis on architecture and environmental planning. *Approaches*, published in 1968 at Oxford University, was concerned with investigating and analysing the philosophy behind avant-garde events.

Among the more politically active, the ironically celebratory *Ronald Reagan*, published in 1968 in London, used the name of the then Governor of California and future President of the United States as the title of a magazine devoted to contemporary, counter-culture poetry. Although not quite a Sixties Underground paper, its graphics and text nevertheless echoed the era's irreverence in being both raucous and anarchic. Similarly, *Mixed Media* from Düsseldorf was published in a newspaper format in 1969 and was also devoted to recent art happenings and concrete poetry. Its ad hoc nature prefigured the DIY (Do-It-Yourself) aesthetics that were to come with Punk in the Seventies.

The Do-It-Yourself ethos derives directly from Dada. And Dada, which may have skipped a few generations but still signalled anti-establishmentism, was decidedly the precursor of Fluxus, the 'Neo-Dada' collective that launched

Opposite, clockwise from top left: **Futura**, cover of no.1, 1965; published by Edition Hansjörg Mayer, Stuttgart. **Die Schastrommel**, cover of no.3, 1970; edited by Günther Brus. **Archigram**, cover of no.8, 1968; edited by Peter Cook. **L'Art Brut**, cover of 'special Adolf Wölfli issue', no.2, 1964; edited by Jean Dubuffet.

Opposite, bottom from left: **Ronald Reagan: the Magazine of Poetry**, vol.2 no.6, 1968; cover with artwork by Pamela Zoline; inside page with artwork by John Sladek; edited by Sladek and Zoline.

Typography was either important or not depending on the statement each periodical wanted to make. *Futura* was bold, *Die Schastrommel* was theatrical, *L'Art Brut* was artless and *Archigram*

was more or less neutral. The British magazine *Ronald Reagan* used Helvetica type, the face of officialdom, to lampoon the ex-movie star and reactionary governor of California.

This page, right and below: **Mixed Media**, cover and spread from 'no.0', March 1969. The German review *Mixed Media* is one of many avant-garde periodicals to exploit and parody the conventional sensationalist newspaper format with its bold gothic type and black and red palette.

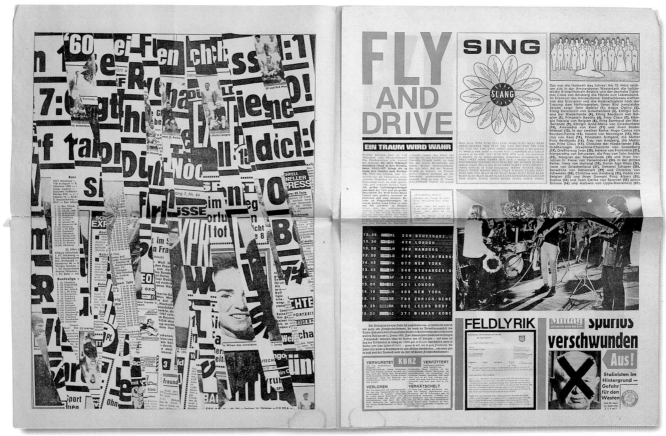

a barrage of anti-art happenings embracing all media, especially periodical publishing. Dada and Fluxus 'both sought to unnerve a complacent, militaristic, decadent society by bringing art into direct confrontation with triviality and aesthetics, and to controvert the idea that art is incapable of effecting social or political change,'[19] wrote archivist John Hendricks.

Fluxus was founded in 1961 by George Maciunas (1931–78) and, given its widespread influence, Maciunas was arguably second to Breton as a cultural instigator. He emerged on the scene at a time when radical shifts in morals and mores were occurring in the United States, Europe and Japan, and were also evident in the emerging visual arts, music and theatre. Artists no longer felt confined to canvas or chained to precedent. Maciunas opened the AG Gallery in New York in 1961 to exhibit abstract art, yet, when it failed, he realized that the art world was moving beyond the old vanguards into a more

radical confluence of popular and alternative cultures. In 1961 in Germany he implemented plans to launch a magazine, in both Europe and the United States, called *Fluxus*, which he would personally design and publish. The initial aim of *Fluxus* was to address new music, and so he planned a series of concerts in European cities that were called 'Fluxus Yearboxes'. The first of these Fluxus events was held in 1962 at the Galérie Parnass in Wuppertal, Germany, which is where Maciunas released the first Fluxus publication, one in a succession of advertisements, missives and periodicals: *Brochure Prospectus for Fluxus Yearboxes, version A*. The Fluxus movement was launched at this musical event and, in its programme, Maciunas introduced himself as editor-in-chief of the new art magazine, which would become the organ of Neo-Dada, anti-art and 'artistic nihilism'. In his first lecture Maciunas states: '… the art nihilist either creates an anti-art or only produces the banal. The anti-art forms are primarily directed against art as a

Below from left: **Fluxus V TRE,** cover of no.10, 2 May 1976, 'Maciunas V TRE: Laudatio Scripta pro George', designed by Sara Seagull, edited by Robert Watts; cover of March 1964 issue. Of all the reams of paper produced by Fluxus – the international consortium of avant-gardists – the broadsheet newspaper was its most common (and inexpensive) format for musings, discourse and experiment. It was edited by George Brecht and George Maciunas and its designers varied. The alternating upper and lowercase typesetting was a Dadaesque use of letter forms, and a breaking of standard typographic convention.

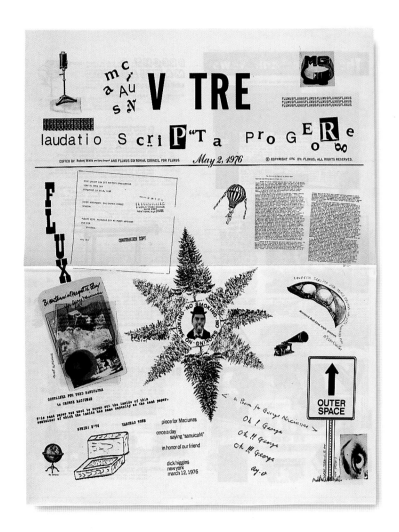

profession, against the artificial separation of producer or performer, or generator and spectator, or against the separation of art and life.'[10]

Fluxus was a collective of artists who created 'happenings' in all media and without formal boundaries. Humour was an important element and the Fluxus notion of creating products (rather than artefacts) was rooted in irony, paradox and cynicism for art-world verities. The initial products were to be anthologies or compendiums that included various loose items: records, films, flip books, original art, metal, plastic and wood objects, scraps of paper, clippings, junk or 'any composition or work that cannot be reproduced in standard sheet form or cannot be reproduced at all', stated the 1962 Fluxus News-Policy-Letter.[11] And, most important, a Fluxus work needed to be cheap and mass producible, although some were, however, expensive and complex.

Since Fluxus was alienated from society, Maciunas built his own alternative universe. The guiding principle was collectivism, uniting under one banner disparate individuals in the US, Europe and Japan, such as Joseph Beuys, Henry Flint, Dick Higgins, Yoko Ono, Naim June Paik, and Emmett Williams. This was influenced in part by the Twenties Russian arts group LEF and its publication, which rallied members through actions, exhibitions and its journal (see Chapter 5). At the outset of the endeavour, Maciunas was frustrated with the delay in producing *Fluxus* 1 due to costly printing and complex editorial issues, so he abandoned plans for the six or seven other Fluxus anthologies and, in 1964, started rapid production of Fluxus newspapers. The newspaper format, printed on high-speed web offset presses, was cheap and immediate, and four appeared in the first six months alone. The titles for the four-page broadsheets regularly changed, but the most common were *Fluxus cc V Tre* or *Fluxus Vacuum TrapEzoid* (a homage to member George Brecht's earlier newspaper, *V Tre*). There was considerable variation in typography (often seemingly

Clockwise from top:
Fluxus V TRE, no.10, 2 May 1976, 'Maciunas V TRE: Laudatio Scripta pro George', centre spread design by George Brecht and Robert Watts, overall design by Sara Seagull, edited by Robert Watts; no.7, 1 February 1966, '3 newspaper eVenTs for the pRicE of $1', spread with collage by Maciunas and 'One Hour' by Jim Riddle; and spread showing 'Yoko Ono & Dance Co.' by Yoko Ono and 'Fiftyeight

Propositions for one page' by Ben Vautier, designed and edited by George Maciunas. Front pages and spreads of *V Tre* were designed in a deliberately ad hoc manner using press type, photo lettering, photos, and clip-art.

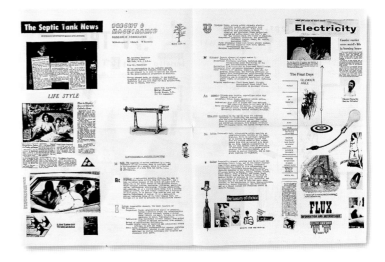

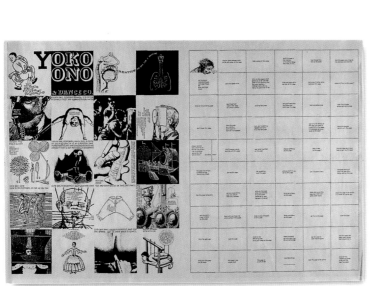

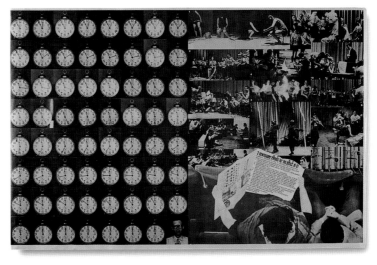

cut from type books or produced by press-down sheets, though the most frequently used Fluxus typeface is a nineteenth-century slab serif. In fact, gothic typefaces abound, and some words were thrown down in a random manner while others purposely echoed tabloid newspapers and Victorian posters. The content varied too, but the newspapers primarily served as advertisements for the ongoing Fluxus happenings. The movement founded by George Maciunas has continued since his death in 1978 through access to its huge archives and the work of former members and recent acolytes.

The Fluxus happenings doubtless influenced the American Surrealist painter William Copley (b.1919; CPLY), who in 1968 conceived the idea of a periodical-in-a-box called *SMS* (Shit Must Stop). This would be a portfolio of multiples created by vanguard artists. In fact, some of the key contributors, including Le Monte Young, John Cage, Ray Johnson and Yoko Ono, were also Fluxus members. Others were masters of Dada and Surrealism such as Nicolas Calas, Meret Oppenheim, Man Ray and Marcel Duchamp, as well as Pop creators like Roy Lichtenstein, Christo, H C Westermann and Dieter Rot. Each used this format to turn 'art into the vehicle of Utopian wishes', as Carter Ratcliff explained in a catalogue for an *SMS* exhibition in 1988. He further noted that *SMS* '... removed all boundaries between the mediums. Everything from poetry to performance to traditional printmaking, received equal treatment ... Moreover, *SMS* bypassed the hierarchical labyrinth of museums and established galleries.'[12]

Following the tradition of Duchamp and other box artists, the publication was mailed directly to subscribers. Every entry therein was an integral artwork independent of all the others. Copley produced six numbers, one every other month for the year 1968; he did not impose a theme, only a vehicle. Each number contained diverse contributions that integrated abstract, Surreal and Pop Art. Lichtenstein's (1923–97) was a folded paper hat made from one of his comic-book parodies of modern art. Claes Oldenburg's (b.1929) was a pamphlet with a felt-pen cover drawing, showing menus for seven quintessentially American meals. Yoko Ono's (b.1933) 'Mend Piece for John' was a box containing materials and instructions for repairing a broken cup with 'this glue and this poem in three stanzas dedicated to John'. And Duchamp's was a seven-minute recording of 'contrepetrie', a word-play based on transposed words and letters.

'As a Surrealist, William Copley believed in the unity of art and life. With *SMS*, he helped generate that unity,'[13] Ratcliff concluded. Although *SMS* was not strictly a journal, it appeared regularly for a limited period. While Copley was not the first to transform a box or use the post, this set a standard for how audacious the form could be as a means of distributing art.

The avant-garde art reviews surveyed in this chapter prefigured, and some paralleled, the rise of the Sixties Underground or alternative press. *The East Village Other*, a pioneer American Underground magazine, was influenced by the Fluxus newspapers in form and sometimes in content. But there were also major distinctions. All these periodicals established philosophies on aesthetic and formal underpinnings directly related to the making of art, poetry and literature. Even the most politicized tracts and manifestos with deep ideological roots expressed themselves through art as a means to change the world. Although some Underground papers supported, utilized and covered the new arts (and even sponsored some of the art happenings of the day), the alternative press was built upon a socio-political foundation. This was ideological – Communist, socialist, anarchist, Students for a Democratic Society (SDS), Black Panther, etc. – and cultural – sex, drugs, rock 'n' roll. While the art press looked at the world in an insular way through the lens of the respective aesthetic movements, the Underground was a radical press which provided news and commentary that the mainstream refused to address.

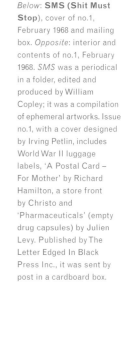

Below: **SMS (Shit Must Stop)**, cover of no.1, February 1968 and mailing box. *Opposite*: interior and contents of no.1, February 1968. *SMS* was a periodical in a folder, edited and produced by William Copley; it was a compilation of ephemeral artworks. Issue no.1, with a cover designed by Irving Petlin, includes World War II luggage labels, 'A Postal Card – For Mother' by Richard Hamilton, a store front by Christo and 'Pharmaceuticals' (empty drug capsules) by Julien Levy. Published by The Letter Edged In Black Press Inc., it was sent by post in a cardboard box.

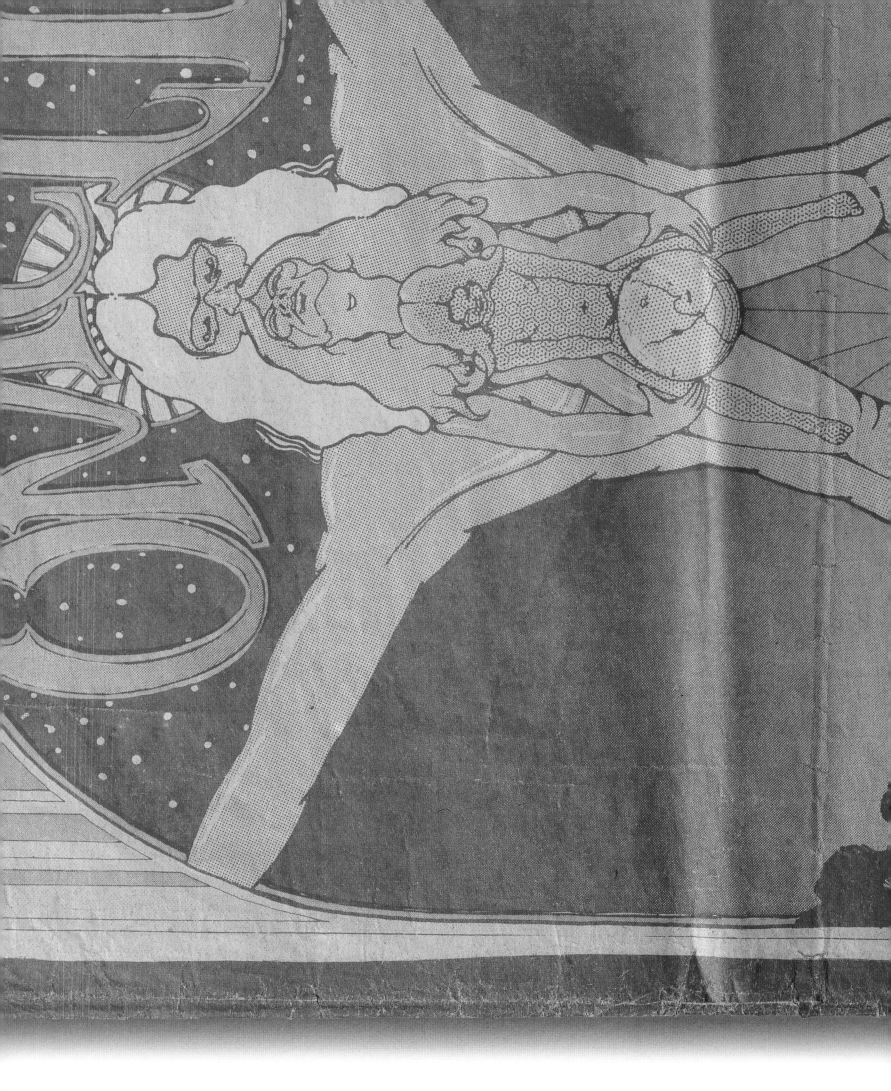

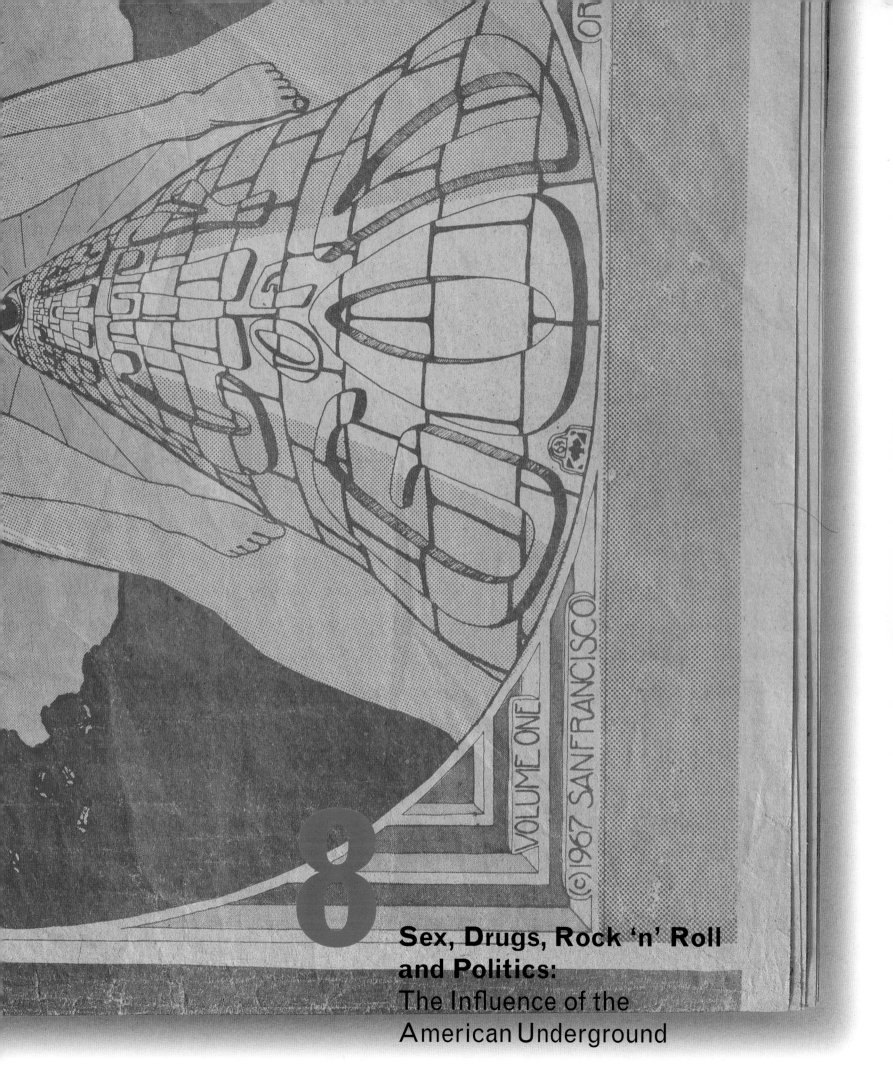

8

**Sex, Drugs, Rock 'n' Roll
and Politics:**
The Influence of the
American Underground

The Sixties Underground press was a fraud. The hundreds of periodicals that came under the 'Underground' umbrella, especially in the United States where the vast majority were published, were not created in dank basements or clandestine hideouts, nor were they concealed from the authorities. Most Undergrounds were produced in storefronts or offices with their logos emblazoned on the door for all to see. Underground was more a state of mind, and given the association with World War II resistance newspapers from Nazi-occupied Europe (notably in France and Holland), it became a romantic conceit.

Yet this does not impugn the Underground press's impact on youth culture or, for that matter, mass culture. It was both influential and threatening. Government agencies in America, including the Justice Department, the armed forces, the FBI and the police, declared these papers contraband. Some legislators called for investigations, and a few editors were legally harassed because they challenged convention with off-kilter ideas and unacceptably subversive words and graphics. Paul Krassner (b.1932), editor of *The Realist*, founded in New York in 1958 and the grandfather of Undergrounds, announced in an editorial of January 1968 in *The Realist* that his goal was to disrupt an insane society.

Underground may not be the most precise terminology but it effectively connotes a distinction between mainstream and alternative presses which, during the late Sixties, was as pronounced as the generation gap was deep. The term 'Underground' underscored the dichotomy between the establishment press with its myriad biases and prohibitions and the counter-culture media that rejected objective journalistic tenets and taboos in favour of subjective mayhem. The Underground press 'doesn't aim to record things that happen, but rather to make them happen. Its writers are doers first and writers second,' wrote the journalist Michael Kernan.[1] The New Left – or The Movement – was a political and cultural entity that espoused revolution, sometimes flirting with the violent overthrow of government but otherwise seeking a more realistic means of challenging policies and mores, including the end to censorship of music and art and the decriminalization of marijuana and LSD. Most importantly, it fought the Vietnam War policy-makers in their own back yard. The clarions of this rebellion were music, theatre, poetry, literature, and weekly, monthly and occasional periodicals sold on news-stands and hawked on the streets. Cheaply printed and hastily composed newspapers were the most volatile media in the counter-culture's repertoire. There was a niche for these papers as long as mainstream publishers failed to meet the needs of youth.

The Underground press, which ran roughly from 1964 (when the *Los Angeles Free Press* was founded) until 1973

Previous page: **The Oracle**, detail of vol.1 no.11, 1967, cover by Steve Schenfer.

Below from left: **The Realist**, no.39, 1962, cover art by Richard Guindon; no.63, 1965, cover art parody of Jules Feiffer by Bob Stewart; no.76, 1967, cover art by Richard Guindon. The logo, designed for Paul Krassner's *The Realist* by John Francis Putnam, was rendered in a calligraphic style that suggested a parody of journalistic appearance, while the contents, including its numerous cartoons, revealed a healthy disrespect for those values.

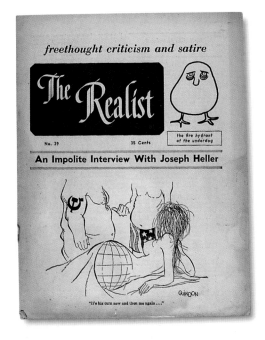

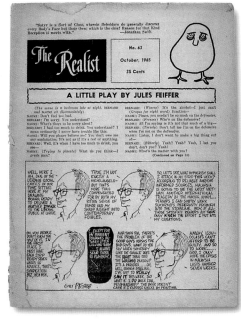

(when most of the radical Undergrounds had folded or transformed into alternative regional newspapers), was a loose-knit confederation of over six hundred small-, medium- and large-circulation periodicals, mostly published in the United States but including noteworthy papers in Canada, Holland and England. Germany, Italy and France had a scattering of such papers but they were not as significant. The United States was the centre of radical activity and youth culture because the Vietnam War and the civil rights movement were essentially US issues. Despite the explosion in youth culture in the UK, which led the way in music and fashion, the US youth culture was a critical mass of disaffection and frustration. The Free Speech movement in the US in the early to mid-Sixties was the fuse on a generational bomb that sought to reject the materialism of the post-war Fifties. Radicalism also grew directly out of the anti-Communist repression in the form of The House on UnAmerican Activities Committee (HUAC) and the unofficial Black List of the early to mid-Fifties that attempted to legislate against and persecute anything that seemed to diverge from status quo, pure Americanism – notably youth music (rock 'n' roll), youth art (comics) and youth culture in general. The response was a minor revolution that was perpetuated through Underground papers which covered and supported new trends in music,

film, theatre, etc. These issues were alive in Europe and Canada, but on a much smaller and less significant scale. The primary reader was between fifteen and thirty years old and most were males. The paper with the largest circulation was the *Los Angeles Free Press* with over 120,000; the San Francisco *Oracle* reportedly had 116,000; and New York's *The East Village Other* (*EVO*) reached a peak of around 90,000 copies per week. A few other high-circulation publications – *The Bird*, *The Chicago Seed* and *Helix* – were in the range of 20,000 to 60,000 (albeit for relatively brief periods). The Underground Press Syndicate (UPS), the umbrella organization that funnelled material to all Undergrounds, estimated that 15 million 'youths' read Underground papers (*Fortune* magazine put the number at one million). But the average number of readers for most other local Undergrounds hovered between 2,000 and 5,000 per issue, with sales fluctuations usually based on the graphics appearing on any given cover.

Photographs of nude women, predictably, sold extremely well, often to males who were not necessarily genuinely involved with youth culture or politics. Political and social cartoons by artists such as Robert Crumb (b.1943) or Ron Cobb (b.1937), and photographs or drawings of rockers such as The Grateful Dead, Jefferson Airplane, Jimmy Hendrix, Janis Joplin and the MC5 also had sales

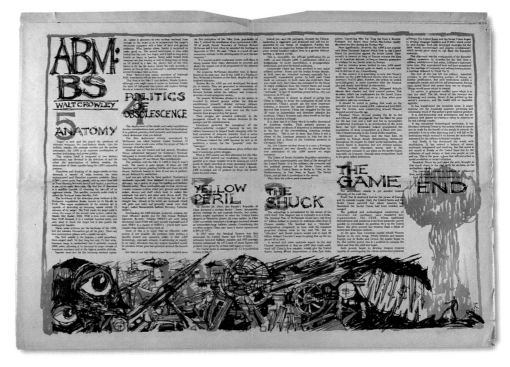

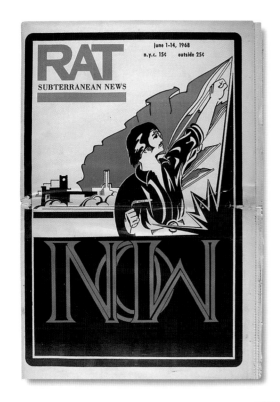
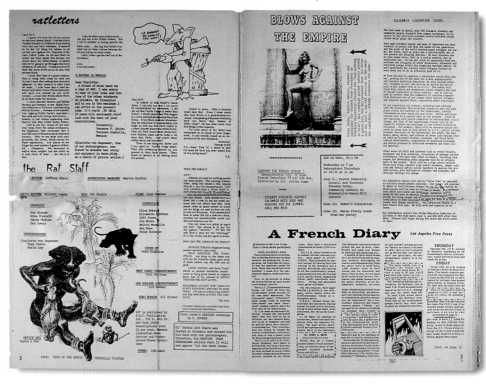

appeal. Poster-like images of timely issues, such as Vietnam wartime atrocities, police 'riots' against anti-war demonstrators, and Black Panther rebels did well too. 'Banned' issues – those confiscated by local authorities for reasons such as sedition, pornography or caprice – were also in demand and boosted the sales of subsequent numbers. In addition to serious editorial content, the personal classified advertisements that appeared in most Undergrounds, promoting weird sexual liaisons, helped to increase the number of copies sold. Graphic design was the least important aspect in terms of sales, unless it was psychedelic design and thus an alluring code for the youth culture.

The Underground Zeitgeist had two roots: one was hippie, flower power and drug culture; the other politically active, radical and New Left. At times they intersected but for the most part the latter 'wanted to change America', according to the journalist Jean Strouse, while the former 'wanted to ignore it'.[2] Drugs took on symbolic as well as recreational importance. The counter-culture vociferously rebelled against the Federal Marijuana Act of 1937 that made weed illegal in the US. While most in the youth culture were not really aware of this specific statute, it underpinned the drug movement. On the political side, as the Vietnam War escalated and racism in America became more untenable, an overriding ethos was built upon a foundation of New Left politics, including anti-war and pro-civil rights protest, which served as an umbrella for sub-groups and so-called 'liberation fronts'. These included Communists, Marxists, socialists, anarchists, Black Panthers, pacifists, feminists, and even high-school 'revolutionaries'. These constituencies may each have viewed their respective missions and philosophies differently but used the same Underground-styled tabloid publishing techniques, such as ad hoc layout, cheap newsprint and inflammatory graphics and text, to get their messages across. The Underground Press Syndicate's statement of purpose was as follows:

- *To warn the 'civilized world' of its impending collapse, through communications among aware communities outside the establishment and by forcing the mass media to pay attention to it.*
- *To note and chronicle events leading to the collapse.*
- *To advise intelligently to prevent rapid collapse and make transition possible.*
- *To prepare American people for the wilderness.*
- *To fight a holding action in the dying cities.*[3]

The majority of Underground papers that subscribed to UPS and allowed their material to be circulated covered a similar *mélange* of fundamental themes, in part because the syndicate supplied all papers with the same basic editorial content on politics, sex, drugs and rock 'n' roll. The most prevalent features addressed the promulgation of free love,

free sex, free marijuana, free LSD and free music, which underscored hippie ideals that further embraced communal living, food dispensaries, health clinics and tribal happenings. Some periodicals were more politically doctrinaire than others, aligned with such radically activist groups as Students for a Democratic Society, Youth Against War and Fascism, the Socialist Workers' Party and the War Resisters' League. Others were somewhere in between: less 'ideologue' and more 'trickster' (as personified in the mythology by Loki, Hermes, Puck, Brer Rabbit, and even Bugs Bunny who up-ended the world through subversive schemes).

These trickster papers issued a diet of pranks aimed to disrupt the establishment's complacency by provoking its young readers to demonstrate against the power structure through civil disobedience. And while the goals of Underground papers may have been similar, the methods varied. The devoutly political papers followed no-nonsense strategies while the tricksters used any means possible. *The East Village Other*'s founder, Walter Bowart, referred to himself as 'libertarian' rather than leftist, and Abe Peck, the former *Chicago Seed* writer and Underground historian, wrote that *EVO* was 'the first Underground paper to be more Groucho Marx than Karl'.[4] *The East Village Other* was born in New York's new Bohemian capital, once called the Lower East Side, but referred to as the East Village, as opposed to Greenwich Village, the historic stomping ground for turn-of-the-century Bohemians and Fifties Beats. The 'Other' was a reference to its alternative stance against the long-standing, conservative *Villager* neighbourhood newspaper and the entrenched alternative *Village Voice*, founded in the late Fifties, which by 1965 represented the so-called 'Old Left'. *The East Village Other* was created to cover the social, cultural and political happenings of the East Village and based much of its early graphic style on Fluxus. Within a couple of years it developed a visual language notable for its employ of collage, comics and raucous typography.

The quality of coverage in Underground newspapers varied according to the talents available to the respective papers. Some artists and photographers were skilled, while most were amateurish. Some of the contributors had serious aspirations as reporters, commentators or artists, yet the majority of them were gadflies for whom the Underground was either a lark or a test-site for experimentation. The mercurial nature of the press was best summed up by Jeff Shero, editor of New York's *Rat*: 'We make up for sloppy writing by verve and passion.'[5] Although the rhetoric was not always grammatically eloquent and hyperbole reigned, it was indeed rousing: 'The Underground press is the mammal devouring the eggs of the dinosaur,' wrote Shero in a *Rat* editorial. 'We lay bare the deformed nature of behemoth America and pierce its scaly armor – the national media.

We are the future, an expression of the youth revolt determined to liberate ourselves and all men.'[6]

The Underground did not possess one iota of the mainstream media's financial or technological resources, money was tight and backers were few. Rumours from the mainstream media that the Underground press was funded by the Soviet Union or the Communist Party of America were ridiculous. Some papers received gifts from sympathetic individuals but rarely enough to ensure publication for more than a few issues. Although some Undergrounds had so-called 'business managers', profit was nevertheless viewed as a capitalist evil. The Undergrounds certainly did not threaten the hegemony of any mainstream medium.

The US Underground press did, however, have a curious licence which was denied the mainstream media. While the major dailies were busy covering quotidian stories, they were also swallowing the hypes of the advertising industry, which allowed the media to distort the reality of events. Conversely, the Undergrounds reported on stories of police brutality, CIA recruitment on college campuses and draft board inequities among races because some of these events were ignored in the mainstream press yet had a direct impact on the Undergrounds' youthful constituents. Certainly many Underground press articles about government provocateurs and spies were based on hearsay and rumour as well as on intuition, but this did not necessarily mean that government-sponsored dirty tricks did *not* occur. A minority of mainstream reporters actually followed leads presented in Underground papers as background for what became substantiated news stories.

The main reason why the overground media looked askance at Underground papers was because they shunned the conventions of traditional journalism, especially in terms of make-up and layout. A notable exception was *The Realist*, which was actually composed by union typographers who adhered rigidly to customary formats. Before phototype was in widespread use in the mid-Sixties, type was set in metal and composed in steel chases, demanding the expertise of craftsmen. This meant that, although the content might be controversial, the paper looked deceptively tame. However, when the next wave began to publish, economic limitations made it necessary to be Do-It-Yourself all the way, and this fundamentally altered how the Underground generation perceived itself in relation to the mass media. 'The new breed of publishers in the Underground press are changing much of the terminology in graphics; yesterday's "craftsmen" have become today's "graphic artists",'[7] wrote the historian Robert J Glessing.

Professional layout was not only a code for the 'system', it was considerably more expensive than alternative

methods. Consequently, the new, non-union printing companies that used photo-offset and cold (or photo) type technologies enabled layouts to be produced without investing in expensive, pre-press equipment, thereby cutting costs by over half. For a few dollars a month, publishers of Underground papers could rent a brand-name typesetting system – Addressograph, Compugraphic or IBM – as well as cameras that made veloxes (or photographic prints) suitable for reproduction. By the late Sixties, compact graphic arts machinery simplified the entire pre-press process so that the work could be done in the office or basement of the Underground paper itself. This also allowed for special effects without incurring the excessive hourly rates of the professional pre-press personnel. Non-union printing firms with web-offset (high-speed, roll-fed, colour-capable) presses, which usually printed supermarket flyers, also charged considerably less than most letterpress printers.

To launch an Underground paper, therefore, vast resources were not necessary. The editors had to know how to edit (at least somewhat), the writers had to know how to write (at least passably), the artists had to know how to draw (or how to do collage or montage, or drip ink on a board) and the graphic designers had to know how to compose, lay out, and paste-up all the visual and textual elements with rudimentary functionality. They also had to be able to operate the typesetting, photostat, photocopying and waxing machines, and to control and manipulate printing effects in order to achieve eye-catching results within minuscule budgets. Given that the majority of the so-called 'designers' or 'art directors' were not formally trained in the nuances of typography, proportion or colour theory, the ersatz 'design' of the vast majority of Undergrounds was no accident.

Although some historians liken the ersatz and anarchic layouts of Sixties Underground papers to Futurist, Dada and Surrealist periodicals, this is at best a coincidence. Attending a paste-up session at *The East Village Other* in 1969, Robert Hughes, who was then *Time* magazine's newest art critic, dubbed what he saw 'a Dada experience', to the bewilderment of the layout team. The deliberate abrogation of typographic standards practised by early twentieth-century avant-gardists as a symbol of their collective rebellion against archaic convention had no direct influence on the Undergrounds. Although Alan Katzman (1937–c.1977), a founding editor of *The East Village Other*, once said that it was the first publication in America to think of a newspaper as an art form, most Underground designers were not well-versed in art history and had little knowledge of past art movements. They may have unknowingly had similar goals to the Futurist and Dadaist typographers – to compose pages that were aggressively free form – but, more likely, they used

Below from left: **The East Village Other**, vol.2 no.8, 15 March–1 April 1966, cover art by Spain Rodriguez, edited by Walter Bowart and Alan Katzman, art-edited by William Beckman; vol.4 no.31, 2 July 1969, cover design by Vaughn Bode; vol.4 no.52, 3 December 1969, cover art by Kim Deitch, edited by Jaakov Kohn. Covers for *The East Village Other* were done on the night that they went to the printer. The decision for a particular edition's cover was based on whichever artist had the work done in time. Its covers were almost always sarcastic or polemical, such as Kim Deitch's 'If Your Heart Is Not In America Then Get Your Ass Out'.

adhesive-backed ruling tapes, 'clip art' and Letraset because these were the only Do-It-Yourself graphic arts tools at their disposal. In any case, not all the Underground papers subscribed to this method. Politically (and comparatively conservative) doctrinaire papers did not want to obscure their messages with disruptive type and layout, so their pages were often packed with uninterrupted columns of type. 'They were more concerned with non-violence than creative page layouts,'[8] wrote Abe Peck.

Conversely, the flower-power, semi-political papers believed that changing all values, including the look of things, was a prerequisite for changing society as a whole. They unquestionably rejected the fundamentals of composition (straight, justified columns of type or headlines and subheads belonging to the same type family) either because they did not know any better or because of the pressure of deadlines. Frequently more than one layout artist, each with differing abilities and 'visions', worked together on the same page or series of contiguous pages, making visual consistency difficult. Moreover, even if a few semi-professional designers had the desire to be consistent, the layout process was viewed as communal and 'personal styles' were encouraged. Perhaps the only publication where this confluence of graphic disparity worked well enough to indelibly define its personality was

the San Francisco magazine *The Oracle*. Founded in 1966, this was the first American Underground paper to introduce the psychedelic (or drug) style to youth culture.

Designed at the Psychedelic Shop in Haight Ashbury, the epicentre of hippie activity in San Francisco, *The Oracle* was an authentic graphic design innovation signalling a distinct departure from previous alternative cultures. *The Oracle*'s most defining trait was souped-up, kaleidoscopic colour. It was printed in multiple or split-fountain hues – in which two different-coloured inks were placed in the inkwells at either end of an offset press so that the colours merged when the rollers revolved at high speed, producing additional prismatic combinations. For one issue, the layout staff actually squirted tomato ketchup into the inkwells (the colour faded soon after printing). Typical illustrations were swerving, swirling, ethereal line drawings and collages that meandered in serpentine fashion around contoured blocks of text (echoing the typography of late nineteenth-century Jugendstil and Vienna Secession; see Chapter 1). The imagery drew further inspiration from the East and from American Indians, *The Tibetan Book of the Dead* and Christian illuminated manuscripts. The pictorial themes that were drawn (often as automatic drawings) while under the influence of hallucinogenic substances are best described as cosmic, fantastic and erotic.

Below from left: **The East Village Other**, vol.5 no.18, 1 April 1970, cover design by Charlie Frick; vol.5 no.51, 17 November 1970, inside spread designed by Charlie Frick. Interior layouts for most Undergrounds were literally slapped together, as this layout attests, with machine-set columns of type, press-down headlines and various halftones and drawings. Individual interior layouts were designed by different artists and amateurs, ensuring that one page never resembled the next.

Opposite: **The Oracle**, vol.1 no.6, 1967, cover by Rick Griffin. The San Francisco-based magazine, *The Oracle* was edited by Allen Cohen and art-edited by Gabe Katz. It was the touchstone for psychedelic design typified by vibrating colours and surrealistic erotic collages and drawings. The rainbow colouring was achieved through a split-fountain printing process.

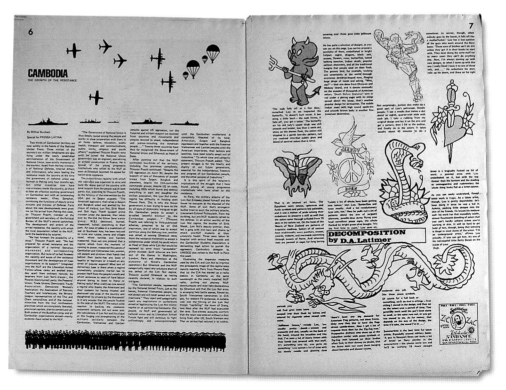

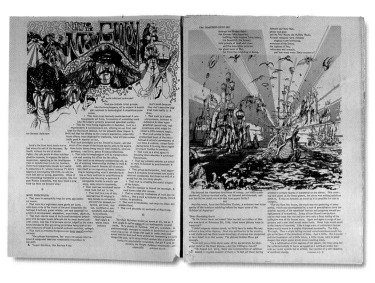

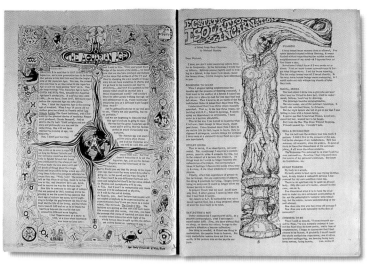

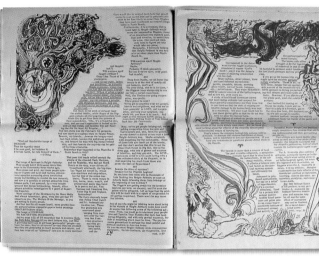

Drugs had stimulated art long before the Sixties, but the new Sixties hallucinogens triggered a uniquely indigenous form of symbolism and Surrealism that incorporated imagery from earlier artistic periods into an aesthetic comprised of sexual and astrological metaphors. The integration of the dissonant graphic components, while occasionally crude, resulted in a seamless entity, a total visual experience, a veritable acid trip in newsprint. A critic writing in the magazine *Editor & Publisher* at the time said that *The Oracle* made standard newspapers look 'about as exciting as the telephone white pages',[9] which is exactly what Allen Cohen (b.1940), the founder of *The Oracle*, had in mind when he said that he wanted to break away from the traditional linear format of newspapers.

The Oracle was a graphic expression of a more conscious, loving, intimate, non-alienated world. And although, with its drug-inspired ethos, it rejected New Left politics in favour of ethereal Aquarian aesthetics, and had published only twelve issues when it closed in 1967, *The Oracle* had a huge influence on subsequent Undergrounds that emulated and expanded the so-called 'rainbow' visual vocabulary. *The Oracle* embodied the hippie aesthetic and sensibility. The text was as eccentric as the graphics and twice as interlaced with purple poetry and drug-induced religious references; this was indeed the verbal and visual language of youth culture. *The Oracle* quoted the leading philosopher-poets (among them Allen Ginsberg and Timothy Leary) and covered the poet-musicians that garnered generational prominence during the 1967 San Francisco Summer of Love. Without the appropriately titled *The Oracle* to lead the way, the psychedelic movement would have found other outlets, but this publication was key to the national dissemination of the new cult. *The Oracle*'s closure was partly due to the fact that its collective creators seriously believed the hippie culture was inextricably linked to the mainstream consumer culture, by which it was viewed as quaint, stylish and profitable. It attained its high circulation numbers (116,000) largely because tourists to Haight Ashbury bought it as souvenirs. Although a subsequent Underground paper adopted the *Oracle* name, it never had the innovative aura of the true psychedelic pioneer.

Perhaps the Underground magazine that owed most to the influence of *The Oracle* was the London-based periodical, *Oz*, which combined the psychedelic look with a more sophisticated cultural/political editorial focus. It bathed the Zeitgeist in Carnaby Street colours yet injected a wry, satirical social commentary into the overall editorial mix. *Oz* was an Underground satirical publication that covered many of the same themes as the American Undergrounds and was persecuted into the bargain. Published in Australia and England from 1963 (actually before *The Oracle*) in a

Opposite, clockwise from top left: **The Oracle**, two inside spreads from vol.1 no.6, 1967, art by Steve Schenfer and Joel Beck (*left*) and Bob Simmons and Niri Rose and Armando Busick (*right*); vol.1 no.7, 1967, art by unknown; two inside spreads from vol.1 no.11, 1967, art by Michael Ferar (*left*), unknown and Eve (*right*); vol.1 no.7, 1967, art by Ami Magill. *Above, clockwise from top left*: vol.1 no.7, 1967, cover photography by Paul Kagan, artwork by Mark DeVries and Hetty McGee; vol.1 no.8, 1967, back cover art by Hetty McGee; vol.1 no.10, 1967, cover art by Bob Branaman; vol.1 no.11, 1967, cover art by Steve Schenfer. *Oracle* layouts owed a spiritual (if not an actual) debt to Jugendstil. The type, lettering and images were completely integrated, often at the expense of legibility.

subdued visual form, *Oz* magazine revelled in social satire and irreverently depicted politicians, royalty and other public figures. Articles of serious political content were usually illustrated with humorous drawings and collages and by the late Sixties psychedelicized comics and graphics. In the early Seventies, however, its editors – Richard Neville, Richard Walsh and Martin Sharp – were charged with violating the obscenity laws of Australia, while over in England, Neville, Felix Dennis and Jim Anderson were arrested and tried for corrupting public morals with the publication of their infamous 'School Kids issue' featuring material deemed unacceptable. Of course, the blown-out criminal trial increased interest in the magazine and forced its designers to up the ante with even more shockingly perverse visuals, including the cover for the 'Special Pig issue' that comically skewers the legal establishment (while again showing the offending cover). *Oz* was further noteworthy for relatively sophisticated typography and a hyped-up colour palette.

The Oracle and *Oz* notwithstanding, the most salient design trait of the Underground press was its resolute sloppiness. Undergrounds obviously did not adhere to modernist grids that determined the order or hierarchy of

Clockwise from top: **Oz**, no.17, cover art by Robert Whitaker; no.35, May 1971, inside spread and cover with art by Ed Belchambler. The London-based magazine *Oz*, edited by Richard Neville and designed by Jon Goodchild, took the Underground aesthetic to the next level. While retaining a raw design look, *Oz*'s type and imagery had a sophisticated finish that toed the line between ad hoc and premeditated.

Right, **Provo**, covers
of no.10, 30 June 1966;
no.11, 15 August 1966.
Amsterdam's *Provo* was
produced in the most ad
hoc manner with typewriter
type and scrawled lettering.
It was edited by Bernard
Holtrop and Roel van Duyn
and designed and printed
by Rob Stolk.

Below from left: **The
Chicago Seed**, vol.3 no.7,
1969, cover with art by
Roslof Hobogritsgraphix
and inside spread.
Psychedelic graphics as
used in *The Chicago Seed*
demanded considerable
skill and patience despite
the fact that they were
probably produced
under the influence of
hallucinogens.

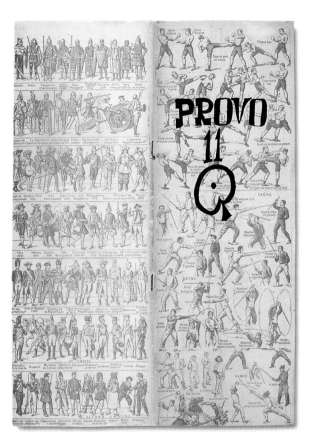

graphic elements. Whichever image made the most compelling or outrageous cover took precedence over a rival theme as the lead story, except when the news demanded undivided attention (such as, say, the 1969 invasion of Cambodia or the subsequent massacre of anti-war protesters by Ohio National Guard troops at Kent State University). Ego also figured in the process. If a layout artist did not like a particular writer, his or her story would not be given exciting graphics – and, depending on the degree of ire, even paragraphs might be mysteriously transposed. In any case, text and picture were pushed, shoved and squashed onto a page and this was true with all the Undergrounds, from *The East Village Other* to *The Chicago Seed*.

Chicago may be called the 'second city' in relation to New York, but *The Chicago Seed* was not a second rate Underground paper. While it adopted a visual language that combined elements of *The Oracle* and *The East Village Other*, it covered socio-political issues unique to Chicago, where in 1968 at the Democratic National Convention a 'police riot' broke out against the thousands of peace demonstrators who had converged on the city to protest against the Vietnam War. For many, watching the Chicago police arrest and beat protestors and innocent civilians on national TV marked a significant turning point in popular antipathy for

the war, and *The Chicago Seed* used this as an opportunity to ratchet up its editorial attacks on the power structure. Visually, the paper adhered to the newly-established youth culture codes – psychedelic lettering, rainbow split-fountain colour printing, satiric collages and ribald comic drawings – but maintained its own identity as well as being a consistent part of the Underground press genre. The raw layout style could also be attributed to the simple fact that many Underground personnel worked under the influence of marijuana, LSD and other drugs. At *The East Village Other*, methedrine, amphetamine and sometimes cocaine were dispensed like snacks throughout the paste-up session. These chemical combinations, combined with sleep deprivation, certainly took their toll on the overall quality of the layouts.

The Underground press was not limited to England and the United States. In Amsterdam, the publication *Provo*, an anarchist magazine which was the mouthpiece of the anti-war Provo movement in the Netherlands during the late Sixties, had an impact on youth culture and alternative politics. Fifteen issues were published, plus one 'extra' bulletin, several of which were quickly confiscated by the authorities. Contributors included Rob Stolk, Roel van Duyn (who became a key figure in the Amsterdam

Below from left: **The East Village Other**, vol.4 no.8, 24 January 1969, cover art by Vaughn Bode; vol.6 no.15, 14 July 1971, back cover with comic strip 'Fabulous Furry Freak Brothers' by Gilbert Shelton, edited by Jaakov Kohn. **Gothic Blimp Works**, no.2, 1969, cover art by Robert Crumb.

Underground comix were one of the most popular features in *The East Village Other*, published by Peter Leggieri and edited by Alan Katzman, evidenced by the Vaughn Bode strip on this cover, that it also published the *Gothic Blimp Works* and devoted it entirely to work by R Crumb, Gilbert Shelton, and other leading comix artists. *Gothic Blimp Works* was edited by Vaughn Bode and art-directed by Peter Mikalajunas.

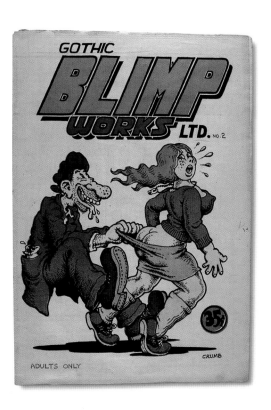

government), Auke Boersma, Hans Korteweg, Robert Jasper Grootveld, Duco van Weerlee, Constant Nieuwenhuys, Bernard Holtrop and many more transitory figures of the Amsterdam scene. The design was even more ad hoc than some of the American Underground publications, relying on typewriter type for text and roughly-scrawled drawings for visual relief.

'Underground comix' were the most original (and have proved to be the most lasting) graphic invention to emerge from youth culture's creative elite. Through an array of characters that got high, had sex, fought cops and otherwise engaged in antisocial behaviour, this genre helped to release the growing frustration of youth in relation to establishment taboos. Among the artists who had given up on the mainstream media's acceptance of their work, and lashed out against the hypocritical attitudes that neutered artistic expression in the pages of *The East Village Other*, were Robert Crumb, Vaughn Bode, Spain Rodriguez, Gilbert Shelton, Kim Deitch, Trina Robbins and Art Spiegelman. Their Underground comix were an emblematic art of alternative culture that emerged during the late Sixties and are still produced in various forms today. Given that copyright notices were either non-existent or ignored, almost every Underground newspaper in America and Europe republished these comic strips and most papers also commissioned new material from a growing troupe of up-and-coming comix artists. So popular were they that *The East Village Other* published a stand-alone monthly called *Gothic Blimp Works*, a tabloid devoted entirely to original comix. Because these were surreal pictorial narratives, they could address an audience with more explicitly controversial themes. Being a newspaper and not a comic book, *Gothic Blimp Works* circumvented distribution channels that were under the thumb of the Comics Code Authority. *Gothic Blimp Works* published only a handful of issues, but forever changed how comic books would be conceived, produced and marketed.

By 1970 the Underground press, like the culture it represented, was at the proverbial crossroads. America has a penchant for absorbing and commodifying the vanguard – outrageous hippie dress becomes expensive ready-to-wear; fine art becomes advertising art; revolutionaries become Wall Street consultants. Papers like *The East Village Other* and the *Los Angeles Free Press* had become so popular that they were, in effect, part of a new establishment. This posed the question as to whether alternative cultures could remain outside the system if it rewarded them with success. Youth culture became a viable market and the alternative music and fashion cultures were marketed by mainstream and hippie entrepreneurs. Even the emotionally-charged peace symbol became a popular piece of jewellery.

Right from top: **Los Angeles Free Press**, vol.9 no.49, 8–18 December 1972, cover art by Ron Cobb. **New York Free Press**, vol.1 no.16, 21 November 1968, cover photograph by George Prince.

The Los Angeles Free Press, edited by Art Kunkin, and *New York Free Press*, edited by S Edwards and designed by Steven Heller, relied on relatively conventional newspaper/magazine formats with standard logos and headline hierarchies. The former used Ron Cobb's cartoons as a regular feature, while the latter occasionally used studio photography such as this. Both publications were more local news-oriented than the other more cultural and political Undergrounds, albeit with an alternative slant on their subjects.

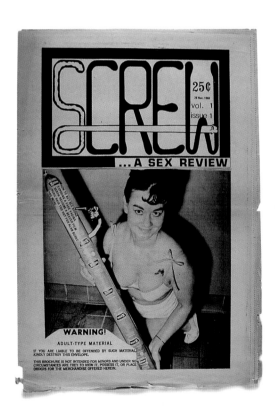

Success was a dubious achievement for the Underground because it implied the onset of maturity, and this in turn demanded a new responsibility towards readers to offer workable alternatives rather than avant-garde ravings. Where once their pages were filled with psychedelic art and rambling essays on rock groups and LSD, some now started running hard-hitting stories on city council candidates, police departments, women's rights, prison conditions and court systems. Some Undergrounds evolved into community or city newspapers, covering many of the same issues as their mainstream predecessors but through a left-of-centre lens. Others struggled to stay afloat. *The Berkeley Barb*, founded in 1966 as a radical Underground, was forced to close in 1980 when, bowing to political pressures within its community, it removed all sex advertising which, in reality, had covered a large percentage of its overheads.

The 'sex papers' were another offshoot of the Underground press which had a life and audience of its own. Spin-offs of the most commercially viable aspect of the radical Undergrounds, the sex papers attempted to balance anti-establishment rhetoric with pornographic words and images. But not everyone viewed them as part of the Underground: 'Certain papers, with tenuous links with the underground, have no scruples about exploiting the human body and the sexual act for profit,' chided critic Roger Lewis. '*Screw* and the *The New York Review of Sex* [published and art-directed by this author] print large uncensored pictures of every part of the body in every conceivable posture. The articles that accompany the photographs are unimaginative, low-grade pornography with nothing to recommend them.'[10] What Lewis does not mention, however, is that these periodicals, along with *Kiss* and *Pleasure*, were published as adjuncts to New York's leading radical Underground papers. *Kiss* was published by *The East Village Other* (and featured artwork by R Crumb), *Pleasure* was published by *Rat*, *The New York Review of Sex* (*NYRS*) was published by the *New York Free Press* and *Screw* originated and was produced in the offices of the same *Free Press*.

Each paper was conceived in response to the growing realization among the Underground publishers and editors that sex was selling their papers much more efficiently than coverage of politics or culture. It is therefore impossible to ignore the sex papers here because of the substantial and unconventional role they played within the rise and fall of the radical press. Moreover, the sex press injected a more professional design aesthetic into the Underground.

Screw, the most original and controversial of them all, was founded in 1968, the very week that Richard M Nixon was elected President of the United States. At the time, the Underground press was in the throes of its first major identity crisis. Would it continue to be 'unacceptable' in form and content, or would it evolve into a quasi-legitimate opposition? Readers were no longer buying every competing paper, but rather choosing to buy one based on their personal loyalty and preference. Only the fittest Underground papers could survive, which meant capturing the influx of advertising dollars from mainstream record companies that were promoting a range of 'alternative' rock groups. This necessitated having a comparatively large circulation and in New York *The East Village Other* had the prime readership – and thus the lion's share of advertising. After a year of success stemming from its visibility as the clarion call of the nationwide student uprisings, *Rat*'s circulation dipped sharply as did that of the *New York Free Press*. To boost readership, the Undergrounds began to publish arty photographs of naked women on their covers. The first *New York Free Press* nude showed a woman from the waist up, wearing only a gas mask (an allusion to the tear-gas attacks to which crowds of demonstrators were then being subjected). However, the *New York Free Press* felt somewhat guilty about what could be construed as sexism, so covers addressing sexual issues became more frequent. The 'End Inequitable Orgasm' cover visited a taboo subject, promised titillation, but did not exploit the female form – or so its editors hoped.

Founded by Al Goldstein (b.1936), a former editor of sensational tabloids, and Jim Buckley (b.1944), the managing editor of the *New York Free Press*, *Screw* had the avowed purpose of presenting adult sexual material in an honest, though acerbic, witty and satirical way. The Underground press had started the job of making sex a household word, but Goldstein felt it did not go far enough. He respected *Eros*, the tastefully designed hard-cover quarterly magazine which, in 1962, had reintroduced the word 'eroticism' into the vocabulary. Despite its elegant typography, created by art director Herb Lubalin (1918–81), sensual photography and smart writing, *Eros* had the temerity to challenge America's sense of prudish propriety and was forced to cease publishing when its founder Ralph Ginzburg was convicted and imprisoned on charges of sexual pandering through the mail.

Goldstein believed, conversely, that Hugh Hefner's *Playboy* magazine and the other copycat 'men's' magazines had over-idealized the female body with airbrushed photographs that made women into mannequins. So, with an Underground bravado, *Screw* attacked the establishment's puritanical moral codes; it ran un-retouched photographs of men and women *in flagrante delicto*, published the first homosexual column (and photographs) in a non-gay publication, and acerbically reviewed porn movies as though they were legitimate films.

Opposite, top row: **Eros**, no.1, Summer 1962, cover photograph by Donald Snyder; no.4, Winter 1962, inside spread photography by Ralph Hattersley. Edited by Ralph Ginzburg, *Eros* was the most alluring magazine of its day (regardless of content). Herb Lubalin's typography was impeccably elegant and layouts of such features as 'Black and White' were artful rather than sensational.

Opposite, bottom row: **Screw**, vol.1 no.1, 29 November 1969, cover and inside spread with photography by Yakoi Kusama. Edited by Al Goldstein and Jim Buckley and designed by Steven Heller, *Screw* was the opposite of *Eros* in every way. It combined the rawness of the Underground with the salaciousness of a Tijuana Bible (pornographic comic booklet from the Thirties) to produce a parody of a genre that became its own distinct genre.

The first issues of *Screw* were sloppily designed because the art director was a novice and the pre-press technology was as inadequate as its budget.[11] Headlines were cut and pasted out of type specimen books and photographs were crudely glued on to pages. Although *Screw*'s pictorial content was tame by the standards of today, it was taboo even in the late Sixties for an under-the-counter publication to show harshly lit photographs of naked men and women simulating sex – and *Screw* was sold on news-stands. Despite the 'Adults Only' warning on the cover, news dealers were surprised to find explicit sexual material inside. Some removed *Screw* from their stands rather than receive summonses (which occurred), but after a while *Screw*'s presence was assured because it sold very well. The resulting publicity stimulated grave concern among the three other leading New York Undergrounds, who feared they might lose their own tenuous hold on sex-interested readers, so each founded their own sex papers that ranged from the acceptably avant-garde to the unacceptably smutty.

The New York Review of Sex sought to bring sexual 'culture' to the Underground with a 'highbrow' alternative to *Screw* and an attempt to follow in the tradition of *Eros*. It was originally supported by Grove Press, the progressive publisher of *Evergreen Review*, a left-leaning journal devoted

Right: **Kiss**, cover of no.1, 12 May 1969. *Below from left:* **The New York Review of Sex**, vol.1 no.7, 15 June 1969, cover and inside spread photography by Mario Jorrin.

Sex sold the Undergrounds as much as politics. But given the pornography laws at the time the covers of *The New York Review of Sex*, edited by S Edwards and designed by Steven Heller, and *Kiss*, edited by Joel Fabricant and Dean A Latimer and designed by Peter Mikalajunas, were prohibited from showing frontal nudity.

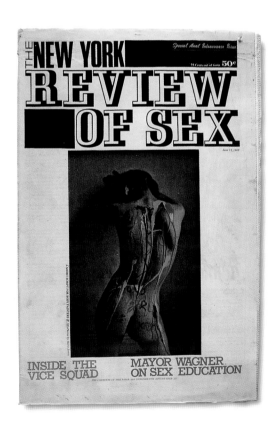

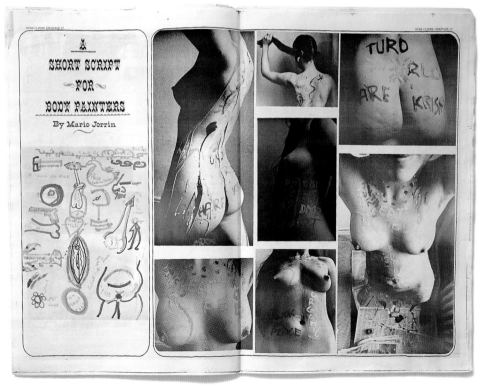

to politics, literature and the arts, which had suffered the legal fallout from its distribution of the Scandinavian erotic film masterpiece *I Am Curious Yellow* and also published serious erotic fiction by the likes of Henry Miller and William Burroughs. *The East Village Other*'s contender, *Kiss*, made no bones about being sexploitative but it did so with characteristic irony by mixing explicit hardcore photography with frames from the raunchy work of its comix artists. In fact, its first 'bust' (arrest) was occasioned by Crumb's cartoon that satirized incest, showing a family engaging in an orgiastic act. *Pleasure*, *Rat*'s publication, forsook any pretence of socially redeeming values, and published a diet of stock photographs designed only to titillate. Each of these publications exploited the body to nourish the body politic by generating much-needed operating income for their host publications. However, the plan failed.

Screw's readership surged as Underground papers generally lost circulation. The circulation gains of *The New York Review of Sex*, *Kiss* and *Pleasure* caused dips in the *New York Free Press* and *Rat* revenues, while *The East Village Other* remained constant for a while longer. After the first few issues of *The New York Review of Sex*, the *Free Press* was forced to fold. A year or so after the publication of *Pleasure*, *Rat* was taken over by radical feminists who were incensed by the magazine's content. But just being a sex paper did not ensure

success, either. Guilty for having caused the demise of its host, *The New York Review of Sex* added the word 'politics' to its name in an attempt to cover cultural and political aspects of the sexual revolution but folded after twenty issues owing to lack of readers and continued legal harassment. Two years after the advent of *Kiss*, the staff of *The East Village Other* decided that a sex paper was not the answer to their woes and threw their energies back into the main paper. However, by 1973, the majority of readers had forsaken it owing to an increasingly schizophrenic editorial direction, and it had also been overtaken by films and television. In 1974, inertia killed *The East Village Other* and most of the other Underground papers as well.

In Amsterdam, the other hotbed, so to speak, of sexual liberation, Willem De Ridder and William Levy published *Suck* in 1970, a *Screw*-inspired sexpaper that injected a more aesthetic sensibility into the mix of sex and sexual politics. Perhaps the most exquisite of its offshoots was a one-off publication called *Wet Dreams Festival*, with plastic-coated paper covers and an extensive collection of explicit texts and photographs documenting the two legendary Wet Dream Festival happenings organized by *Suck* magazine and held in Amsterdam in November 1970 and October 1971. William Levy and designer Anthon Beeke also published a special issue of *Suck*, titled *The Virgin Sperm Dancer*, an ecstatic journey photographed by Ginger Gordon of a boy transformed

Below from left: **The Virgin Sperm Dancer**, cover and inside spread from 1970 issue, with photography by Ginger Gordon. *The Virgin Sperm Dancer* was edited by William Levy. It was an offshoot of the Dutch magazine *Suck* and was designed by Anthon Beeke to have the same cinematic impact as a film.

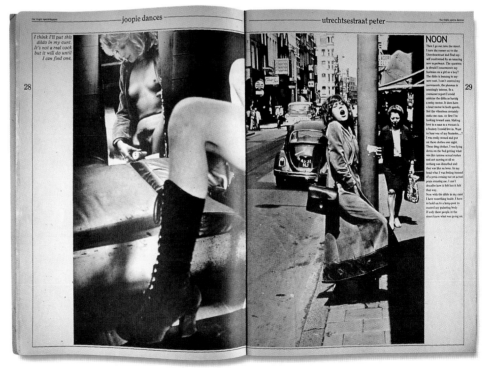

into a girl for one day only, and 'her' erotic adventures in Amsterdam.

After almost ten years of insurgent publishing of both Underground and sex papers, there was a brief interregnum between the death of one and birth of the next wave of alternative periodicals. Into the vacuum came thousands of 'zines' – small, independent, handmade, photocopied publications produced to satisfy the quirky and obsessive passions of individuals reaching out to other like-minded souls (and the subject of many books already). Parallel to the rise of zines, a few novice publishers began a post-Underground publication renaissance with niche newspapers and magazines that covered the developments within the new subcultures. The most outrageous of these was the Punk movement – a late twentieth-century aesthetic and political, social and philosophical revolution against the status quo. The movement was reactionary in its rejection of the left/hippie idealism and aesthetics and was defined by nihilism, anarchy and a quasi-religious devotion to the concept of 'DIY' (Do-It-Yourself) as the solution to all problems on all levels.

Although guitar-powered rock 'n' roll and angst-laden lyrics defined Punk rock, periodicals such as *Punk*, *Slash*, *Sniffin' Glue*, *Search and Destroy* and *The Rocker*, as well as countless quick copy shops that produced inexpensive offset printing, also propagated Punk poetry, aesthetics and celebrity. Punk zines were the embodiment of the 'Anybody can do it! You don't need them!' attitude in visual form, and Punk graphics are what established the Punk aesthetic. Torn paper edges and misspelled typewriter typography were the visual equivalent of a loud, out-of-tune, slashing power chord or stained clothes from the charity shop.

The term 'Punk' was arguably coined by the flagship of the movement, *Punk* magazine, which premiered in New York in January 1976. *Punk* was a clarion and a provocateur. Its co-founder and designer, John Holmstrom (b.1953), says the magazine used the word 'Punk', which denoted petty thugs and jailhouse paramours, to distinguish its music from syrupy pseudo-psychedelic hippie pop of the post-Sergeant Pepper era. 'Without *Punk* magazine there probably would have been no "Punk rock" and no Punk movement,' says Holmstrom, insisting that his co-founder, Legs McNeil, had only a vague knowledge that it was already a musical term. 'Legs audaciously called himself a "Punk". And, through the magazine, he mapped out a lifestyle that defined what a punk is: the dress and values. The English Punk movement was inspired by our look and ideas.'[12]

English punks will certainly argue that bands were in the Punk mode before The Ramones hit England. Malcolm Maclaren and Vivienne Westwood caused a stir with The

Clockwise from top left: **Punk**, vol.1 no.3, April 1976, cover art by John Holmstrom; vol.1 no.4, July 1976, cover art by John Holmstrom; vol.1 no.10, Summer 1977, cover art by Bobby London; vol.1 no.12, January 1978, cover art by John Holmstrom; vol.1 no.8, March 1977, cover art by Steve Taylor. *Opposite*: vol.1 no.1, January 1975, cover art by John Holmstrom. *Punk*, designed and edited by Holmstrom, was borne of a comic strip sensibility. The covers and interiors were almost entirely hand-lettered in a DIY manner. Although its design was linked to that of the Underground press, *Punk* sought to distance itself from hippie culture following instead a stark urban-graffiti style.

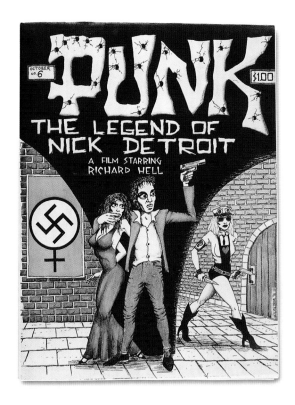

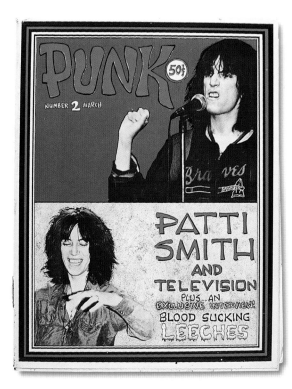

Sex Shop as early as 1974. But in America *Punk* was the glue that held the disparate traits together under one banner. *Punk* was quintessential DIY, produced for less than nothing and fuelled by the sweat of its founders. Since they could not afford typesetting, the lettering was methodically rendered by hand – every word in every article, caption and advertisement – in a comic-book style by John Holmstrom. The cover of issue no.1 featured Holmstrom's cross-hatched, comic drawing of Lou Reed as Frankenstein, which established the magazine's bawdy illustration style. The overall design format was clunky – as stiff as the brittle, heavy white newsprint on which it was printed – yet it had a visual energy all its own. *Punk* did not start the torn-paper, ransom-note mannerism that eventually became the hallmark of British Punk. With Holmstrom's precisionist hand-lettering, it was a cross between an Underground paper and a fanzine.

Holmstrom tried to make *Punk* look different by rejecting Underground design elements. In contrast to flowery lettering, *Punk* interiors employed a stark, simple, black-and-white look – the look of urban graffiti. As a counterpoint to hippie illustrations, which were airbrushed, over-rendered and silly – naked women with butterfly wings and caterpillars puffing on hookahs on top of mushrooms –

Holmstrom's crude drawings contributed to what he calls a 'crummy-looking' magazine. However, he did not sacrifice legibility and used 'a lot of straight lines' in layouts to make the hand-lettering look orderly. He insisted that the magazine must not look as if anything was done unintentionally. And, most importantly, it had to echo the music: fast, primitive and loud. Despite his antipathy for the hippie style, he wanted *Punk* to look as dirty and disreputable as the leftist newspapers of the Sixties. 'I wanted to take chances. I wanted the magazine to be as unpredictable as the early MAD comics – you'd never know what format *Punk* would be printed in, or what weird thing might appear in it.'[13]

The photoplay comic genre, which helped to give *Punk* its personality, was borrowed from Spanish-language, pulp-romance magazines. The form allowed *Punk*'s artists to create a unique cinematic sensibility using punk rockers and their friends as the cast of characters. *The Legend of Nick Detroit* (*Punk* no.6) was a feature-length gangster movie on the printed page. There was no rock writing, no record reviews, no music news, no interviews in the issue – just photos, drawings and captions. And it was all in black and white. It failed miserably at the news-stands. Nevertheless, it was a coup.

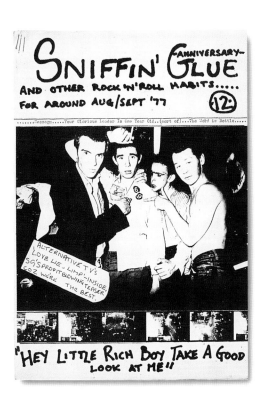

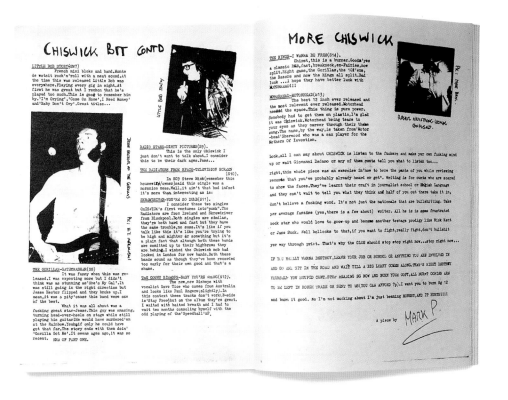

American Punk was more cultural than political, while British Punk steered towards the hardcore Left. Even so, *Punk* magazine stubbornly refused to change its emphasis from rock to politics. Holmstrom claims, 'We were right-wing at the time, mostly because the status quo was left-wing. It was one more hippie thing we were rebelling against.'[14] But the main thrust was always the music as a panacea for all ills. Punks took a music culture that had become sedate and boring and injected excitement and energy into it. They knocked down the barriers that kept people from creating their own music and art, and encouraged them to do it themselves. But DIY was not a priori amateurish. DIY and professionalism were mutually exclusive. In fact, *Punk* went from a two- and three-colour quarter-fold to a standard magazine format with a slick four-colour cover, and by the end of its run it was printing 25,000 copies, with sales of around 15,000. In early 1979, three-and-a-half years after it began and on the eve of its anniversary issue, *Punk* magazine folded due to financial difficulties as well as the changing times. *Punk* so resolutely defined the Punk scene that it left no room to morph into something more lasting.

Strands of Punk DNA were also found in such DIY periodicals as *Sniffin' Glue,* published in England in 1977 and edited by Mark Perry, which became the archetype of British Punk style because it was resolutely unprofessional, completely handwritten in a raw, scratchy scrawl without any of the tutored nuances that Holmstrom had invested in *Punk*. Produced essentially on a photocopier, *Sniffin' Glue*'s pages were haphazardly laid out, without an iota of concern for legibility. Similarly, the San Francisco-based *Search & Destroy: New Wave Cultural Research* (which eventually evolved into *RE:Search*), edited by V Vale from 1977 to 1979, revelled in its total disregard for design tenets. Its pages, with type composed on an IBM Selectric typewriter, looked similar to the broadsheets posted on lamp-posts and US mailboxes raving about government conspiracies and UFOs.

At the other end of the design spectrum *Wet*, which began in San Francisco in 1976 (lasting until 1981) as a four-page zine with a design 'grid' by designer John Van Hamersveld (b.1941), developed a graphic style which, while alternative, clearly aspired to be professional. 'To my mind, *Wet* definitely was not punk,' states Leonard Koren (b.1948), the publisher and editor, adding that he 'strove for a kind of sensuality and sense of absurdity that was too self-aware for Punk. If anything, *Wet* was proto-New Wave.'[15] Koren does, however, admit to a kinship with DIY: '"Cheap is good" were, in fact, *Wet*'s guiding bywords.'

Los Angeles's first Punk paper, *Slash*, published by Steve Samiof (b.1950), began eighteen months after *Wet*. Although *Wet* did not overtly inform *Slash*'s aesthetic, which was more akin to Underground press design, Koren believes that *Wet* contributed to Samiof's decision to go off in the publishing direction. The anti-design of the Sixties pervaded *Slash*, and to any outsider whose reference is from that era it appeared to be a less political offshoot. Yet it included its own latter-day Underground comic strip, 'Jimbo' by Gary Panter (b.1950), who by virtue of this platform established his 'ratty line' as the quintessential Punk comic style.

Punk influenced a wide range of cultural activity from music, such as Grunge, Hip Hop and Heavy Metal, as well as films like *The Road Warrior* (1982), to fashions (leather and torn shirts), to toys (action figures), and even professional wrestling. Holmstrom grandiloquently speculates that the whole 'bad taste' trend in movies was Punk-inspired. However, as Punk fashion was co-opted by marketers and entrepreneurs, not unlike the fate of the hippie lifestyle, *Punk* and other seminal periodicals in the US and England relinquished the field to contemporary diehard esoteric descendants such as *Maximum Rock 'n' Roll*, *Punk Planet*, *Hit List* and *Ray Gun*, one of the bibelots of the digital age.

The periodicals addressing politics, sex, drugs and rock 'n' roll met one of three fates: either they closed because they were too outrageous, or because they had outlived their period of outrage; or survived because the culture now accepts what was once outrageous. Just like novelty itself, the avant-garde has a limited shelf-life before it is taken over by the society it had wanted to shock. In a consumer society, where the flow of ideas through the media is increasing as new technologies expand, it is predictable that the predominant themes of the Sixties Underground movement would ultimately become a recipe for acceptability.

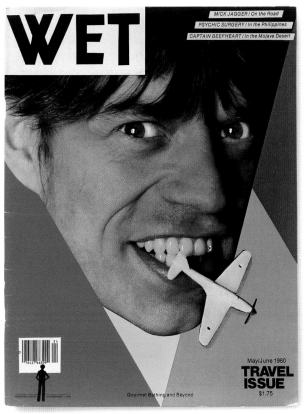

EMIGRE No19

Starting Fro

Zero

Price: $7.95

EMIGRE

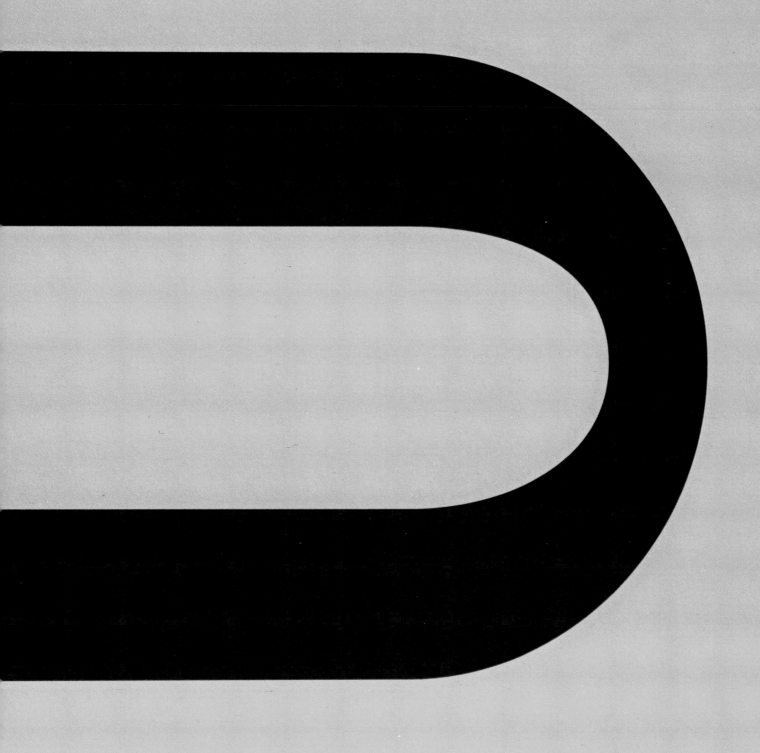

9

Pixel Pirates:
The Desktop Era

By the mid-Eighties it was increasingly difficult for alternative periodicals to be truly unacceptable. Mass media had eclipsed the former 'Underground press' as a source of taboo. Films, television and video had become the vehicles for what had earlier been a cultural underbelly. The sexual revolution was the most mainstream of the formerly aberrant counter-culture movements. Previously such contraband periodicals as *Eros* and *Screw* were subject to harassment and arrest, but by the Nineties subject matter that was equally or more extreme was not only apparent in films from major Hollywood studios but also on television – first on cable and then network TV – when programmers became aware of the public's increasing tolerance of voyeurism and salaciousness. What was once offensive is now vernacular; what was once odious is now common popular fare.

After the Sixties Underground died, alternative periodicals were no longer fuelled by revolutionary rhetoric, political bombast or even lewd pornography. 'Alternative' simply meant they were not being published by mainstream publishing houses. Although social critics spoke of culture wars between the haves and the have-nots, religionists and secularists, conservatives and liberals, these conflicts were fought in mass media and mainstream venues, including on public television and in daily newspapers and intellectual journals. Arguably Sixties anti-establishment periodicals had succeeded so well in altering the standards of acceptability that very little remained shocking in terms of form or content. The typical news-stand (in many large cities, at least) had become a veritable smorgasbord of slick magazines with content that had once been considered offensive and unsavoury.

This did not mean that alternative periodicals had given up as laboratories; it just implied that the essence of experimentation had changed from what it was during the Dada or Surrealist epochs (see Chapters 3, 4 and 7). The newer wave of independent periodicals, to be surveyed in this chapter, may not have been as politically motivated but they were passionately concerned with formal issues, notably type and composition. With the onset of mass computer technology, many of the standards and tenets that had governed graphic design and typography were becoming available to all. Experimenters were required to make sense of the new technologies and their effects on page design and composition – and this ultimately reflected political and social shifts in art, culture and mass communications.

Alternative periodicals founded between the mid-Eighties and the mid-Nineties may not have threatened social or political disruption, but a few of them upset the fundamental rules that governed graphic design and advertising, and in this sense they extend the legacy of the rational modernists (see Chapter 5). Radicalism in print was about destabilizing a post-war design ethic or 'rightness of form' that was built on a foundation of rationalism, minimalism and modernism. This was known as New Graphic Design (or the Swiss International Style because it started in Zurich) and it proffered a so-called universal graphic vocabulary built on grid systems. This approach was eventually adopted throughout the corporate world because it had the virtue of neutrality in an increasingly multinational (and multilingual) corporate culture. As a counterpoint, young designers rejected such regimentation in favour of relaxation of grids, provocative clutter and visual anarchy – a critical mass of reaction that became a symbol of the information age.

The impulse to break steadfast rules was, of course, not new. Every action fosters reaction, and each new methodology invites its opposite. The Bauhaus rejected archaic tradition just as Sixties Underground designers eschewed the rational New Typography. In many of the periodicals surveyed in earlier chapters, form was consequently altered as a means of symbolizing *and* expressing new ideas. During the Eighties, new technology ushered in a need for change while the personal computer arrived at a propitious moment in the history of typography. As a consequence, altered and degraded type and typography was made possible through handy computer programs. The results were something of a frontal attack on a perceived power elite that was symbolically represented in the media by official typefaces and sanitized layouts.

Facing bankruptcy as an aesthetic system, the International Style was under attack by those designers who, tired of its monotony, sought new ways of guiding the eye over a page as well as developing alternative textual hierarchies. In Basel during the Seventies, the designer Wolfgang Weingart (b.1941) developed a system of typographic reordering that pushed graphic design into its next philosophical and stylistic stage by creating shifts in weight and size to re-exploit type's expressive potential. On the surface his approach appeared chaotic yet it was built on logic. Words and sentences were emphasized within a phrase through abrupt changes in type-size and colour that helped guide the reader towards the essence of a particular message. Weingart's experiments were often laboriously rendered using hot metal or phototype composition, but it was a signpost for the computer advancements that would soon arrive.

Phototype enabled designers to tinker freely with size, shape and spacing but the real impact of change was not completely felt until the advent of Apple's designer-friendly Macintosh desktop computer and such design programs as PageMaker, Quark, Fontographer and others. Technology has a greater or lesser consequence in many of the publications

Previous page: **Emigre**, detail of no.19, 1991, cover design by Rudy VanderLans, with type design by Barry Deck.

Opposite, top: **Hard Werken**, no.7, May–June 1980, cover art by Henk Elenga. Holland's *Hard Werken*, a pre-digital review that combined Punk and New Wave design styles was edited by Gerard Hadders, Rick Vermeulen, Henk Elenga and others. It espoused innovative methods and ideas that would emerge with the new technology.

Opposite, bottom: **Fetish**, vol.1 no.2, Fall 1980, cover with photography by Jere Cockrell and inside spread. *Fetish* was one of a handful of 'culture tabs' that prefigured the typographic gyration and discordance, combining Dada and Constructivism, that became common during the digital age. *Fetish* was designed by Jane Kosstrin, Terence Main and David Sterling, edited by Susan Klein and art directed by Doublespace, Inc.

discussed in this book, but the revolutionary impact of the computer exceeds the more incremental evolutionary shifts from hot metal to cold type. The new hardware and software truly transformed the ways in which graphic designers interacted with content. The word 'interact' (the mantra of the digital age) is indeed apt because a new breed of graphic designer, working with digital tools, could compose type on the screen without the aid or interference of other craft persons. This, most importantly, enabled the designer to be both manipulator of form and author of content.

At the outset of the digital revolution in the mid-Eighties, print and multimedia platforms became hothouses of experimentation as the primitive aspects of the new technology, such as raw bitmapped type, saw technological weakness turn into viable applications. Over time, improved technology and experimental activity merged into a visual language that was at once metaphorical and functional. Moreover, a new style emerged that was characterized by multiple layers of discordant typefaces, sometimes integrated with imagery. While this discordance was akin to Victorian typography of the late 1890s, when jobbing printers deliberately mixed dissimilar typefaces together in the service of fashion and function, the new digital typography was concerned with stretching the definition of legibility and readability. This led to a method known as

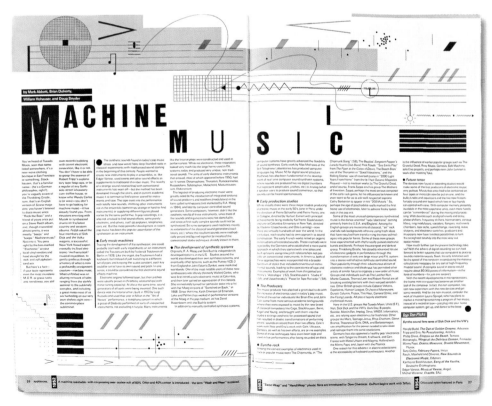

Deconstructive typography: a style inspired by contemporary linguistic theory that proffered an analytic breakdown of texts visualized through changes in typographic size and composition for the purpose of showing disparities in many social and cultural standards. Texts were not actually deconstructed in a literary sense but designers created a style that used certain computer programs to produce type that looked as if it had been through a Magimix. This approach was common with so-called 'culturetabs' (local and national tabloid newspapers and magazines devoted to arts and culture), such as Holland's *Hard Werken* and New York's *Fetish*, which were crossed between the Do-It-Yourself ad hoc-ism and postmodern New Wave-ism that preceded the digital aesthetic to come, once designers felt more comfortable with the personal computer. Both periodicals addressed cultural phenomena and artistic developments of their time. Each represented 'auteurship', whereby designers who were presumed to provide design services to editors and publishers were, in fact, taking on the roles of editor, publisher and content provider. Both magazines suffered from a lack of professional editorial expertise but conversely were compelling because they were unfettered by the rules. They further established a visual language that served as a bridge between the end of the New Wave and the beginning of the new computer age. These magazines were ripe for experimenting with new technologies yet each folded within a few years of the Macintosh's invention.

Initially the Macintosh was used with the timidity of a child playing Etch-A-Sketch but gradually designers, impatient to surmount barricades, geared up for a radical shift in their practices. The Macintosh provided a tool for the average designer but for visionaries it offered the potential for creating new visual languages. In this sense it enabled entrepreneurial designers, such as Rudy VanderLans (b.1955) and Zuzana Licko (b.1961) to create their own magazine, *Emigre*.

The most progressive of the digitally composed magazines, *Emigre* began in 1984 as a tabloid covering the arts in northern California. It was neither culturally nor politically rebellious in an ideological sense, and comparisons to Dada periodicals would be inaccurate. But it was the first dedicated graphic design journal of the digital age to address the need for change in graphic design. Unlike Jan Tschichold's one issue of *Typographische Mitteilungen*, which attempted the same goal in 1925 (see Chapter 6), *Emigre* published four times yearly (in this incarnation)[1] for over a decade and eventually developed a unique typographic style originally based on primitive bitmapped, default typefaces endemic to the new Macintosh. But as a general publication *Emigre* limped along, perfecting its typographic

Below: **Shift**, cover of vol.3 no.4, 1989. The arts journal *Shift* was edited by Anne Marie MacDonald. Designer Rudy VanderLans introduced Zuzana Licko's experimental digital typeface Matrix, destined to become one of the emblematic typefaces of the era, to the magazine.

Opposite, left: **Emigre**, cover of no.4, 1986, study 'Time Transmission' for a stage photo event by Henk Elenga (1985). This early issue of *Emigre*, which was published and art directed by Rudy VanderLans, is a bridge between the culture tabloid and design clarion it became, and introduces the first bitmapped typeface, designed by Zuzana Licko.

Opposite, right: **Emigre**, cover of no.24, 1992, type design by Barry Deck. By no.24, Licko and other type designers were regularly contributing to the magazine. The 'Neomania' addressed how the new typography was being integrated into popular culture.

primitivism for a handful of issues until VanderLans and Licko decided to recast the magazine into a dedicated graphic design journal, a fanzine for type and typography. At the time VanderLans pointed out that he was more of an admiring onlooker than a trendsetter. None the less *Emigre* became the crucible of unconventional and anti-modernist graphic design.

VanderLans and Licko were intrepid entrepreneurs. They had already designed a number of periodicals, including *Shift*, an arts magazine that made VanderLans realize that to publish his own was double the fun because he was able to make all the important decisions. So, they founded *Emigre* magazine; three years later (from 1987–9) Emigre Graphics (later incorporated in 1994 as Emigre Inc.), was used to sell

and promote typefaces developed for the magazine. They also started a digital type foundry, which they called Emigre Fonts. *Emigre*, the magazine, promoted their typographic wares and propagated their design faith; Emigre Fonts introduced some of the earliest and quirkiest dot-matrix and, as the technology improved, high-resolution digital typefaces. *Emigre* magazine showcased the leading proponents and exponents of anti-modernist typography as well as student designers who challenged the canonical rules of modernism by busting pages into illegible, abstract fragments.

Emigre was a significant phenomenon in graphic design because it provoked both militant opposition and slavish

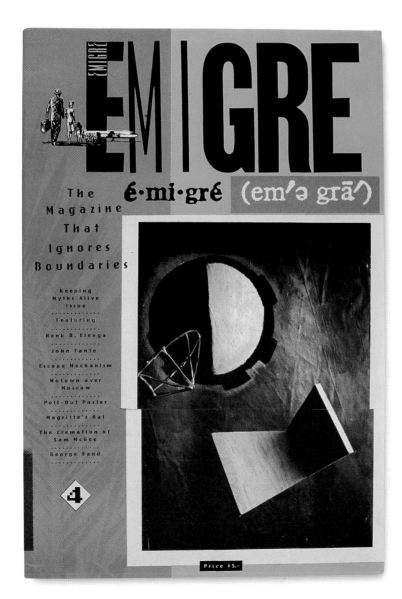

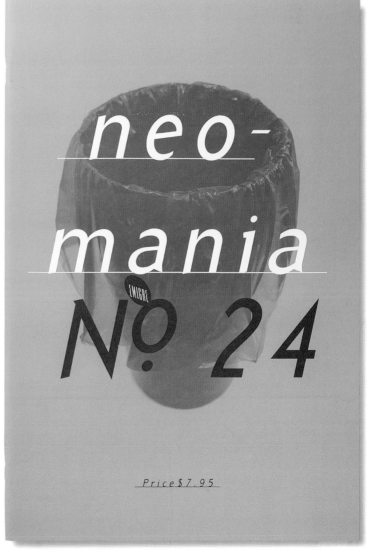

EMIGRE Nº19:
Starting From Zero

Emigre

Ó

Startin
g From
Zero

and standardization. In the past, it had been claimed that the machine was used to express the fables of fashion victims who chose historical motif for ornament. A truly utilitarian art, they argued, would be based on an accurate appraisal of mechanical production in order to develop the truest, purest mechanical aesthetic. Standardization and streamlining were the key to this approach.

Towards a new order

Walter Gropius is the best known ideologue of the International Style, but he was only one of a phalanx of artists espousing the new art. He promoted a new unity where architecture became the center. Here, the fine arts served the crafts, which furnished the building with all its fittings and ornament. Theo van Doesburg was an important theorist. Neo-plasticism was concerned with the hard-line geometric truth behind all human production - both artistic and industrial. El Lissitzky and Laszlo Moholy-Nagy were two of the major practitioners of the new Neo-plasticism or Constructivism. What they shared was the desire to transcend national styles, a response to a new technology through their art. Early in the Modern movement, these artists were still developing what can be identified as parochial styles. But their theory was well ahead of their practice. They were working towards a new order even through the anarchy of Dada and the concrete poets.

In 1928, which was early in the development of Modernism, the first major manifesto on modern design was published by Jan Tschichold, called Die Neue Typographie. As with most radical movements, their more extreme ideals were emerged first only to be watered down in practice. In Tschichold's case, he was to become one of the finest classical designers, overturning nearly all of his early theories. His propaganda for the International Style, however, was to remain influential in Europe and even the USA long after the war. Die Neue Typographie advocated a new approach to typographic design, because modern designers were working in a new age. Tschichold rejected the printed tradition from the position of style, however, not of function. So what was the new typography according to Tschichold?

KEITH ROBERTSON
Zero The will to eradicate the past with a new set of values and establish a new age in the Modernist mythology we inherit in the art books. The Modernists were political ideologues who rewrote history with a new brush. It was the Bauhaus groupies and Constructivists who designed a radical new workers' paradise and these movements helped create a new age; a future where the past would no longer be recycled because the new theory exposed the past as corrupt and outmoded. Theory was above all a belief that justified action. Starting from zero was not the obsession of the Dada anarchists nor the naive optimism of the Futurists. 'Starting from zero' was the catch-phrase of one of the most influential, opinionated and ultimately conservative groups of architects and designers who were ideologically working out theories of functionalism in design. Here was design governed by an idea.

Much of the nineteenth century had to do with coming to terms with the Machine Age. John Ruskin and William Morris criticized nineteenth century British design and manufacture for their destruction with the materials of manufacture and utilitarianism. Reeling after the death and destruction of the First World War, it is not surprising that the next generation should take a harder line, apply the Modernist theory to their art, and be suprement creating a bold new future. They, after all, created the new Modernism and called it the 'International Style' - it was international because it transcended the parochial national styles and traditions. It was the new art that repressed that which was universal in the world - the new technology of mass production

1. It was essentially simple and pure design in harmony with the modern world.
2. Asymmetry replaced symmetry because it was more functional, reflecting the more complex rhythms of the modern age.
3. Only sans serif typefaces were efficient communicators of modern information. Serifs were relegated to the historians' scrap heap.
4. Where greater emphasis was needed, he insisted on using different weights of type (e.g. bold, demi-bold, light) rather than different faces and even point sizes.

There was also emerging a new emphasis on "objective" and "scientific" approaches to the page grid - one planned less by tradition (the golden section) and more by mathematics. The mathematical grid can be most clearly identified in the early designs of Theo Ballmer. The radical beginnings of the Modern movement started with the mad fruit salads of point sizes and faces of Dada and the bold asymmetry of Tschichold, Bayer and Moholy-Nagy. Slowly, however, there was a formalization and ossification of the Modern movement, culminating in Switzerland after the war.

Helvetica Hel-

---

fairly simple messages to convey, the philosophical approach, complicating them, makes them more interesting. Another approach to design when you have very complex messages to convey is to synthesise and simplify them. **Kathy:** Every project is different and requires a different kind of treatment. Once you leave Cranbrook, you have to be capable of doing the range of design approaches. **Ed:** Right! And nobody is advocating this 'overstating' approach for a manual. For, let's say, brain surgery. This 'overstated' approach frequently is done for things that are cultural messages that would include a time, place, date and mood, and where there isn't really anything in the information that's very complicated. But the culture that surrounds it, the context, is very complex, and that is what's put into these pieces. **! Baby cries !**

Emigre: Part of the work produced at Cranbrook is explained as a reaction against Modernist ideas. In the book Cranbrook Design: The New Discourse, it is stated that there are "serious doubts about the function of the International Style as a means of visual communication," and that students have "challenged the sterility of this 'universal design'." But most of the work that you do here, in a reaction to Modernist ideas, is work that is played out in very ideological projects. It is not played out, for instance, in corporate identities, which is really where, in your eyes, Modernism has failed. The Cranbrook book shows posters for the most part; there is not one corporate identity shown. **Kathy:** In the above part of the book there are several logotypes. But yes, we really chose to publish the more polemical work. People came to Cranbrook after doing very systematic, program-driven work as professional designers. The idea is that during the two years at Cranbrook you can involve yourself in more personal, more culturally oriented work. One thing that might not show up, but is certainly embedded in my own personal process, and I think it probably comes out in a lot of the critiques I give of work, was in an ongoing project called the 'Vernacular Message Sequence.' This project was more or less the foundation of our approach to graphic design, although we didn't show too many examples of this in the book. This project's sequence goes from the extremely analytical, reductivist approach, where you are working on a message analysis and running up with hierarchies of importance to the entry point, before proceeding to the more creative expressive personal phases of the project. The project covers the full range, from the highly objective to the highly subjective. I believe that today, everybody learns this in undergraduate school, or has learned it on the job, before they come to Cranbrook, so we don't spend too much time doing that anymore. It's interesting to have this thinking. It might not be visible in the final manifestation, but hopefully, as you approach the context, as you are reading it, you will get an intuitive sense of that structure. Nobody is following grids much, correctly, but that thinking is embedded in our students' methodologies.

Scott: Are you saying that it might be interesting to see some work produced here that would challenge a more systematic approach? **Emigre:** Yes, I would find it interesting to see the experimental work that is done here be applied to, let's say, a huge corporate identity, instead of posters only. **Scott:** I think it is possible. It's one of many things possible, but it doesn't necessarily have to be studied here. Many of us have come to Cranbrook to more or less de-professionalize, and that means also ceasing to work on systematic projects for a while, to give our brain cells a little bit of a break and to look into other directions. **Kathy:** Scott Santoro has taken the experiments of his student work and is beginning to apply them to his professional work. Of course it is not quite as radical, but that is because he is working with different parameters, with strict program criteria. **Emigre:** But most of the work done by Cranbrook graduates is still for art institutions or culturally oriented projects. **Kathy:** Not all of it is, but yes, you will see that an awful lot of the work in the book is for somewhat culturally connected clients. One thing we talk about a lot here is the message, and how it is the designer's duty to take somebody else's message and give form to it, and how your design is only as interesting as the message. So one thing that people do when they leave here is look for the interesting clients who have something worth saying, as opposed to, for instance, discount shoe stores. If it's banal going in, it's going to be banal coming out, no matter how fine a designer you are. So on the one hand it's a process of natural selection. The work of the people that leave here is more appropriate for culturally connected things, but they're also very consciously seeking out interesting, worthy clients.

For prior orientations, you are at.

Page 1
8 »»

(Where continue)

Henk Elenga is one of the founding members of the Dutch design group Hard Werken. He moved to California in 2011 to open the "L.A. Desk" of Hard Werken in Hollywood. Although he became a well-known figure for his operations in graphic and interiors design, Elenga has been involved in theatre, video performance art, and photography. His photographic works have been published around the world. Among the many projects that make Elenga's work so unique, he has designed numerous album covers.

"Creativity at its deepest, is a return to a primary pro-cess rather than a response to external stimuli. My choice of using photography, in the artistic process, is only for formalization and styli-zation.

Henk
Elenga

»

the end

devotion, spawning fierce argument and uncompromising loyalty: 'The debate about the future of graphic design and typography ignited within its pages has traveled to the farthest outposts of the profession, and the landscape would look very different without it,' wrote design critic Rick Poynor.[2]

VanderLans's policy was to celebrate experimental forms of typography that the established trade magazines, *Communication Arts*, *Graphis* and *Print*, overlooked either by ignorance or design. Yet *Emigre* was more than a *salon de refusé*; instead, it featured the work of progressives such as Ed Fella, Nick Bell, Barry Deck, Mr Keedy and others who refused to accept convention. In issue no.19 of 1991, for example, VanderLans asked the question: Does all experimentation in graphic design eventually lead to the simplification of graphic design? In this issue, which was entitled 'Starting from Zero', he provided an answer. The entire publication was set in only one typeface, the emblematic font of the Nineties, Template Gothic designed by Barry Deck (b.1962). All the copy was ranged left, which was VanderLans's gesture towards Swiss modernism. Otherwise this was a uniquely daring typographic issue that seemed to parody the modernist spirit of economy.

VanderLans did not exercise conventional editorial control over *Emigre*'s content. Because editing would compromise the integrity of the material, contributors had a free hand in word and design. He never rejected work on aesthetic grounds (only from personal preference) which, as Poynor points out, made the magazine 'exciting and unpredictable; it also makes it tremendously variable'.[3] VanderLans's *laissez-faire* editorial policy resulted in rambling interviews and portfolios by neophyte designers who had yet to test their mettle. He also celebrated veterans who had turned from the tried-and-true towards the experimental. In issue no.17, 1991, Fella, a former 'commercial artist' who had worked for the automobile industry in Detroit and who in retirement had developed a uniquely artful form of hand-lettering and type design, became *Emigre*'s resident guru. Working alongside Fella was an international array of rising stars: VanderLans devoted entire issues to students from hothouse art schools such as Cranbrook (issue no.10, 1988), and daring young mavericks such as Alan Hori (issue no.12, 1989). Critics said that *Emigre* was disjointed and indulgent, yet the comparatively sizeable readership for a design magazine (hovering around 36,000) did not seem to mind.

Massimo Vignelli (b.1931), the veteran modernist designer, dismissed *Emigre*'s typography as 'garbage' and even this author wrote it off as a blip in the continuum of graphic design history.[4] Such antipathy was not entirely a knee-jerk reaction to the new, but it nevertheless revealed the growing schism between young and old, modernist and postmodernist generations. While the criticism focused on *Emigre*'s formal and utilitarian application, the real agenda was discomfort with change because it signalled unnerving changes in the profession. The *Emigre* 'style' trumpeted the obsolescence of older methods. Its message was that stasis is the hobgoblin of creativity and progress in art and design is axiomatic, even if the baton is not smoothly passed. The new approaches promoted by *Emigre* encouraged a re-evaluation of older aesthetics and the magazine became a touchstone for progress.

Eventually, though, the magazine provided templates for mimicry. Regardless of how determined *Emigre* was to forge new directions, VanderLans and Licko were incapable of preventing appropriation. And, as proprietors of a type foundry, they relied on such appropriation to earn their living. The cultural feeding frenzy that overtook the *Emigre* 'style' was predictable. What *Emigre* initiated was taken up by scores of mainstream, fashion-conscious media – from magazines to MTV. Eventually, *Emigre* outgrew its experimental cocoon. The style became the common way to communicate with the youth of the time. For some, this was the goal; for others, becoming acceptable was an insurmountable barrier to expressive development.

In 1995, after more than a decade of continuous independent publishing, VanderLans pre-empted *Emigre*'s own obsolescence and thwarted an internal economic crisis by radically changing the size of the publication from an expansive (and expensive) tabloid to a smaller, more conventional news magazine format. For the first time, *Emigre* accepted outside advertising and added more advertisements promoting its own typefaces. In short, *Emigre* became a catalogue for Emigre Fonts with its editorial content sandwiching the promotion. In an attempt to sell more typefaces the magazine was also mailed free to subscribers.

Given the slick paper, the new *Emigre* covers took on a more professional look and feel. While retaining many of the experimental typographics, notably Elliott Earls's issue no.48, some covers, such as issue nos. 40 and 48, reflected the *au courant* styles (which *Emigre* helped to foster). Issue no.56 even looked like a high-tech computer catalogue. In fact, the entire issue was devoted to all the computer equipment that *Emigre* had used and discarded during the past decade – an ironic and curiously poignant mini-history of the digital revolution.

Since the change in size, *Emigre* has struggled to find a distinct editorial identity; it has, however, matured and is more strictly edited at the expense of its earlier anything-goes experimental stance, and has become more polished as a result. VanderLans continues to design each issue independently of the next, never sticking to a single, overriding graphic format. He also routinely develops

Opposite: **Emigre**, no.19, 1991, cover, inside spreads and back cover designed by Rudy VanderLans, with type design by Barry Deck. After covering a few years of graphic complexity spawned by the computer, *Emigre* devoted an issue to the question 'Does all experimentation in graphic design eventually lead to the simplification of graphic design?' Issue no.19, set entirely in Deck's Template Gothic, metaphorically wiped the slate clean and started from zero.

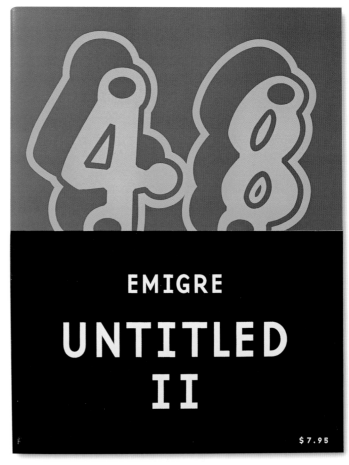

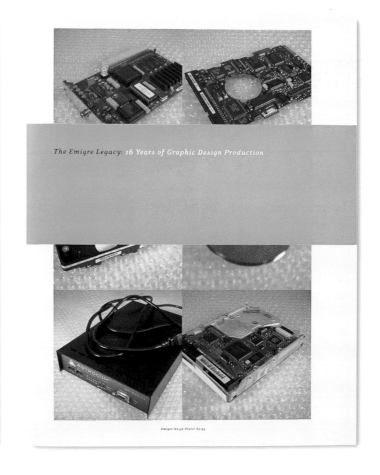

The Emigre Legacy: 16 Years of Graphic Design Production

Emigre No.50 Price: $7.95

surprising themes (notably one issue was replete with VanderLans's own, mysterious photographs of Southwestern deserts). In 2001 he shrunk the magazine even further and inserted a music CD. Today *Emigre* is a vehicle for distributing the new music that VanderLans produces. The magazine no longer projects the same urgency as when it was the standard-bearer for experimental digital typography. Nevertheless, VanderLans and Licko have continued to retain their independence in a world where mavericks are frequently absorbed by conglomerates. Still not satisfied to follow tradition, they have created a tradition of their own.

During the time that *Emigre* was trying to find a road less travelled, the task of testing the limits of typography using state-of-the-art technology rested with a decidedly experimental 'journal' called *Fuse*, founded and edited in 1991 by English designers Neville Brody (b.1957) and Jon Wozencroft (b.1958). *Fuse* merged various novel ideas: it was difficult to define in terms of existing publishing formats. It was issued periodically, although it was not a periodical *per se*. It was distributed by subscription through FontShop International, rather than sold on news-stands or in bookstores. It included a print component that was a series of folded posters rather than collated pages. It was digital but only insofar as its basic content was stored on a diskette. It did not come stapled between covers but rather in a brown corrugated box with a spare typographic label that changed colour each issue.

Each individual issue was always based on a particular social or cultural theme. *Fuse* was a radical departure in form, whose content was designed to alter how people – and especially its targeted audience of graphic designers – perceived type design and typography. It presented type not so much as a vessel of meaning as a collection of prototype alphabets, sometimes abstract conglomerations of signs and symbols that stimulated new interpretations more akin to jazz improvization than conventional type-play.

Brody's reason for founding *Fuse*, he once explained, was because he saw that, with the personal computer, 'there was an opportunity to democratize the fiefdom of typographic design'.[5] Brody realized that virtually overnight it was within the capacity of people who had sophisticated computers to create unprecedented type. *Fuse* enabled him to work with people to explore ideas that challenged the core notions of what typographic language should be. Its editorial concept was based on the idea that designers could design typefaces in an abstract manner. Brody and Wozencroft have acknowledged their debt to a litany of progressives: Dadas, Surrealists, William Burroughs, Mark Rothko, Josef Beuys, Brion Gysin. They describe *Fuse* as a hybrid between *Die Aktion* (1911–32), a Punk fanzine, and a Twenties type catalogue.

Opposite, clockwise from top left: **Emigre**, covers of no.40, 1996, type design by Zuzana Licko; no.48, 1998, type design by Licko and Elliott Earls; no.56, 2000, photography by Rudy VanderLans and type design by Rodrigo Cavazos; no.49, 1998, type design by John Downer, all covers designed by Rudy VanderLans. These smaller magazine sized issues marked a transition from a design 'zine' to a more critical design journal.

Below from top: **Emigre**, inside spreads from no.51, 1999, with poem by Captain Beefheart, type design by John Downer; no.56, 2000, type design by Rodrigo Cavazos. The photography and design of both issues is by Rudy VanderLans.

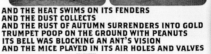

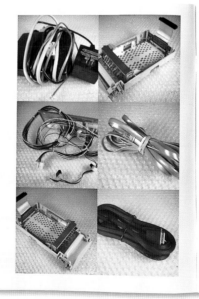

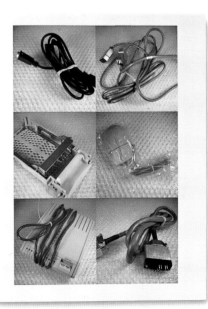

Fuse proposed the far-fetched notion of separating the words from sentences, thus allowing the individual writing components to be the content. Brody was interested to discover the degree to which form itself affects content, and *Fuse* was both a forum for debate and an experimental workshop where people were invited to pursue this exploration. In fact, what Brody and Wozencroft proposed was a typography devoid of words. Rick Poynor described it as 'an organized set of abstract digital marks that carry no linguistic meaning and bear only a passing resemblance to the alphabets we know'.[6] For all its experimental aesthetic, *Fuse* was always intended to concern itself with a particular stage in the development of human languages and their use.

The goal was not to create usable fonts – although many of the designers invited to contribute did produce fonts that were, perhaps in spite of themselves, available for sale through FontShop. The standards that determined inclusion or rejection were taste and dogma. *Fuse* had no criteria as such, but it did have a creed: 'The only criteria was to be as questioning of convention as possible,' Brody explained. 'But beyond that, it's impossible to police.'[7] Yet even *Fuse*'s editors admitted that the company put out very bad fonts and very good fonts all in the name of research.

Given the unprecedented nature of the project, contributors were not always prepared for the expectations that came with freedom. Type was a means to an end, not an end in itself. In fact, the results were dubious. But Wozencroft anticipated that *Fuse* would take a long time to hit the right chord, and from the first issue the editors tried to balance trendy typefaces with experimental dysfunctional ones. Wozencroft cited typefaces that seemed very cutting edge when they first appeared, such as Lushus and Caustic Biomorph in *Fuse* no.4, yet had very quickly exhausted their commercial potential. Others, like the abstract contributions to the free-form theme of *Fuse* no.10, seem more radical as time goes by.

Design critics reproached *Fuse* for being a catalogue of Grunge-style decoration, a pretentious intellectual excuse for what in the end was commercial novelty. Brody complained that some of the *Fuse* designers instinctively went in the fashionable direction: 'It's not always easy to work with a designer, to get them to the heart of an idea rather than to respond decoratively. That may be the result of an exploration. But we [were] trying to get people to get to the idea behind that rather than the surface effect.'[8]

By virtue of the obsolescence of the diskette on which *Fuse* was made available, the eighteen extant issues (out of a planned twenty) are arguably throwbacks to a primitive stage in the digital revolution (although plans to use DVD have been contemplated). Yet the questions *Fuse* has posed

regarding the limits of type and visual language are not entirely bound by new technology. *Fuse* halted production with issue no.18 because of a lack of funds but the two last issues in the original series remain on the drawing-board, with the goal of further challenging the very essence of typography.

Emigre and *Fuse* promoted unconventional design to those primed to accept it. But the real test of their ideas would be in the market-place. One of its most intrepid exponents was designer David Carson (b.1956) who, in 1990, was art director of *Beach Culture*, a fairly traditional magazine of West Coast water sports (particularly surfing) that had been a supplement to an advertising catalogue called *Surf Style*. Under Carson's auspices, this new entity became something of a cult design journal when it emerged as a winner in design competitions. Later Carson art directed *Ray Gun*, a post-Punk alternative rock 'n' roll magazine, which featured page layouts with an array of bawdy typography that took the *Emigre* model a few steps closer to the edge.

Beach Culture was full of design indulgences and technological trickery and included expressive photography and illustration by artists such as Geof Kern, Marshall Arisman, Milton Glaser, Matt Mahurin, Steve Byram and Henrik Drescher. It was often unreadable, yet, given its context, conventional readability was not the goal. Following in the footsteps of Wolfgang Weingart, Rudy VanderLans and Neville Brody, David Carson began his own expedition into new realms of visual presentation. His spin on typographic anarchy was different from that of his predecessors. He not only infused his pages with wit and irony; he believed that since a magazine page is destined to be pulped anyway, whatever happens is ephemeral. In one issue he ran an article in three conventional columns of type, but rather than reading vertically down it read horizontally across, with each sentence jumping from one column to the next. On another page he designed the page numbers larger than the main headline – a joke in itself – and when the editor changed the order of the pages, Carson retained the original out-of-sequence page numbers. *Beach Culture* may have been spiritually Dadaesque but nevertheless it was an example of a new generation of self-conscious experimental graphic design.

Carson also took the premise of typographic illegibility to the extreme by obliterating most headlines through overlapping, overprinting, smashing and covering letter forms in black, abstracting words and phrases until they appeared to be paint scrawls by Jackson Pollock. All this was achieved by courtesy of Pandora's digital box, the Macintosh. Carson had witnessed the way in which the defaults and mistakes translated into print, and intuitively

understood how these effects could be stretched. He also believed that his audience would rather subscribe to a publication that looked 'cool' rather than read well. This was the critical trade-off, a gamble that a generation raised on TV and video games could relate to visual codes that expressed chaos and confusion. He was right, yet *Beach Culture* met an abrupt end in 1990 because it did not make a profit. However, Carson had released the new typography into the mainstream of youth culture and for almost a decade there was no holding it back. In 1993 he became art director for *Ray Gun* and here he pushed the envelope of print typography as far as it could be pushed at the time – without losing any utility.

Ray Gun was founded by photographer and publisher Marvin Scott Jarrett in 1993. The older *Rolling Stone* had long since evolved from its Underground origins into a mainstream pop magazine, and Jarrett astutely realized that new sounds and attitudes required a new mouthpiece. *Ray Gun* was never intended to be avant-garde in the ascetic sense – it sought an audience to attract advertising to make profit – but it was de facto avant-garde by virtue of its alliance with the emerging counter-culture. Jarrett brought in Carson who created a visual language which, like psychedelic graphics before it, would appeal to the young audience and serve as a distinct code. With *Ray Gun* Carson's graphic design more ostentatiously challenged the conventions of legibility – its words were reduced to textures on pages that seemed more like abstract canvases than manuscripts. This was not some arcane fanzine with a minuscule readership but a leading competitor on the news-stand next to *Rolling Stone* and *Spin* (the former a perennial award winner for its innovative, though less radical, typography). In addition to featuring young musicians ignored by the mainstream press, *Ray Gun*'s provocative and tenacious graphic design set the standard for a generational style of typographic goofiness which became the fashion with countless other alternative-culture publications and on posters, packages and the covers of music videos.

Between *Ray Gun*'s covers, traditional type hierarchies (i.e., headlines, subheads, body text and page numbers) were rejected in favour of apparent randomness. The Macintosh computer was the supercharged engine that made this production possible, allowing experiments (and tricks) that took earlier Underground layout artists untold hours to achieve. Even designs that were anathema to accepted tenets had a certain authority. In at least one issue of *Ray Gun* the page numbers were blown up large and positioned in the middle of each page. In other issues, text type was bled off the page in the middle of a paragraph. Instead of communicating ideas, the pages created auras

From left: **Ray Gun**, no.9, September 1993, cover photography by Lisa Spinder; no.11, November 1993, cover photography by Stefan Ruiz and typography by Calef Brown. *Below:* no.19, September 1994, inside spread designed by Martin Venezky. *Ray Gun*, the magazine of alternative music, was a veritable canvas on which David Carson virtually painted with typography of all kinds. Whether his audience read the text was irrelevant to the avant-garde code that the composition elicited. *Ray Gun*'s publisher and editor-in-chief was Marvin Scott Jarrett, and David Carson was the art director.

spew

conver-
sation
music
art fiction
fashion film

$4.50 $6.00 Canada
fall 97

7 25274 87781 2   73>

that gave an impression of expression. Despite some protests from angry writers, *Ray Gun* continued to showcase layout that created an unapologetic identity for the magazine and the generation that read it. It was not the first to test the limits of typographic tolerance, and it will not be the last. It did, however, do its job with fairly expensive production values – full colour, slick paper – and contained considerable advertising to pay for it.

If *Emigre* was the grandfather, *Ray Gun* was the father, as it were, of subsequent edgy, consumer-targeted culture magazines including *XLR8R*, *Lava*, *Pulp*, *Huh* and *Speak*. These were the most unique of their genre for they took computer-driven typography to new levels of

challenged readability. A typographic genre rooted in, but not exclusive to, editorial design born of *Emigre*, extended by *Ray Gun*, and customized by various designers who adopted the fundamentals of the overarching vision and spawned a generational code symbolizing rebellion, not dissimilar to what Futurism and Dada did earlier in the century. Once the floodgates were open – and the style caught on among the targeted youth audience – there was no stopping the innovations. Moreover, as the need grew so too the computer applications increased to meet demand. These culture magazines became veritable canvases on which type and image were no longer neutral vessels of content, but equal to it as a means of conveying messages

Opposite: **Speak**, Fall 1997, cover photograph by Martin Venezky. *Below*: no.3, 1996, inside spread designed by Venezky. *Speak*'s typographic vocabulary is a synthesis of Dada and Futurism, with an *Emigre* accent. Venezky pushed his work to the next and last expressive stage of digital type manipulation. *Speak* was edited and published by Dan Rolleri and art directed by Martin Venezky.

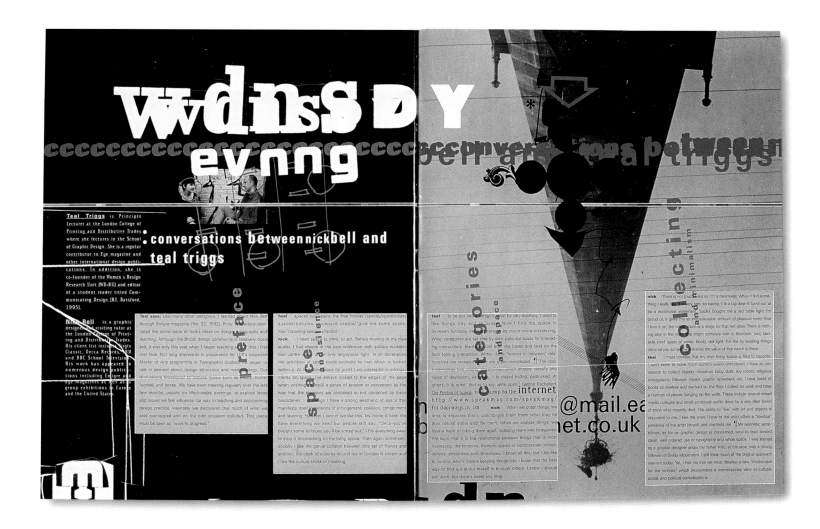

and 'attitudes'. Marvin Scott Jarrett, who published *Ray Gun*, built a publishing stable upon an 'in-your-face' design ethic that attacked any semblance of typographic neutrality as antiquated and uncool. He hired the British typographic experimentalist and record sleeve designer, Vaughan Oliver, to design *Huh* intentionally to explore the lengths to which type and image could express new values without becoming tired and overdone. Whereas David Carson practised brute expressionism, Oliver's marriage of type and image was more rigorous yet curiously impressionistic, sometimes ethereal. Then, in *Ray Gun*'s wake came *Speak*, published by Dan Rolleri, originally designed by Carson before the baton was passed to

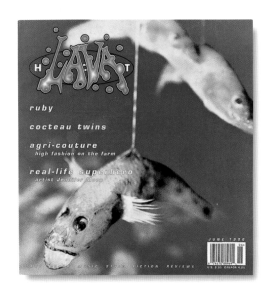

Martin Venezky (who earlier designed pages for *Ray Gun*), which effectively upped the typographic volume (or some critics might say noise). *Speak* was a more general alternative culture magazine than *Ray Gun*, but it was a similar canvas on which layers as well as chunks, of brutishly designed typographic material violently and digitally intersected with editorial text. The design was not merely a frame but endemic to the overall content of the magazine – it was not simply a format but a language.

Against the frenetic experimentation of these and other magazines following raucous typographic mannerisms, *Ray Gun* served both as a model and touchstone. For some it represented total liberation from the strictures of modernism, for others it was an instantly encrusted style – a brief moment of popularity – that formented a new rebellion against chaos and clutter in favour of simplicity and minimalism. *Ray Gun* was indeed avant-garde for a moment, then was absorbed into the melting-pot of progressive commercial culture, where it remained until it played itself out. Carson's self-described 'end of print' style inevitably evolved into a brand that, when bound together with the approaches proffered by *Emigre*, *Fuse* and other proponents of expressive typographic-technics, has certainly defined a design Zeitgeist. But like all fringe sensibilities that are eaten up by commercial culture the line toed between unacceptability and warm embrace is often very thin and entirely mutable.

The plethora of brute typography in periodical and countless other design media soon became commonplace, removing its key attribute – unpredictability. The end of this design movement was marked by the return to new sobriety (not unlike the transition from Futurism to Bauhaus) that many of the digital revolutionaries had earlier rejected. Marvin Scott Jarrett admitted that once he accepted that the typo-centric trend made it difficult to clearly convey information, he turned to relative simplicity and has asserted that the current stage of magazine design is emphasis on economy and legibility.[9] Likewise, Rudy VanderLans radically shifted *Emigre* away from the explosive typographic splatter of its formative years into a more systematized, yet free-form format. While he continues to experiment and routinely changes the magazine's shape, size and content, *Emigre*'s typography is now more circumspect in its relation to the word. With this current direction only time will tell whether simplicity is a momentary detour or the long road. With the increasingly ambitious pyrotechnics of the web looming as 'the next big thing', it is unclear how print, especially magazine, designers will respond.

Opposite, top: **Pulp**, Winter 1988, cover photograph by Francisco Caceres. *Opposite, middle*: **Huh**, cover of no.6, February 1995; no.20, April 1996, inside spread with photography by Alison Dyer; *Opposite, below*: **Hot Lava**, vol.2 no.10, June 1996, cover photography by Sean Murphy and inside spread. Art direction/ design by Jennifer Tough.

Below: **XLR8R**, cover of no.27, July 1997. During the late Eighties and Nineties scores of 'little' arts and culture magazines used digital design technology to produce a variety of experimental venues for designers and type designers. They included *Pulp*, edited and designed by Nicholas Pavkovic; *Huh*, editor-in-chief Marvin Scott Jarrett, creative director

Vaughan Oliver/V23; and *XLR8R*, published and edited by Andrew Smith, design director Richard Hansen. Critics argued that the new avant-garde emphasized illegibility as the cornerstone of digital eccentricity. But these layouts provided readers with new pathways. *XLR8R*, for instance, began its lead story on the cover, cropping off some of the lead paragraph which continues on the inside.

The future of avant-garde periodicals should be the theme of an epilogue, but not *this* one. The avant-garde publications discussed here are something of a paradox since they are new ideas presented in old forms. Most are produced using time-honoured materials – type and ink on paper – but the more advanced, indeed the most culturally significant, use these media in unprecedented ways. Moreover, any attempt to predict the next stage of 'avant-gardery' would require more vision than I possess.

The periodicals discussed in this book stood alone from the artistic and political establishments of their respective times as clarions of change, instruments of revolution and laboratories of experimentation. Some of them busted norms, albeit temporarily; others created new ones in art, literature and design. The advent of digital media and the World Wide Web has obviously changed the future of the publishing field, offering unknown opportunities for as yet unformed avant-gardes. But rather than prognosticate on the nature of a paperless future, this postscript surveys five periodicals which, owing to their unique characteristics, do not fit into any of the previous chapters. Before doing so, it is useful to revisit what constitutes a 'periodical' avant-garde and why this book has covered the ground that it has.

The periodicals included here were selected because they are indelibly written into the historical record. Understanding the cultural upheavals of the twentieth century cannot be accomplished without appreciating the role which many of these publishing activities have fulfilled. *Dada* no.3, *Jedermann sein eigner Fussball*, *Bauhaus* and even *The East Village Other* are holy grails of the movements for which they stood. Their progressive intentions were clear, yet their ultimate status in the cultural pantheon was an unknown quantity until they had ceased publication. Since they were printed on cheap acidic papers they were destined for the dustbin. Yet a few of these documents are now as important as the works of art or cultural events that they originally covered.

Fervency was the requisite for launching and maintaining an alternative periodical but even this degree of commitment did not ensure an avant-garde result. In fact, many aspiring vanguard reviews failed miserably through trying too hard to be cutting-edge, while others were posing in avant-garde skins. Arguably, *Minotaure* was too well produced to fit the mould of the avant-garde and, despite the unprecedented use of modern photomontage by progressive Russian designers, *USSR in Construction* was a tool of state-sanctioned propaganda. By the time that *Minotaure* folded, Surrealism had already been tamed by mainstream advertising's appropriation of its style and some of its followers.

So why have I chosen to include these publications? If the definition of avant-garde is confrontation, with intent to disrupt the status quo, *Minotaure* and *USSR in Construction* could be disqualified. But, then again, distance is necessary to assess the overall importance of each avant-garde journal. The truly radical journal that attacked accepted tastes and mores with unacceptable form and content must be analysed together with those that simply flirted with nonconformity, since synergy often existed between them. *Minotaure*, for example, exposed the Surrealists to a broader audience and introduced them to other art forms, while *USSR in Construction* gathered together the remnants of radical design before Stalin totally eviscerated the Soviet avant-garde in 1934.

Different publications either expressed the aspirations of specific cultural vanguards or mirrored the Zeitgeist. One might ask whether, for example, the Sixties magazine *Avant Garde* (which has not been previously discussed in this book) had a greater counter-cultural impact than its sister publication *Eros* (see Chapter 8). The latter introduced a prudish, censorious society to taboo eroticism and sexual

Epilogue:
A Few Loose Ends

politics, which enabled certain radical pioneers (as well as crass pornographers) eventually to push the boundaries even further. Conversely, *Avant Garde*, despite its provocative title, merely followed *Eros*'s innovative lead by using sexual content in a manner deliberately designed to allure and provoke. Although both were published and edited by Ralph Ginzburg, *Eros* was a trailblazer with a permanent impact on American morals (and its publisher paid the price with imprisonment). On the other hand, *Avant Garde*, which like *Eros* was designed by Herb Lubalin, contributed fewer new ideas and did not face the same legal peril.

Although *Avant Garde* was not sold in basements by subversives – but rather distributed through the US mail and available on news-stands – it reported and codified the sexual and political revolutions of the times. In so doing, it was a building block in alternative culture's inevitable elevation towards public acceptance. Invariably, 'culture-vultures' (marketers and trendsetters) assimilated the most advanced yet acceptable characteristics of the avant-garde into the mainstream, and *Avant Garde* magazine can be seen as bridging the divide between what was taboo and what was fashionable.

As we have seen, the life expectancy of an avant-garde periodical can vary from a month to several years, from one to dozens of issues, but rarely do they last for long before the avant-garde edge is worn off. With the notable exception of *Emigre* (see Chapter 9), which is still publishing, since it began in 1984, and frequently reinvents itself, most magazines discussed in this book were played out over a relatively short period. Some foundered due to a lack of funds or a surfeit of interference, while a few lasted longer than they should have done. *Ray Gun* was one that went through an 'experimental' stage and then settled into an 'establishment' period a couple of years later.

It is fruitless to preordain just how long a magazine should continue publishing. If the purpose of an avant-garde periodical is to leap ahead of the pack, its accomplishment must be measured by the amount of dust it kicks up during its lifespan rather than by its longevity. A propitious time for a magazine to fade into the stacks is when it no longer challenges an audience's expectations. An avant-garde periodical that outlives its ability to disrupt has lost its *raison d'être*, even if it has miraculously retained its circulation.

For alternative periodicals to survive, they cannot succumb to the demands of the market-place. An avant-garde publication is doomed the moment it compromises its editorial integrity by accepting advertising. Of course, what constitutes advertising is relative. Dada and Surrealist publications of the Twenties and Thirties accepted advertisements for other Dada and Surrealist publications and also served to promote kindred movements and exhibitions. Sixties Underground newspapers accepted whatever advertising was offered but on their own terms. In fact, the music and clothing companies that advertised in Underground newspapers saw these outlets as conduits to reach targeted audiences – a symbiotic relationship which benefited both parties. But another model exists: during *Emigre*'s first ten years, it did not advertise anything other than its own products. Eventually, soaring production and mailing costs forced Rudy VanderLans to accept outside advertisements to cover its operating expenses. Today, the expense of paper, printing, publishing and distributing demand that even avant-garde publications, unless they are cheaply laser-printed 'zines', address the economic bottom-line. Money is the key obstacle towards sustaining an alternative periodical, so a magazine must find ways of achieving fiscal solvency.

This prompts me to mention one avant-garde publishing venture not discussed elsewhere in this book but which serves as a textbook case. Indeed, one of the most innovative alternative periodicals of the Eighties ignored economic imperatives despite the costs incurred by its superior

Below from left: **Avant Garde**, no.10, January 1970, cover photography by Thomas Weir; inside spread from no.5, November 1968. Herb Lubalin designed *Avant Garde* in an unprecedented (at least in the Sixties) yet professional manner. The typography was bold but it was meticulous and elegant, not as in the typically raw experimental journal. *Avant Garde* was edited by Ralph Ginzburg.

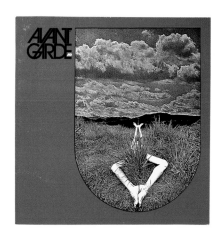

printing values – quality paper, generous use of colour, multiple inserts and special effects. This was *Raw*, the first 'experimental', post-Underground comix magazine, published and edited in New York from 1980 to 1991 by Art Spiegelman (b.1948) and François Mouly (b.1955). Underground comix were born in the late Sixties as an adjunct to the Underground press (see Chapter 8) and were the most original graphic arts of the hippie era. Like the alternative newspapers in which they originally appeared, alternative comic books were cheaply produced and inexpensively priced, but *Raw* broke that mould. It was not a comic-book format, but rather a large tabloid with heavy paper stock. It eschewed many of the well-known Underground artists in favour of newer and younger American comix artists interspersed with European veterans who had had no previous exposure in the United States. And the Underground thematic trinity of sex, drugs and rock 'n' roll was swapped for more introspective, psychological and satirical graphic narratives. Spiegelman, who had previously edited *Arcade*, an Underground comics review, used the new magazine to make comics into a more mature visual/literary form. Towards this aim he published instalments of his own comic-strip memoir 'Maus: A Survivor's Tale', an account of his Jewish family's life in Nazi Europe. *Raw* was an ambitious project that initially survived on the passion and ingenuity of its editors, who used mostly personal capital and unorthodox means to keep it afloat.

Raw is a hybrid among hybrids but has the distinction of being innovative in the field that grew up around it. It falls under the rubrics of art, literature and design, and its contributors addressed politics, culture and society through, alternately, absurdity, fantasy and autobiography. It was also influential beyond the world of comics, as evidenced by a rise in circulation from an initial few thousand to twenty thousand in just over eight issues. When *Raw* came into being, there were other large-size cultural tabloids, including *Wet*, *Fetish* and *Interview*, covering Seventies and Eighties art and celebrity. The only thing that *Raw* had in common with them was the designation 'New Wave', a generic label that spoke more for the contemporary look than for the content of each publication – a post-Underground/Punk but pre-digital anti-modernist sensibility. The look hinged on not appearing Do-It-Yourself and yet eschewed predictability as well. Spiegelman believed that a magazine of this size would signal a new approach to comics, and he was right. As for the title, he and Mouly wanted a three-letter name in the tradition of *Mad* (the vintage humour magazine). To their chosen title *Raw*, which Spiegelman defines as 'having vital juices intact',[2] they added different evocative subtitles for each issue, including

Below from left: **Raw**, vol.1 no.1, Fall 1980, cover art by Art Spiegelman; vol.1 no.3, July 1981, cover art by Gary Panter; vol.1 no.6, May 1984, cover art by Mark Beyer. *Opposite, from top*: vol.1 no.3, July 1981, inside spread and insert with artwork by Mariscal (*left*) and Art Spiegelman (*right*); vol.1 no.6, May 1984, inside spread with artwork by Mark Beyer. *Raw* magazine was founded in 1980 to change the common perception of comics. To accomplish this, Art Spiegelman and François Mouly rejected the typical comic-book format in favour of a tabloid, with covers by Spiegelman, Beyer and Panter. *Raw* was printed on heavy stock with a generous number of special effects, including the insert, *Maus*, in issue no.3.

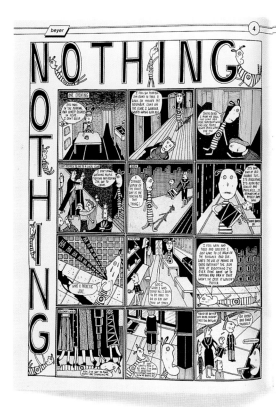

'The Graphix Magazine for Damned Intellectuals', 'The Graphix Magazine of Abstract Depressionism', 'The Graphic Aspirin for War Fever' and 'The Graphix Magazine that Overestimates the Taste of the American Public'.

Graphic design in *Raw* was a mix of New Wave decoration and expressive typography. Each page was crowned with a running head in which the artist's name appeared and a page number dropped, somewhat inelegantly, out of a circle – this was *Raw*'s signature design motif. Each table of contents was artwork in its own right, with overprints, drop-outs and other printing concepts echoing the Punk DIY aesthetic that was introduced a few years earlier. *Raw* no.1 was printed on heavy white paper and included a small comic book by Spiegelman titled *Two Fisted Painters* (one of many strips devoted to a satirical analysis of the formal traits of comics). The front cover had a colour panel pasted on to it, adding a further dimension to Spiegelman's stark black-and-white illustration of a man reading the same first issue of *Raw*. A lot of attention was paid to its physical presence.

Raw was a Mecca for a coterie of visionary artist/storytellers. Among them, Gary Panter (b.1950) already enjoyed a cult following for the comic strip 'Jimbo' which appeared in the West Coast Punk review *Slash*. Charles Burns (b.1955) became known for his meticulously-drawn ironic interpretations of Fifties horror and love comics. Jerry Moriarty (b.1938) was the creator of 'Jack Survives', a subtle, Surrealistic view of everyday banalities, and Mark Beyer (b.1950) contributed tales of urban depression that were rendered in the manner of outsider art. *Raw* also published the cream of the European comic-strip artists. Among the most noteworthy were the painstakingly lettered and composed kinetic sequences by Joost Swarte (b.1947) from Holland and Ever Meulen (b.1946) from Belgium, the explosive erotic graphic fantasies of Pascal Doury (1956–2001) and the *noir* storytelling of Jacques Tardi (b.1946) from France, as well as the seductive eccentricities of Javier Mariscal (b.1950) from Spain. To separate *Raw* from the Underground verities, Spiegelman published brand-new stories by the masters of the older genre – Robert Crumb (b.1943), Kim Deitch (b.1944), Justin Green (b.1945), and Bill Griffith (b.1944) – because the field had changed and so had they. He further provided a forum for political artists including Sue Coe (b.1951) who produced some of the most strident polemical visual commentaries in *Raw*.

Raw published irregularly for eight numbers in a tabloid format and then, after a short hiatus when two issues appeared as a quarto-sized paperback, it ran out of steam. The reasons for *Raw*'s suspension had as much to do with Spiegelman and Mouly turning their attention towards other projects as it did with soaring production costs and

the rise of additional *Raw*-like publications that sapped the uniqueness of the original. Although *Raw* could easily have been absorbed by mainstream publishing because it garnered a good press and encouraged the widespread acceptance and appreciation of sophisticated comics in a broader popular culture, Spiegelman and Mouly would not allow the magazine's integrity to be violated.

One of the most unique of all hybrids was *Spy*, which had its audience and advertising base in the mainstream yet retained an avant-garde spirit. *Spy* was founded in New York in 1985 by writers Graydon Carter (b.1949) and Kurt Andersen (b.1954) on the premise that a progressive magazine combining satire and reportage with acerbic political and social commentary could hold its own in the market-place without kowtowing to advertisers or demographics. Andersen once noted that the two founders spent 'a year over lunches dreaming up "our favourite magazine", a magazine that we would love to read, that would be an antidote to pandemic Eighties puffery – but without any serious intention of starting it.'[3] Nevertheless, pipedreams were the genesis for many avant-gardes. Although launched from the margins of the periodical publishing industry, *Spy* (the name was taken from a gossip magazine in the film *The Philadelphia Story*) did not exactly fit the profile of an avant-garde magazine because it was not associated with a radical movement or ideology.

The plan was to combine real journalism and fresh information with a satirical sensibility and report on institutions, trends and people that did not normally attract rigorous press coverage. 'The slogan we invented – Smart. Fun. Funny. Fearless – sums up the intention,'[4] Andersen explained. And it lived up to the promise. Within a few issues, *Spy* became *the* magazine that New Yorkers were compelled to read (and quote). It tapped into and helped to develop a New York attitude of intelligent irony and it also ignited a revolution in magazine design.

Spy had conventional pagination, including a cover, regular columns, sidebars and features – but within these confines its designer, Stephen Doyle (b.1956), who had previously worked on *Rolling Stone* and *Esquire* magazines, developed a quirky format. He introduced text with varying column-widths and different typefaces in multiple weights and sizes on a single page to represent the cacophony of *Spy*'s varied voices. Using multiple type-styles on the same page, even in the same sentence, was not new; in fact, Doyle credited a sixteenth-century polyglot bible as his inspiration. None the less, for *Spy* he designed a separate, narrow column of small 'factoid' type along the outside margin, placed beside two columns of more standard feature text. The factoids and the longer narratives congealed into a dense mass of information illustrated by humorous

Opposite, clockwise from top left: **Spy**, October 1986, cover photography by Chris Callis; December 1986, cover photography by Bert Sternn; inside spread from December 1986 issue; inside spread with map from December 1989 issue. *Spy*, edited by Kurt Andersen and E Graydon Carter, was designed by Stephen Doyle, of Drenttel Doyle Partners, with all the traits of a slick mainstream magazine. However, it was based on avant-garde shock principles of multiple type-styles that allowed for various editorial voices.

(though utterly factual) charts and graphs that presented a broad swath of real and comic information. As functional as the charts may have been, they were also caustic commentaries on conventional, complex and often unnecessary 'information graphics' that were regular features of mainstream weekly news magazines. Through frequent usage in *Spy*, these graphs became a biting comic genre. Another emblematic conceit were tiny, silhouetted head-shots of people discussed throughout the magazine. Andersen noted that 'the collision of dissimilar elements and approaches, and parodic subversions of magazine clichés',[5] brought *Spy* spiritually closer to Twenties Dada journals, which had attacked the journalistic establishment through stories that both parodied and undermined the biases of state-sanctioned papers.

Spy did not remain in the margins for long. In attacking the culturati, glitterati and social world, its surging popularity among twenty-to-forty-somethings in New York and elsewhere in the US made the magazine a prime venue for fashionable advertisements for alcohol, food, cars and clothes. Although its editors provided a regular critique on cultural and political *bêtes noires*, what started as a means to fill an intellectual void itself became a publishing institution. So, when after four years *Spy*'s founders sold the magazine to a larger publishing company that planned a more mainstream circulation drive, and ultimately disassociated themselves from the publication, the end was in sight. *Spy* proved, however, that mainstream avant-garde is an oxymoron.

To remain avant-garde means rejecting the allure of mainstream success and embracing the margins. Indeed, another hybrid that combines both print and sound in one package, revels in its marginal space. *Unknown Public*, an 'audio journal', conceived in London by editors John Walters (b.1953) and Laurence Aston (b.1947), was born out of a dissatisfaction with conventional methods of distribution for non-commercial music, and a belief that regular magazine journalism could not do justice to the more esoteric areas of jazz, contemporary, electronic and other music. They were also frustrated that there was no generic term to describe the music or the audience which they wanted to reach. Since much of the music in their sphere was literally indescribable, they used the term 'creative music' to distinguish the new material from 'repertoire music' – and it was on this foundation that the magazine was constructed.

The title, *Unknown Public* (*UP*) was taken from a *Guardian* interview with Pierre Boulez, which describes the audience as the 'listenership'. There had been LP and cassette journals before, and there had been boxed magazines – notably the American *Aspen*, which included booklets, records and posters (much like *SMS*). But Walters

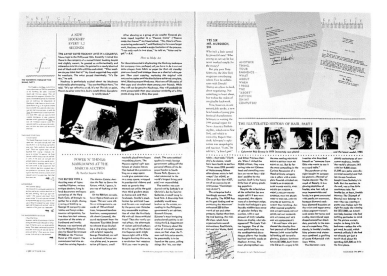

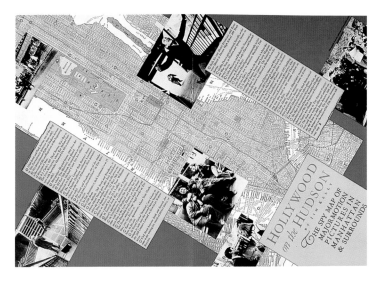

chose *his* box because he realized that with the emerging technologies of lower-cost CDs, DAT, MiniDisc and DAC (now obsolete), the new magazine could not commit to one format or shape. It was therefore decided that a box was the ideal solution to contain the various music-delivery formats.

The English designer John Warwicker (b.1955), who later founded the progressive design office Tomato, designed a logo that already looked familiar, based on the typeface Gill Sans in a brick red rectangle. The first dummy, which became the opening issue, had looseleaf pages designed by a student, Graham Wood. Walters and Aston launched *UP01* in late 1992, and numbers continue to come out on an irregular basis, mainly supported by subscribers. As *Unknown Public* evolved, its issues contained content and design other than music: postcards by Terry Howe, folded posters, and caricatures of Michael Nyman and Frank Zappa by Richard Kemp (b.1958). *UP03* (1993) featured a complex 'scratchpad' poster – all superimposed type and thick black rules.

After *UP08* Walters engaged a series of guest designers: Richard Hollis, Stuart Bailey, Lucy Ward and Jon Barnbrook. The brief to each was that almost anything was possible within the constraints of the budget and the brown kraft-covered cardboard box with its standardized labels. Advertising is only possible in the form of leaflets inserted in the box – which subscribers could choose to ignore. Of course *Unknown Public* has such broad design freedom because it sells through subscription. Yet the graphic design, which is far from obtrusive, is not meant to draw attention away from the content: music.

Unknown Public began as looseleaf pages and postcards in a box, but with *UP13* the box has been jettisoned in favour of another form (this one more like a book) and a digital conveyance is not far off. Probably the World Wide Web, with its ability to deliver high-fidelity

sound, cannot be ignored. And maybe this will be the direction in which other avant-garde periodicals will eventually move. The Web serves all the requirements of an independent publisher – access, economy, effects, mutability, etc. – and presumably it will always be with us.

But, as yet, a new chapter in avant-garde publishing and progressive design has not been written. In recent years the bridge between avant-garde and popular culture has been steady and direct. Often what purports to be avant-garde is so quickly consumed by the mass media that there is little chance to determine its relative worth. Today there is no paucity of independent magazines on subjects that once would have been the province of an avant-garde, but a truly progressive alternative press that challenges complacency does not really exist, or is not yet obvious (a paradox in itself). A twenty-first-century avant-garde periodical must somehow redefine old assumptions of what is avant-garde, and the advent of new media – the convergence of print, video, digital and sound transmitted through various electronic devices – is a major consideration in any such new development.

The Web is home to much fascinating and shocking (and sometimes distasteful) material, but I have yet to experience a 'webzine' avant-garde movement. This may be a function of being too close, or not close enough, to the vortex of avant-garde activity. But if the function of an avant-garde magazine, newspaper or website is its ability to inspire and incite action, perhaps the overwhelming quantity of media – print and Web – has made this goal considerably harder to achieve. None the less, whatever the future holds for paper or pixels, it is safe to assume that individuals and groups with alternative agendas will continue to issue some kind of periodical-like manifestation that will attack convention and alter perceptions.

Below from left: **Aspen**, cover sleeve and inside contents of no.4, 1967. A magazine is a storehouse of ideas despite its format. *Aspen*, edited by Phyllis Johnson and designed by Quentin Fiore, came as a box filled with individual articles and features.

Opposite, from top: **Unknown Public**, interior/contents of no.8, 1993, designed by Jason Kedgley and John Warwicker of Tomato, poster by UPD; mailing boxes of no.10, 1998–9, designed by Stuart Bailey; no.8, 1996, designed by Jason Kedgley and John Warwicker of Tomato; no.11, 2000, designed by Lucy Ward. *Unknown Public*, a boxed magazine with various features, including a CD, is designed to give the reader a tactile experience while providing a range of editorial experiences. *Unknown Public* comes in a plain cardboard box with the logo pasted to the front and spine. The box allows for a variety of contents in differently designed formats. It may not be the Internet but it offers as many levels of complexity and ingenuity. *Unknown Public* is published by Laurence Ashton and edited by John L Walters.

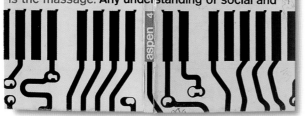

unknown public opinion

Q: must contemporary creative music always be 'spiky' or 'alienating'? can new music evoke more pleasurable sensations without descending to banality? can abstraction be sexy?

A: we're slowly moving away from 'the u... ...etter' and thank...

A: pleasure is a subjective experience ... all creative music has potential pleasurability

A: the curves c... be as powerf...

sensuality: essence

○ thanks to everybody who replied to the question ○ poster published by Unkn...

Notes

Introduction

1　Bertrand Russell, *Unpopular Essays*, George Allen & Unwin, London, 1950.

Chapter 1

1　Ralph Shikes, *The Indignant Eye: The Artist as Social Critic in Prints and Drawings from the Fifteenth Century to Picasso*, Beacon Press, Boston, MA, 1969, p.198.
2　Quoted in Christian N Nebehay, *Ver Sacrum 1898 to 1903*, Rizzoli International Publications, Milan, 1978, p.23.
3　Ibid., p.22.
4　Ibid., p.23.

Chapter 2

1　F T Marinetti, *The Founding and Manifesto of Futurism*, quoted in translation from http://www.unknown.nu/futurism/manifesto.html.
2　Quoted in Christine Poggi, 'Lacerba: Interventionist Art and Politics in Pre-World War I Italy', in Virginia Hagelstein Marquardt, ed., *Art Journals on the Political Front 1910–1940*, University Press of Florida, Miami, FL, 1997, p. 27.
3　Ibid., p.28.
4　Quoted in *Ex Libris Catalogue no.6: Constructivism and Futurism: Russian and Other*, text by Arthur Cohen, T J Art Inc., New York, 1977. Cohen's catalogues for the Ex Libris antiquarian bookstore were among the earliest sources of information on avant-garde publications. Even now, long after the business has closed, these catalogues offer rare insight into the quality, quantity and overall editorial significance of these journals.
5　Wyndham Lewis, *Blast*, no.1, reprint: Black Sparrow Press, Santa Barbara, CA, 1981, p.143.
6　Wyndham Lewis, *Blast*, no.2, 'The War Number', reprint: Black Sparrow Press, Santa Barbara, CA, 1981, p.24.
7　Ibid., p.5.
8　Wyndham Lewis, *The Enemy*, no.1, The Arthur Press, London, 1927, p.ix.

Chapter 3

1　Quoted in the Introduction to Lucy Lippard, ed., *Dadas on Art*, Prentice Hall Inc., Englewood Cliffs, NJ, 1971, p.1.
2　Michel Sanouillet, 'Dada: A Definition' in Stephen C Foster and Rudolf E Kuenzli, eds., *Dada Spectrum: The Dialectics of Revolt*, Coda Press, Madison, WI, 1979, p.25.
3　Quoted in Robert Motherwell, ed., *The Dada Painters and Poets: An Anthology*, The Belknap Press of Harvard University Press, Cambridge, MA, 1951, p.25.
4　Quoted in 'Dada', Zurich, 1966–7, in Lippard, *Dadas on Art*, p.36.
5　Arthur Cohen, 'The Typographic Revolution: Antecedents and Legacy of Dada Graphic Design' in Foster and Kuenzli, eds., *Dada Spectrum*, p.73.
6　The primary content was the same; different articles were sometimes included in different editions.
7　Quoted in Lippard, *Dadas on Art*, p.44.
8　Kurt Schwitters, 'Merz', published in *Der Arart*, Munich, 1921, quoted in Lippard, *Dadas on Art*.
9　After the war the British had brief control over the permits given to publishing houses.
10　Quoted in 'Cahiers d'Art, 1932–34', excerpted in Motherwell, *The Dada Painters and Poets*, p.157.

Chapter 4

1　Originally published in *Cahiers d'art*, vol.7, nos.1-2, 6-7, 8-10, 1932, and reprinted in Motherwell, *The Dada Painters and Poets*, p.141.
2　Ibid., p.146.
3　Quoted in Lippard, *Dadas on Art*, p.54.
4　Quoted in Motherwell, *The Dada Painters and Poets*, p.39.
5　Quoted in Lippard, *Dadas on Art*, p.48.
6　George Grosz and Wieland Herzfelde, *Die Kunst ist in Gefahr*, Malik Verlag, Berlin, 1925, quoted in Lippard, *Dadas on Art*, p.85.
7　Wieland Herzfelde, *John Heartfield: Leben und Werk*, Verlag der Kunst, Leipzig, 1962, quoted in Lippard, *Dadas on Art*, p.93.
8　Quoted in the Introduction to the exhibition catalogue of *The Malik Verlag*, Goethe House, New York, 1983, p.23.

Chapter 5

1　László Moholy-Nagy, *Malerei, Fotografie, Film*, Bauhausbücher no.8, Albert Langen Verlag, Munich, 1927.
2　Alston Purvis, *Wendingen: A Journal for the Arts, 1918–1932*, Architectural Press, Princeton, New Jersey, 2001, p.20.
3　Irina Subotić, 'Zenit and Zenitism', *Journal of Decorative and Propaganda Arts*, no.17, Fall 1990, Wolfsonian Institution, Miami, FL, p.15.
4　Interview with Steven Heller, September 1996.

Chapter 6

1　Virginia Smith, *The Funny Little Man*, Van Nostrand Reinhold, New York, 1996, p.8.
2　Frank H Young, 'Modern Layouts Must Sell Rather Than Startle', in *Advertising Arts*, no.1, New York, 1933.

3　Percy Seitlin, *AD* editorial, The Composing Room, April–May 1942, p.37.
4　Interview with Steven Heller, December 1992.
5　Ibid.
6　Ibid.
7　Ibid.
8　Ibid.

Chapter 7

1　Quoted in André Parinaud, ed., *Conversations: The Autobiography of Surrealism*, Marlowe & Company, New York, 1993, p.120.
2　Ibid., p.133.
3　Albert Skira, Introduction to *Minotaure: Authorized Reprint Edition*, Arno Press, New York, 1969, p.4.
4　Catrina Neiman, 'Introduction: View Magazine: Transatlantic Pact', in Charles Henri Ford, ed., *View: Parade of the Avant-Garde 1940–1947*, Thunder's Mouth Press, New York, 1991, p.xiv.
5　Ibid., p.xvi.
6　Quoted in Parinaud, *Conversations: The Autobiography of Surrealism*, p.156.
7　Albert Skira, Introduction to *Labyrinthe* reprint, Arno Press, New York, 1968, p.3.
8　David Crowley, 'Detach, Détourne & Consume: Alienation Sells!', *Eye*, Hearst Corporation, London, vol.11 no.42, Winter 2001.
9　John Hendricks, Foreword to *Fluxus Codex*, Harry N Abrams Inc., New York, 1988, p.21.
10　George Maciunas, quoted in Hendricks, *Fluxus Codex*, p.23.
11　Ibid., p.92.
12　Carter Ratcliff in *SMS* exhibition catalogue, Rhinehold Brown Gallery, New York, 1988.
13　Ibid.

Chapter 8

1　Michael Kernan, 'Radical Press: Underground Energy', *Washington Post*, 1970.
2　Jean Strouse in *Eye*, Hearst Corporation from 1967 to 1969.
3　Quoted in Abe Peck, *Uncovering the Sixties: The Life & Times of the Underground Press*, Pantheon Books, New York, 1985.
4　Ibid.
5　Quoted by Jean Strouse in *Eye* magazine, 1969.
6　Quoted in Peck, *Uncovering the Sixties*.
7　Robert J Glessing, *The Underground Press in America*, Indiana University Press, Bloomington, IN, 1970, p.48.
8　Abe Peck, *Uncovering the Sixties*.
9　Quoted in Glessing, *The Underground Press in America*, p.40.

10　Roger Lewis, *Outlaws of America: The Underground Press and its Context: Notes on a Cultural Revolution*, Pelican, Harmondsworth, 1972, p.34.
11　In 1968 Steven Heller (author) was art director of *Screw* for the first five issues. He left to found the *New York Review of Sex* in 1968, before returning to *Screw* two years later.
12　Interview with Steven Heller, January 2001.
13　Ibid.
14　Ibid.
15　Interview with Steven Heller, 2001. The designation 'New Wave' did not emerge until *Wet* had been publishing for at least two and a half years.

Chapter 9

1　In 1995, with issue no.33, *Emigre* changed its size and editorial focus from experimental laboratory to critical journal. In 2001, with issue no.60, it revamped again to an even smaller format complete with CD, as a venue for new music.
2　Rick Poyner, 'Into the Digital Realm' in *Design Without Boundaries: Visual Communication in Transition*, Booth-Clibborn Editions, London, 1998, p.211–13.
3　Ibid.
4　'The Cult of the Ugly', *Eye*, vol.9 no.3, September 1993, p.52.
5　Interview with Steven Heller, January 2000.
6　Rick Poyner, 'Rub Out the Word' in *Design Without Boundaries*, p.156.
7　Interview with Steven Heller, January 2000.
8　Ibid.
9　Interview with Steven Heller, August 2002.

Epilogue

1　In the Thirties the American industrial design pioneer, Raymond Loewy, referred to MAYA (Most Advanced Yet Acceptable) as an explanation of how the avant-gardisms were adopted by the mainstream.
2　Interview with Steven Heller, May 1995.
3　Interview with Steven Heller, October 2001.
4　Ibid.
5　Ibid.

Edward Abrahams, *The Lyrical Left: Randolph Bourne, Alfred Stieglitz and the Origins of Cultural Radicalism in America*, University of Virginia, Charlottesville, 1986.

Dawn Ades, *Dada and Surrealism Reviewed*, Arts Council of Great Britain, London, 1978.

Jaroslav Andel, *Czech Modernism 1900–1945*, Bulfinch Press, Boston, 1989.

Wayne Andrews, *The Surrealist Parade*, New Directions, New York, 1988.

Umbro Apollonio, *Futurist Manifestos*, Viking Press, New York, 1970.

H H Arnason and Marla Prather, *History of Modernism*, 4th ed., Harry N Abrams Inc., New York, 1998.

Neil Baldwin, *Man Ray: American Artist*, Da Capo Press, Cambridge, MA, 1988.

Hugo Ball, *Flight Out of Time*, Viking Press, New York, 1974.

Alfred H Barr Jr, *Cubist and Abstract Art*, MOMA Press, New York, 1936.

Alfred H Barr Jr, *Fantastic Art, Dada, Surrealism*, MOMA Press, New York, 1946.

David Batchelor, Briony Fer, Paul Wood, *Realism, Rationalism, Surrealism: Art Between the Wars*, Yale University Press, 1993.

Stephen Baum, ed., *Documents of Twentieth Century Art: The Tradition of Constructivism*, Viking Press, New York, 1974.

John I H Baur, *Revolution and Tradition in Modern American Art*, Harvard University Press, Cambridge, MA, 1958.

John Berger, *Arts and Revolution*, Pantheon, New York, 1969.

Lewis Blackwell, contributor, *The End of Print: The Graphic Design of David Carson*, Chronicle Books, San Francisco, CA, 1996.

Rudi Blesh, *Modern Art USA: Men, Rebellion, Conquest 1900–56*, Knopf, New York, 1956.

Szymon Bojko, *New Graphic Design in Revolutionary Russia*, Praeger, New York, 1972.

John Bokult, *Documents of Twentieth Century Art: Russian Arts and the Avant-Garde*, Viking, New York, 1976.

Jean Cassou, Emil Langui, Nikolaus Pevsner, *Gateway to the Twentieth Century*, McGraw-Hill, New York, 1962.

Joseph Harris Caton, *The Utopian Vision of Moholy-Nagy*, UMI Press, Ann Arbor, MI, 1984.

Monique Chefdor, ed., *Modernism: Challenges and Perspectives*, University of Illinois Press, Urbana, IL, 1986.

Arthur Cohen, *ExLibris Catalogue no.6: Constructivism & Futurism: Russian and Other*, T J Art Inc., New York, 1977.

Arthur Cohen, *Herbert Bayer: The Complete Work*, MIT Press, Cambridge, MA, 1984.

Wanda M Corn, *The Great American Thing: Modern Art and National Identity 1915–1935*, University of California Press, Berkeley, 1999.

Anne D' Harnoncourt, *Futurism and the International Avant-Garde*, Eastern Press, New Haven, CT, 1980.

Marius de Zayas, *How, When and Why Modern Art Came to New York*, ed. Francis Naumann, MIT Press, Cambridge, MA, 1996.

Wolf-Dieter Dube, *Expressionism*, Praeger, New York, 1972.

Carol Eliel, *L'Esprit Nouveau: Purism in Paris 1918–1925*, Harry N Abrams Inc., New York, 2001.

Stephen Escritt, *Art Nouveau*, Phaidon Press, London, 2000.

Charles Henri Ford, ed., *View-Parade of the Avant-Garde 1940–47*, Thunder's Mouth Press, New York, 1991.

Stephen Foster, ed., *DADA/Dimensions*, UMI Press, Ann Arbor, MI, 1985.

Stephen Foster and Rudolf Kuenzli, eds., *Dada Spectrum: the Dialectics of Revolt*, Coda Press, Madison, WI, 1979.

Marcel Franciscono, *Walter Gropius and the Creation of the Bauhaus*, University of Illinois Press, Urbana, IL, 1971.

Waldo Frank, ed., *America and Alfred Stieglitz: A Collective Portrait*, Literary Guild, New York, 1934.

James Fraser and Steven Heller, *The Malik Verlag*, exhibition catalogue, Goethe House, New York, 1983.

Matthew Gale, *Dada and Surrealism*, Phaidon Press, London, 1997.

Robert J Glessing, *The Underground Press in America*, Indiana University Press, Indianapolis, IN, 1970.

Roselee Goldberg, *Performance Art: From Futurism to the Present*, Thames & Hudson, London, 2001.

John Golding, *Visions of the Modern*, University of California Press, Berkeley, 1994.

Edward M Gottschall, *Typographic Communications Today*, MIT Press, Cambridge, MA and London, England, 1989.

Camilla Gray, *The Great Experiment: Russian Art 1863–1922*, Harry N Abrams Inc., New York, 1962.

Martin Green, *New York 1913: The Armory Show and the Paterson Strike Pageant*, Scribner, New York, 1988.

George Grosz and Wieland Herzfelde, *Die Kunst ist in Gefahr*, Malik Verlag, Berlin, 1924.

Andy Grundberg, *Brodovitch*, Harry N Abrams Inc., New York, 1989.

Mikhail Guerman, *Art of the October Revolution*, Harry N Abrams Inc., New York, 1979.

Steven Heller, *Paul Rand*, Phaidon Press, London, 1999.

Steven Heller and Seymour Chwast, *Graphic Style: From Victorian to Postmodern*, Harry N Abrams Inc., New York, 1988.

John Hendricks, *Fluxus Codex*, Harry N Abrams Inc., New York, 1988.

Wieland Herzfelde, *John Heartfield, Leben und Werk*, Verlag der Kunst, Leipzig, 1962.

Richard Hollis, *Graphic Design: A Concise History*, Thames & Hudson, London, 1994.

Pontus Hulton, *Futurists and Futurism*, Abbeville, New York, 1986.

Marcel Jean, ed., *Documents of Twentieth Century Art: Autobiography of Surrealism*, Viking Press, New York, 1974.

Nicholas Jenkins, ed., *By, With, To and From: A Lincoln Kirstein Reader*, Farrar, Strauss & Giroux, New York, 1991.

Hans L C Joffe, *De Stijl*, Harry N Abrams Inc., New York, 1971.

German Karyinov, *Rodchenko*, Thames & Hudson, London, 1979.

Donald H Kershan, *Archipenko*, Westview Press, Colorado, 1974.

Maiakovskii Khudozhnik, V V, Soviet Union, 1963.

Hilton Kramer, *The Age of the Avant-Garde, An Art Chronicle 1956–72*, Farrar, Strauss & Giroux, New York, 1973.

Rudolf E Kuenzli, ed., *New York DADA*, Willis, Locker and Owens, New York, 1986.

Jean-Clarence Lambert, *Cobra*, Abbeville, New York, 1983.

Maud Lavin (curated by) *Montage and Modern Life 1919–1942*, MIT Press, Cambridge, MA, 1992.

Martijn F Le Coutre, *Wendingen A Journal of Arts 1918–1932*, Princeton Architectural Press, New York, 2001.

Barbara Lekatzas (compiled by), *The Howard L and Muriel Weingrow Collection of Avant-Garde Art and Literature at Hofstra University: An Annotated Bibliography*, Greenwood Press, Westport, CT, 1985.

Helena Lewis, *The Politics of Surrealism*, Paragon House, New York, 1988.

Roger Lewis, *Outlaws of America: The Underground Press and its Context: Notes on a Cultural Revolution*, Pelican, New York, 1972.

Wyndham Lewis, *Blast*, no.1 (reprint), Black Sparrow Press, Santa Barbara, CA, 1981.

Wyndham Lewis, *Blast*, no.2, 'The War Number' (reprint), Black Sparrow Press, Santa Barbara, CA, 1981.

Wyndham Lewis, ed., *The Enemy*, no.1, The Arthur Press, London, 1927.

Lucy Lippard, ed., *Dadas on Art*, Prentice Hall Inc., Englewood Cliffs, NJ, 1971.

Lucy Lippard, ed., *Six Years, The De-materialization of the Art Object from 1966–72*, Praeger, New York, 1973.

Lucy Lippard, ed., *Surrealists on Art*, Prentice Hall Inc., Englewood Cliffs, NJ, 1970.

Giovanni Lista, *Le Livre Futuriste*, Editions Panini, Modena, 1984.

Alan and Isabella Livingston, *Thames & Hudson Encyclopaedia of Graphic Design and Designers*, Thames & Hudson, London, 1992.

Christina Lodder, *Russian Constructivism*, Yale University Press, New Haven, CT, 1983.

Virginia Hagelstein Marquardt, ed., *Art Journals on the Political Front 1910 –1940*, University Press of Florida, Miami, 1997.

Marianne W Martin, *Futurist Art and Theory 1909–15*, Clarendon Press, Oxford, 1968.

J H Matthews, *Introduction to Surrealism*, Penn State University Press, Pennsylvania, 1965.

Liz McQuiston, *Graphic Agitation: Social and Political Graphics Since the Sixties*, Phaidon Press, London, 1993.

Philip B Meggs, *A History of Graphic Design*, 3rd ed., John Wiley & Sons, New York, 1998.

John Milner, *Vladmir Tatlin and the Russian Avant-Garde*, Yale University Press, New Haven, CT, 1983.

Robert Motherwell, ed., *The Dada Painters and Poets: An Anthology*, Harvard University Press, 1951.

Josef Müller-Brockmann, *A History of Visual Communications*, Teufen, Switzerland; Verlag Arthur Niggli, New York; Visual Communication Books, Hastings House, 1971.

Maurice Nadeau, *History of Surrealism*, Macmillan, New York, 1965.

Francis Naumann, *Making Mischief: DADA Invades New York*, Whitney Museum, New York, 1996.

Dorothy Norman (foreword by), *291 (Numbers 1–12) 1915–1916*, Arno Press, New York, 1972.

Amedee Ozenfant, *Foundations of Modern Art*, Brewer, Warren, Putnam, New York, 1931.

Krisztina Passuth, *Moholy-Nagy*, Thames & Hudson, London, 1985.

Abe Peck, *Uncovering The Sixties: the Life & Times of the Underground Press,*

Pantheon Books, New York, 1985.

Roland Penrose, *Man Ray*, New York Graphic Society, Boston, 1975.

Gaetan Picon, *Surrealists and Surrealism, 1919–1939*, Skira/Rizzoli, New York, 1977.

Susan Noyes Platt, *Modernism in the 1920s: Modern Art and New York*, UMI Press, Ann Arbor, MI, 1985.

Renato Poggioli, *The Theory of the Avant-Garde*, Belknap Press, Harvard, MA, 1968.

Sue Ann Prince, *The Old Guard and the Avant-Garde: Modernism in Chicago 1910–1940*, University of Chicago, Chicago, 1990.

Kerry William Purcell, *Alexey Brodovitch*, Phaidon Press, London, 2002.

Vieri Quilliei, *Rodchenko: The Complete Works*, MIT Press, MA, 1986.

Tony Richardson and Nikos Stangos, eds., *Concepts of Modern Art*, Harper and Row, New York, 1974.

Hans Richter, *Dada: Art and Anti-Art*, Harry N Abrams Inc., New York, 1965.

Gail Harrison Roman and Virginia Hagelstein Marquardt, eds., *The Avant-Garde Frontier: Russia Meets the West, 1910–1930*, University Press of Florida, Gainesville, FL, 1992

Eberhard Roters, *Berlin 1910–1933*, Rizzoli, New York, 1982.

William S Rubin, *Dadaists, Surrealists and their Heritage*, MOMA Press, New York, 1968.

James Rye, *Futurism*, Dutton, New York, 1972.

Roger Sabin, *Comics, Comix and Graphic Novels: A History of Comic Art*, Phaidon Press, London, 1996.

Nachma Sandrow, *Surrealism: Theater, Arts, Ideas*, Harper and Row, New York, 1972.

Barbel Schrader, *The Golden Twenties: Art and Literature in the Weimar Republic*, Yale University Press, New Haven, CT, 1988.

William C Seitz, *Art of the Assemblage*, MOMA Press, New York, 1969.

Peter Selz, *Beyond the Mainstream*, Cambridge University Press, Cambridge, England, 1997.

Peter Selz and Mildred Constantine, eds., *Art Nouveau*, MOMA Press, New York, 1959.

Klaus-Jurgen Sembach, *Style 1930*, Universe Books, New York, 1971.

Meyer Shapiro, *Modern Art, 19th and 20th Centuries, Selected Papers*, George Braziller, New York, 1978.

Terry Smith, *Making the Modern: Industry, Art and Design in America*, University of Chicago Press, Chicago, 1993.

Kristian Sotriffer, *Modern Austrian Art: A Concise History*, Praeger, New York, 1965.

Ladislav Sutnar, *Visual Design in Action*, Hastings House, New York, 1961.

Martica Swain, *Surrealism in Exile and the Beginnings of the New York School*, MIT Press, MA, 1995.

Dickran Tashjian, *A Boatload of Madmen: Surrealism and the American Avant-Garde 1920–1950*, Thames & Hudson, London, 1995.

Dickran Tashjian, *Skyscraper Primitives: Dada and the American Avant-Garde 1910–25*, Wesleyan University Press, Middletown, CT, 1975.

S K Tillyard, *The Impact of Modernism and the Visual Arts in Edwardian England*, Routledge, London, 1988.

Rudy VanderLans and Zuzana Licko (with Mary E Gray), *Emigre: Graphic Design into the Digital Realm*, Van Nostrand Reinhold, New York, 1993.

Peter Veres, *A Selection from the Arts of Kenneth Patchen: The Argument of Innocence*, Scrimshaw Press, Oakland, CA, 1976.

Willy Verkauf, ed., *DADA: Monograph of a Movement*, George Wittenborn, New York, 1957.

Nicholas Wadley, *Movements in Modern Art: Cubism*, Hamlyn, London, 1970.

Rose-Carol Washton, ed., *German Expressionism: Documents*, Macmillan, New York, 1973.

Jeffrey Weiss, *Popular Culture of Modern Art: Picasso, Duchamp and Avant Gardism*, Yale University Press, New Haven, CT, 1994.

Frank Whitford, ed., *The Bauhaus*, Overlook Press, Woodstock, 1992.

Robert C William, *Artists in Revolution: Portraits of the Russian Avant-Garde 1905–1925*, Indiana University Press, Indianapolis, IN, 1977.

William Carlos Williams, *A Recognizable Image: William Carlos Williams on Art and Artists*, New Directions, New York, 1978.

Eddie Wolfram, *History of the Collage*, Macmillan, New York, 1976.

Jon Wozencroft, *The Graphic Language of Neville Brody*, Rizzoli, New York, 1988.

Larissa Aleksecuna Zhadova, ed., *Tatlin*, Rizzoli, New York, 1988.

Piet Zwart and Fridolin Muller, *Visual Communication Books*, Hastings House, New York, 1966.

Acknowledgements

Many years ago I read in a book by the newspaper and magazine historian, Frank Luther Mott, that even by 1920 over a million different magazines and newspapers had been published in the United States and Europe. At the time this number seemed incredibly inflated until I understood that this included countless short-lived magazines. When I began researching these independent, alternative and avant-garde periodicals for this book, I realized that Mott's estimate was conservative. Every time I thought I had a grasp on a particular period or movement I would find dozens more long- and short-term journals that had been published on a variety of themes. Although I chose to ignore a large number because they were poorly designed or historically tangential, I was astounded by how many significant publications there actually were.

When I initially proposed this book to my editor at Phaidon Press, Vivian Constantinopolis, I had no idea what was in store for me over the next three years. This has been one of the toughest books I have ever written. Vivian was a tough task-master but a wonderful collaborator during the development of a project that, owing to its enormity, simply did not want to end. My heartfelt thanks go to Vivian, who left Phaidon before the book's completion, for her good humour, excellent suggestions and loyal support.

Others were integral to this project and this acknowledgement is a small reward. Thanks to Jeff Roth, my chief researcher and friend, without whom I would not have found a third of the publications discussed in this volume. Everyday for months he would return from various forages to libraries and collections with hands full of familiar and unfamiliar journals. His dogged devotion was both saving grace and torment. Every time he found a new publication I knew I would have to spend even more time learning, understanding and deciding whether or not to include it. Jeff obtained access to The Howard L and Muriel Weingrow Collection of Avant Garde Art and Literature at Hofstra University, Long Island, New York, the most extensive assembly of avant-garde periodicals and artefacts I have yet come across.

I am in debt to Dr Barbara Kelly, Victoria Aspinwall, Bronwyn Hannon and Debra Willet of the library and Weingrow Collection at Hofstra for allowing us free access to the collection. Also other collectors have made a great contribution to this book. Elaine Lustig Cohen has always been an incredible resource and friend, and during the research of this book

she gave much needed counsel. Much gratitude goes to Jan Van Der Donk of Jan Van Der Donk Rare Books, Inc., in New York for generously loaning many of the publications herein. June and Bob Leibowits also generously opened up their astounding collection to supplement my original holdings. Material was also loaned (or sold) by many friends and colleagues, including Irving Oaklander, Oaklander Books, New York; Barbara Moore, Bound and Unbound, New York; Warren Lee, Nijhof & Lee, Amsterdam; Rich West, Periodessy, East Hampton, Mass.; Steven Lamazow; Mirko Ilic; Lisa Naftolin; Rudy VanderLans; Rick Poynor; John Walters; Neville Brody; Kurt Andersen; Art Spiegelman and François Mouly; Jaroslav Ander; Seymour Chwast; Marion Rand; Dr James Fraser; Victor Margolin; and Radislav Sutnar. My friend Jordi Duro did important supplementary research on the avant-garde in Barcelona, Spain. Last, but certainly not least, deep thanks to Michael Dooley for his generosity, knowledge and quick responses to scores of frantic emails.

In addition, I want to thank the following for granting permission to use magazines that they either published, edited, art directed, designed or illustrated: Marvin Scott Jarrett, Jaclynn Jarrett, Stephen Doyle, Dan Rolleri, Martin Venesky, Jon Wozencroft, Nicholas Pavkovic, Paul Krassner, Geof Kern, Stephen Byram, Steve Brower, Rick Vermeulen, David Sterling, Martin Fox and John Walters.

I am extremely grateful to my colleagues at Phaidon Press including Victoria Clarke, editor, and Charlotte Garner, assistant editor – thank you both for service above and beyond the call of duty, without you there really would be no book – and Emma Brown, picture researcher. Thanks to Alan Fletcher, who was behind the scenes but ever-present, and to Richard Schlagman, publisher, who has had a special and important interest in this project.

Back in New York, Tony Cenicola did most of the photography for the book. And in Kent, England, Hans Dieter Reichert, the designer, created a splendid format that gives this book its form and structure. I cannot say enough about his contributions. Thanks also to his assistants Paul Spencer and Paul Arnot who added much needed support.

Finally, I must pay homage to those who published, edited and designed these and other alternative magazines. Thank you for adding another dimension to the publishing world and for creating publications that have been an inspiration.